The Atlantic World

Essays on Slavery, Migration, and Imagination

Wim Klooster
Clark University

Alfred Padula
University of Southern Maine

PEARSON
Prentice
Hall

Upper Saddle River, New Jersey 07458

Library of Congress Cataloging-in-Publication Data
The Atlantic world: essays on slavery, migration, and imagination / [edited by] Wim
Klooster; Alfred Padula.
  p. cm.
  Includes bibliographical references and index.
  ISBN 0-13-183915-2
  1. America—History—To 1810. 2. Slavery—America—History. 3. Africans—
Migrations—History. 4. America—Ethnic relations. 5. Ethnicity—America—History.
6. America—Emigration and immigration—History. 7. Europe—Emigration and
immigration—History. 8. Europeans—Migrations—History. 9. Europe—Colonies—
America. 10. America—Intellectual life. I. Klooster, Wim. II. Padula, Alfred.

  E18.82.A848 2005
  909'.09821—dc22

                                                                      2004044447

Editorial Director: Charlyce Jones Owen
Executive Editor: Charles Cavaliere
Editorial Assistant: Shannon Corliss
Director of Marketing: Beth Mejia
Executive Marketing Manager: Heather Shelstad
Managing Editor: Joanne Riker
Production Liaison: Marianne Peters-Riordan
Manufacturing Buyer: Tricia Kenny
Cover Design: Bruce Kenselaar
Cover Illustration/Photo: Theodore de Bry, *America*, vol. IV (Frankfurt am Main, 1594). Ship plying
the Atlantic Ocean. Courtesy of the Osher Map Library, University of Southern Maine.
Photo Researcher: Sheila Norman
Image Permission Coordinator: Joanne Dippel
Composition/Full-Service Project Management: Lithokraft/Marty Sopher
Art Production Manager: Guy Ruggiero
Printer/Binder: Courier Companies, Inc.
Cover Printer: Phoenix Color Corp.

Credits and acknowledgments borrowed from other sources and reproduced, with permission, in this
textbook appear on appropriate page within text or on page 177.

Pearson Education LTD.
Pearson Education Singapore, Pte. Ltd
Pearson Education, Canada, Ltd
Pearson Education–Japan
Pearson Education Australia PTY, Limited

Pearson Education North Asia Ltd
Pearson Educación de Mexico, S.A. de C.V.
Pearson Education Malaysia, Pte. Ltd
Pearson Education, Upper Saddle River,
  New Jersey

10 9 8 7 6 5 4 3 2 1

ISBN 0-13-183915-2

CONTENTS

PREFACE

This book began its life as a lecture series that we convened at the University of Southern Maine in the academic year 2000–2001. We paired scholars in the same subfield of Atlantic history on four occasions and asked them to transform their presentations into book chapters. These chapters shed light on the manifold connections between the Old World and the New in the early modern period. The first set of essays looks at the role of specific port cities in Atlantic history. Subsequent sections explore European migration, the African dimension, and the ways in which the Atlantic world has been imagined.

We would like to thank Dorothy Rosene for bringing us in touch with Prentice Hall, and Charles Cavaliere, the History editor at Prentice Hall, for his enthusiasm for the book project. We are also grateful to Patricia Finn for her tireless administrative support, and George Carhart and Yolanda Theunissen of the Osher Map Library for their assistance in the selection of illustrations. Thanks are also due to the reviewers of the manuscript for their useful remarks: Ida Altman (University of New Orleans), Gayle Brunelle (California State University, Fullerton), Nicholas Canny (National University of Ireland, Galway), Graciella Cruz-Taura (Florida Atlantic University), Alison Games (Georgetown University), and John Thornton (Boston University).

Wim Klooster
Alfred Padula

NOTES ON CONTRIBUTORS

Rosalind Beiler is an Associate Professor of History at the University of Central Florida in Orlando. Her essays on German migration to the British American colonies have appeared in *Pennsylvania History, Business and Economic History*, Lehmann, Wellenreuther and Wilson, *In Search of Peace and Prosperity* (University Park, Pa., 2000), and in Finzsch and Lemkuhl, *Atlantic Communications* (Oxford, forthcoming). She has been a fellow at the Charles Warren Center for Studies in American History at Harvard University and a Senior Fulbright Scholar at the Free University of Berlin.

Jorge Cañizares-Esguerra received his PhD in the History of Science at the University of Wisconsin Madison in 1995. He is an Associate Professor of History at the University at Buffalo (SUNY-Buffalo). Cañizares-Esguerra has been a NEH, SSRC, and Harvard's Charles Warren Center fellow, as well as member of the Institute for Advanced Study at Princeton. He is currently a Mellon Research Fellow at the Huntington Library. His book *How to Write the History of the New World. Histories, Epistemologies, and Identities in the Eighteenth-Century Atlantic World* (Stanford, 2001) won two AHA awards in 2001: the Atlantic History and the Spanish and Latin American History Prizes. He is now completing a new book tentatively titled *Nature Narratives and Identities in the Atlantic World, 1500–1900*.

Meaghan N. Duff's historical research interests focus on the social history of colonial South Carolina, the place of the Lower South in the early modern Atlantic World, and the uses of cartography in North American colonization. Her book-length manuscript, "Carolina By Design: The Social and Geographical Construction of an English Colony, 1663–1719," reconsiders the settlement of South Carolina in continental and transatlantic contexts. The project examines the social and geographical factors shaping English plantation development in the Atlantic World—in Ireland, the Chesapeake, New England, the Caribbean, and Georgia—using proprietary South Carolina as a baseline for comparison and contrast. Dr. Duff is presently the senior manager for Global Services at Blackboard Inc., an education software and services company.

David Eltis obtained his PhD at the University of Rochester in 1979. He is currently Woodruff Professor of History at Emory University and Research Professor at the University of Hull in England. He has held visiting fellowships at Harvard, Yale, and All Souls, Oxford. He is currently working with Ugo Nwokeji on a database of the names and descriptions of 67,000 Africans recaptured from slave ships by British naval cruisers in the nineteenth century, a project aimed at establishing the identity of peoples forced into the slave trade.

Wim Klooster is an Assistant Professor of History at Clark University. He has held fellowships at the John Carter Brown Library, the Charles Warren Center at Harvard University, and the National University of Ireland. His publications include *The Dutch in the Americas, 1600–1800* (Providence, RI, 1997) and *Illicit Riches. Dutch Trade in the Caribbean, 1648–1795* (Leiden, 1998). The working title of his current book project is *The Dutch in the Atlantic World: Expansion and Contraction in the Golden Age.*

Paul E. Lovejoy is Distinguished Research Professor at York University and holds a Canada Research Chair in African Diaspora History. He is also a Fellow of the Royal Society of Canada and is Director of the Harriet Tubman Resource Centre on the African Diaspora, which is affiliated with the UNESCO Slave Route Project. He is the author of numerous books and articles, including *Transformations in Slavery: A History of Slavery in Africa*, 2d ed. (Cambridge, 2000), which received a Certificate of Merit from the Canadian Historical Association, and (with Jan Hogendorn), *Slow Death for Slavery. The Course of Abolition in Northern Nigeria, 1897–1936* (Cambridge, 1993), which received the Howard K. Ferguson Award.

Alfred Padula began his professional career as a servitor of the Cold War, first in Naval Intelligence and thereafter in the State Department. His work as Cuban analyst precipitated a lifelong interest in that country. Receipt of a Ford Foundation Fellowship for the Study of Revolutions led him into academia, specifically at the University of Southern Maine (USM) in the seaport city of Portland, where he could also indulge his interests as a small boat sailor. At USM, Professor Padula taught Latin American history, and produced numerous papers, reviews, and articles on Cuban issues, climaxing in a volume on women and the Cuban revolution: *Sex and Revolution. Women in Socialist Cuba* (Oxford, 1995).

Mark Peterson is an Associate Professor of History at the University of Iowa, where he teaches courses on North America and the Atlantic world from the sixteenth to the nineteenth centuries. He is the author of *The Price of Redemption: The Spiritual Economy of Puritan New England* (Stanford, 1997) and of "Puritanism and Refinement in Early New England: Reflections on Communion Silver," *William and Mary Quarterly* 58 (April 2001), which was awarded the Woodrow Wilson Prize by the Presbyterian Historical Society. He is currently at work on a book on Boston in the Atlantic World, 1630–1860, for which he has been awarded a Burkhardt Fellowship from the American Council of Learned Societies.

Benjamin Schmidt is an Associate Professor of History at the University of Washington in Seattle. He is the author of *Innocence Abroad: The Dutch Imagination and the New World* (Cambridge, 2001), which won the Renaissance Society of America's Phyllis Goodhart Gordan Best Book Prize for 2002. He has published widely on early modern European culture and Atlantic World history, and is currently working on a study of geography, imperialism, and cultural production in Baroque Europe,

"Inventing Exoticism: The Project of Geography and the Production of Globalism circa 1700."

Timothy Walker completed his doctorate in early modern European and colonial American history at Boston University (2001). He lives and works part of each year in Portugal, teaching American history at Lisbon's Universidade Aberta. He has held numerous research grants and fellowships, and conducted research in Portugal, India, Brazil, Germany, Austria, and Great Britain. In the Boston University Maritime Education Program, Walker teaches courses on Atlantic World Maritime History, focusing on European exploration and colonization.

Introduction: The Rise and Transformation of the Atlantic World

Wim Klooster

BEGINNINGS

Al-Mas'udi, a Baghdad geographer of the tenth century, called it the green sea of darkness.[1] Sailors feared to venture beyond the sight of shore. However, beginning in the late thirteenth century, the Atlantic was gradually transformed from an ocean that divided continents to one that connected them. The first stage of Europe's thrust into the Atlantic was marked by two developments: first, the forging of lines of maritime communication in the late thirteenth century between the Mediterranean and Northwestern Europe; and second, from the early fourteenth century, the creation of a zone of navigation between the Azores in the north, the Canary Islands in the south, and the Iberian and African coasts in the east.[2]

After a Genoese galley sailed through the Strait of Gibraltar and thence along the European coast to Flanders in 1277, a feat facilitated by the recent Christian occupation of Islamic territories in the Iberian peninsula, several Italian states began to use this sea route as an alternative to the long-standing routes to England, France, and Flanders by way of the Alps and the Rhone, Seine, and Rhine rivers.[3] The growing intensity of this traffic into the eastern Atlantic led to technological innovations in seafaring. New ship types were introduced, including the *caravel,* which dominated both Portuguese expeditions to Africa after 1440 and Spanish voyages to the Caribbean before 1550.[4]

The small size of the *caravels* and other ships that plied the ocean in the late medieval and early modern period is astonishing by modern standards. The overall habitable space of between 150 and 180 square meters on Spain's fleets in the sixteenth century breaks down to a mere 1.5 square meters for each man on board. The sixteenth-century sailor had to content himself with the lack not only of space, but of hygiene and chairs or any other type of comfort.[5] Nor did conditions dramatically improve over the next three centuries. An English author noted in the eighteenth century that being in a ship was like being in jail with less room and with the chance of drowning.[6]

Navigation to the islands in the eastern Atlantic was also opened up by a Genoese initiative. In the midst of the fourteenth century, Lanzarotto Malocello, sailing south along the African coast, found one of the Canary Islands. In the following century other Atlantic archipelagoes were discovered. Colonization of these fell to the Portuguese, who began to populate and exploit the Madeiras, Azores, and the Cape Verde Islands in the 1420s, 1440s, and 1460s, respectively. The Canaries became a Castilian territory.

The Portuguese next initiated the exploration of the African coast by attacking the walled Moroccan city of Ceuta at the mouth of the Strait of Gibraltar in 1415. In this war with the "Moors," the Portuguese combined the quest for land and wealth with the need to create career opportunities for aspiring young noblemen. Demographic decline at home had brought about economic and fiscal problems and made it difficult for the Crown to maintain its patronage of noblemen. The conquest of Ceuta and its defense in the following decades did not solve the financial malaise, but enabled nobles to gain both a reputation and knighthood.[7] One of these noble-man was the twenty-one-year-old son of King João I, Prince Henry (1394–1460), known since the nineteenth century as "the Navigator" for his contributions to Portuguese expansion.

In Prince Henry's day, Portuguese navigators, well-positioned and highly-motivated, took it upon themselves to sail down the African coast. In 1455–1456, two successive popes granted Portugal a monopoly of navigation southward and eastward to the Indies, the legendary lands of spices and untold wealth.[8] Finding the Indies was, of course, a tall order. Atlantic navigation had presented challenges from the start, since sailing from coast to coast, as occurred in the Mediterranean, was no longer possible. In the uncharted waters of the Atlantic, the sailor had to navigate by the stars.[9] He measured the altitude of the Pole Star, which indicated how far south he had gone, and once he found the right altitude, he would sail east or west until he reached land. This method presented Portuguese sailors with difficulties off West Africa, since the Polar Star would vanish at about latitude 9° north. The other obvious option was to measure the position of the sun, but until the late fifteenth century there was no instrument to do so with any accuracy. The invention of an astrolabe in 1497 that could be used on board ships changed that. The inventor, Abraham Zacuto, a Jewish astronomer in Portugal, had earlier developed a calendar that gave the sun's declination for the day. The astrolabe and the calendar together allowed the navigator to determine his latitude.[10]

Portuguese expansion was both economically and religiously motivated. The Portuguese were determined to carry a Christian holy war to the very heart of Islam, and recapte Jerusalem from the Muslims. Thus, the battle over Ceuta had overtones of a crusade. In their subsequent reconnaissance of the West African coast, the Portuguese searched for both a route to India and for the legendary Christian kingdom of Prester John. The two were linked, for although Prester John was believed to be the Emperor of Ethiopia, there was such a confusion between India and Ethiopia in the late Middle Ages that the Portuguese hoped that tracing John to West Africa would coincide with the discovery of a passage to India.[11]

Asia was associated with fabulous wealth: spices from India, Ceylon, Java, and the Moluccas, as well as silk and porcelain from China, captured Europe's imagination. Trade in these items had blossomed after the end of the Crusades, owing to the rule of the Great Khans of the Yüan dynasty after 1272, which enabled Europeans to bypass Muslim merchants.[12] The arrival of the plague in the mid-fourteenth century, the fall of the Mongol empire in 1368, and the expansion of the Ottoman empire spelled the end of this long-distance trade. Bypassing the Muslim world now required a more radical solution: rounding Africa, whose exact shape was still a mystery to Europeans.

Another, perhaps even more important, reason to explore the African coast was the lure of gold. During Europe's "Middle Ages," camel caravans carried gold dust washed from rivers and streams south of the Sahara across the great desert to North Africa, where it was transshipped to Spain and other parts of Christian Europe. In 1324–1325 the king of Mali made a pilgrimage to Mecca carrying such large amounts of gold that Europeans were astonished. When it arrived in Egypt, Malian gold caused the price of gold—which was increasingly becoming Europe's currency—to fall by twelve percent.[13]

Yet it was not until the Portuguese voyages of exploration that Europeans became actively involved in the gold business, purchasing the coveted metal on the Guinea coast and the Gambia River. The Portuguese presence off West Africa caused a diversion of the traditional flow of gold from its traditional trans-Saharan route to the coast. Some of the gold originated in the mines of Bambuk on the upper Senegal River and Bouré on the upper Niger, but a growing amount was obtained from the more southern Akan fields, dominated by the Akan of present-day Ghana and Ivory Coast. A trading nation called the Wangara controlled the gold flow to the market town of Jenne (Mali). Their slaves carried salt imported from the western Sahara, as well as cloth, brass, and copper by headload to the gold fields, where it was bartered for the coveted gold dust.[14]

In order to tap into the West African gold trade, the Portuguese established the fort of São Jorge da Mina, or Elmina (in modern Ghana), in 1482, on the southern fringe of the Akan country. The castle, the first European building in the tropics, soon became a major gold-gathering station. As the Portuguese learnt that their silks, woollens, and linens were not in high demand, they began to market textiles from North Africa. Before long, another solution was found, as the Portuguese discovered that slaves (from other parts of West Africa) could be traded against gold. Even as the slave trade gained pace, the Portuguese never came to monopolize the Akan gold trade, and their access to gold was frequently blocked because of wars between African nations.[15] Still, since ocean shipping proved cheaper than camel caravans across the desert, the Portuguese and subsequent European settlers on the coast obtained more West African gold by the seventeenth century than the Saharan merchants. Gold remained the main export item of Atlantic Africa until the end of the century, when its value was surpassed by that of slaves.[16]

In 1487, five years after Elmina was built, the Portuguese navigator Bartolomeu Dias rounded the Cape of Good Hope. Eleven years later, Vasco da Gama, following in Dias' tracks, sailed around the Cape and on to India. He returned to Portugal with an enormously valuable cargo. The next fleet bound for India, commanded by Pedro Álvares Cabral in 1500, sailed so far west into the Atlantic to pick up favorable winds, that it touched the shores of Brazil. The exploitation of Brazil, however, was postponed for several decades, as India lived up to its reputation, and fleet after fleet returned to Lisbon laden with riches.

The Portuguese reserved colonial trade for themselves, excluding foreigners such as the Genoese, whose political power waned in the fifteenth century. Archenemy Venice defeated Genoa in a series of wars over commercial access to the Middle East, blocking Genoese access to spices, while the Ottoman Empire seized its colonies in the Black Sea. Genoa's merchants were now in bad need of outlets for their capital. The fact that it was a Genoese who suggested an alternative, western, route to

India should thus not come as a surprise. When Christopher Columbus (1451–1506) failed to convince Portugal's King João II of the feasibility of his bold plan to sail west across the ocean to India, his logical next step was to turn to the Catholic rulers of Spain, Isabella of Castile and Ferdinand of Aragon. Spain and Portugal had been Atlantic rivals for many decades. Every step that was made by one side, every island conquered, was contested by the other. Intermittent warfare thus characterized the colonization of the Canary Islands from 1425, and an outright war erupted in 1475, when Castile challenged Portugal's monopoly over trade with, and navigation to, Guinea. Four years later, this first colonial war ended with Castile's defeat.[17]

Despite Columbus' outrageous promise to find Asia 3,000 miles to the West of Spain, which was unlikely given the accepted circumference of the earth, Ferdinand and Isabella did not dismiss him. However, only after their victory against Granada, the last Muslim kingdom in Iberia, in 1492 did the Catholic rulers decide to finance Columbus' visionary project. With three ships and eighty-eight men, Columbus left Andalusia on August 3 and sailed west via the Canary Islands. For hundreds of years, Spain's transatlantic navigators would use this route.

Reaching the Bahamas on October 12, thirty-three days after leaving the Canaries, Columbus made his first sighting of the Americas. He was convinced he had discovered a faster sea route to Asia. He would die believing that. What unfolded after his triumphant return to Spain the next spring was not merely the beginning of Spanish colonialism in the New World. While the Vikings and other adventurers may have preceded Columbus,[18] it was he who established a continuous exchange of people, ideas, germs, commodities, and flora and fauna between both sides of the Atlantic. The spread of American plants in the following centuries was without precedent. In a slow process, they completely transformed African and European diets. By the late eighteenth century, potatoes, beans, and maize had become staple foods all over Europe, while by 1900 beans, tomatoes, sweet potatoes, peanuts, and cacao were grown throughout the African continent. Conversely, this so-called "Columbian exchange" saw the introduction to America of wheat, onions, oranges, and bananas, to name just a few Old World plants.[19]

Columbus and subsequent conquistadors did not, of course, come to grow crops; they arrived to seize land and find gold. The Windward Antilles, where the trade winds carried their ships, were the first focus of activity (Map 1.1), but after the conquests of the awe-inspiring Aztec (1519–1521) and Inca (1533–1535) empires, the emphasis shifted to the mainland. The lightning speed with which the Spaniards conquered American lands and subjected entire empires begs for an explanation. Many reasons have been suggested. Some historians have pointed to the superiority of Spanish weapons. The steel swords, pikes, and lances were more effective than the wooden spears, clubs, axes, or bows and arrows of the native Americans. Cannon and firearms are said to have provided the troops of Hernán Cortés (in Mexico) and Francisco Pizarro (in Peru) with an additional advantage. While fierce dogs were reliable allies of the Spanish, the terror inspired by the horse, its rider encased in steel armor, was far greater. Still, this threat should not be exaggerated, since Cortés had only sixteen horses with him. Other factors in Spanish favor were native mythologies which prophesied the arrival of white gods, and the lack of native unity, which presented the Europeans with willing allies in both Mexico and Peru.

Woodcut from the "Columbus Letter," showing Caribbean islands with Spanish names that would not last. Christopher Columbus / C. Verardus, *De insulis nuper in mari Indico repertis* (Basel, 1494). *Courtesy of the Osher Map Library, University of Southern Maine.*

Crucial, however, in victories of Spain and other European states was disease. As the biologist Jared Diamond has explained, over millennia, the Europeans had become immune to the diseases harbored by their domesticated animals such as sheep, pigs, goats, and cows.[20] The high level of genetic homogeneity among Native Americans facilitated the rapid spread of the diseases and their destructive consequences. The most deadly epidemics in early America were smallpox and measles.[21] Smallpox is estimated to have killed between one-third and one-half of the native population of Hispaniola in 1518–1519. It was also smallpox that struck the Aztec capital of Tenochtitlán at a key moment, just as Cortés and his men had been repelled in 1520. The spread of the epidemic, which affected all classes and ages and left the population without care-givers, enabled the Spanish to regain control.[22] Likewise, an unidentified disease may have been responsible for the death of 90 percent of some

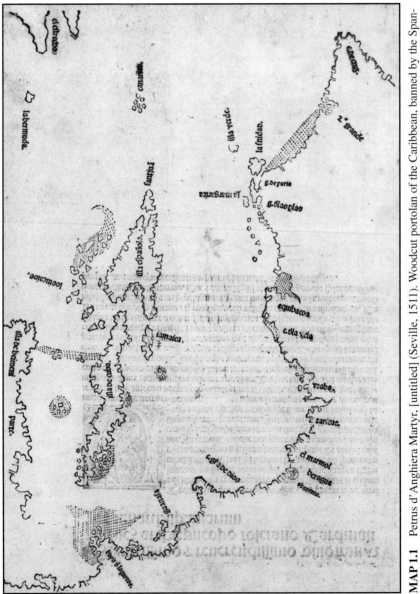

MAP 1.1 Petrus d'Anghiera Martyr, [untitled] (Seville, 1511). Woodcut portolan of the Caribbean, banned by the Spanish Crown for the secret information it conveyed. The representation of the Strait of Gibraltar on the right side makes the Atlantic seem much smaller than it actually is. *Courtesy of the Osher Map Library, University of Southern Maine.*

groups of New England Indians within just four years (1616–1620).[23] These are staggering figures. When the Black Death ravaged Europe in the mid-fourteenth century, about one-third of the continent's people died.[24] The overall loss of life in the New World after the first encounter with Europeans was far larger. Central Mexico's population declined from 5–10 million (1519) to 2.7 million (1568), Peru's from 9 million (1532) to 1.3 million (1570), while on Hispaniola a mere 2,000 natives were left in 1542. The only disease that the New World exported to the Old was syphilis, first identified in Italy one year after Columbus' return in 1493.

On that first return trip Columbus took back seven natives from Cuba. Thinking that he was in the vicinity of India, Columbus called them "Indians." The term stuck. By employing some of these Taínos as translators, the Admiral emulated the slave-interpreter system he had seen at work among the Portuguese in West Africa, a system that would facilitate European exploration and colonization in all of America.[25]

The Indians' perspective on early contacts with Europeans is recounted in some oral histories. The Micmac of New England relate that when "there were no people in this country but Indians, and before any others were known, a young woman. . . . dreamed that a whole island came floating in towards the land, with tall trees on it, and living beings–among them was a man dressed in rabbit-skin garments. . . . It was the custom in those days, when anyone had a remarkable dream, to consult the wise men. . . . These pondered over the girl's dream, but could make nothing of it. The next day an event occurred that explained it all. Getting up in the morning, what should they see but a singular little island. . . . which had drifted near to the land and become stationary there!"[26] The Europeans had arrived.

In many parts of America, native surprise and curiosity soon gave way to fear and anger, as the strangers employed violence to achieve their objectives. Columbus sent scores of Indians to Spain. He envisioned a regular exchange of natives for seeds, cattle, and provisions. Although the Crown suspended this trade almost immediately, the enslavement of Indians did not stop. Classical philosophers seemed to provide a justification for slavery. In *Politics,* Aristotle argues that "from the hour of their birth, some are marked out for subjection, others for rule." The same principle governing the rule of a nation applied to the rule of slaves. Although Aristotle admitted that some "affirm that the rule of a master over slaves is contrary to nature, and that the distinction between slave and freeman exists by law only, and not by nature," his work was used to defend the enslavement of Indians and, later, Africans.[27] Still, it did not answer some fundamental questions about the "primitive" people in central and southern America: Did people living in a state of nature have property rights? If so, did Europeans have the right to enslave them? Did people who seem to live like animals have souls? If so, shouldn't they be converted to Catholicism rather than exploited? In Spain, this discussion was only resolved in the mid-sixteenth century when it was decided that Indians did, indeed, have legal rights and souls.

Slavery was replaced with forced labor systems, like the *mita* and *repartimiento,* which allotted workers to mine operators, landowners, and other entrepreneurs when the latter needed them. After the job had been done, which might take weeks or months (central Mexico), or at least a year (Andes), the workers returned home with their wages. The monetary reward made this arrangement a curious mixture of the free labor market and a forced labor system. In a completely free market, wages would have been significantly higher, but power relations between the victorious Spaniards and subdued natives enabled employers to pay low wages.[28]

Some groups, such as the Caribs or Kalinagos in the Lesser Antilles, forcefully resisted the Europeans until well into the seventeenth century, when they were overpowered by the French and English. Similarly, the Araucanians in Chile managed to keep the Spanish north of the Bío Bío River. For others, the shock of invasions, epidemics, violence, forced relocations, coercive labor laws, and the evident incapacity of native gods and cultures to resist the Europeans was devastating. In many native societies migration to escape disease and taxation became a widespread phenomenon, whole sections of pre-Columbian society (state leaders, priests, merchants) disappeared, work lost its value as a sacred act, and old habits and traditions lost their meaning.[29] By forcing men to travel to Potosí and other mines, the labor draft in Bolivia and Peru robbed the Andean highlands of many of their workers at harvest time. Under the circumstances, the *ayllu* (kin group with right to land) disintegrated. This had serious consequences for women. Under the old system, male and female labor had been equally valued and daughters had been able to inherit property from their mothers. Henceforth, women's domestic chores were no longer viewed as vital, but as ancillary.[30]

Similarly, in New England where Eastern Abenakis had once worked together, the growing participation of men in the fur trade created a new role for the women. They stayed at home, processing pelts, cultivating crops, and devoting themselves to community affairs. The popularity of European tools and utensils accelerated this process among the Micmac. Men now used the time previously spent manufacturing traditional tools to hunt.[31]

Not everywhere in America did the first European incursions set the stage for the withering of Indian cultures. If settlers did not follow in the wake of explorers and merchants, natives and Europeans often lived peacefully side by side for extended periods of time.[32] Some Europeans, like the French fur hunters in Canada or sailors in the Caribbean, went native, marrying indigenous women and leading the lifestyle of their host societies.[33] Where natives declined in number, a growing group of newcomers, the African slaves, contributed to a process of accommodation.

In addition, sexual contacts between people from different continents produced whole new ethnic denominations. Thus we have the *mestizoes,* the offspring of Europeans and Indians, who are the dominant population group in Latin America today. *Mestizoes* frequently suffered discrimination because they did not belong to any recognized ethnicity. In official documents they were branded as vagabonds, in part because they were rejected by both Indians and Europeans.[34] It was difficult for them to climb the ranks of society. Few of them, for example, were included among the officers of Spain's American army at the sergeant level.[35]

European Impressions

How was Europe affected by its encounters with unknown lands and peoples in Africa and the Americas? The number of pamphlets and books dealing with Africa before the middle of the sixteenth century is remarkably small, partly because of the

Portuguese Crown's attempt to control the flow of information on the discoveries. The publication by Venetian Giovanni Battista Ramusio in 1550 of the first volume of his collection of overseas travel accounts marked the dawn of a new era. Descriptions of Portuguese expansion henceforth proliferated. The purely Atlantic content of these accounts was modest, for the treatment of explorations in Africa was usually overshadowed by the portrayal of Portuguese encounters with the more advanced Asian societies. The Dutchman Jan Huygen van Linschoten and the Englishman Richard Hakluyt, who popularized the non-European world for their countrymen, also made the Indian Ocean rather than the Atlantic the centerpiece of their work.[36]

Information about sixteenth-century America spread through various channels: the spoken word, the correspondence of envoys and papal nuncios at the Spanish court, letters between Spanish merchants and foreign colleagues, handwritten newspapers, exotica, pictures, maps, and of course, printed works.[37] The fabled city state of Venice was the leader in publishing books about the newly-discovered lands in America and Asia. However, this dominance was undone by the Inquisition and the Church's Index of Prohibited Books. As the center of world trade moved from the Mediterranean to the Atlantic, Antwerp, and later Amsterdam, took over as the premier sites of European book publishing.[38]

Maps of America and Africa were continuously updated, as knowledge about the world's geography improved dramatically. When the Portuguese explorer João Gonçalves Zarco reached the Senegal River in Africa, the chronicler Gomes Eanes de Zurara, traveling in his company, wrote that this site was far beyond the lands that Alexander the Great had known. The maps of Greek map-maker Ptolemy and their derivations, which had dominated cartography for a millennium, were revealed to be patently wrong.[39] "The simple sailors of today," argued French explorer Jacques Cartier in 1545, "have learned the opposite of the philosophers by true experience."[40]

Classical authors were not ignored, however. In representing Africa on his world map of 1507, the German cartographer Martin Waldseemüller not only used recently obtained Portuguese knowledge about Africa's coastline, he was also indebted to the classical tradition, using Ptolemy's terms for the continent's lakes and rivers.[41] Waldseemüller's map was published along with a globe, both of which gave the name "America" to the West Indies, honoring Americo Vespucci, the Florentine navigator who had twice sailed to the New World. The map is one of three printed world maps that stand out in the sixteenth-century European representation of the Americas. The other two are the copperplate map which the Italian map-maker Francesco Rosselli published in Florence in 1506, which was the first printed map containing clear information on the location of the newly-discovered lands (Map 1.2); and the 1570 map produced by Spain's court geographer, Abraham Ortelius, which referred to both the north and south of the New World with the name that Waldseemüller had first introduced. The popularity which Ortelius's map enjoyed contributed to "America's" endurance.[42]

The news from America and Africa was, nevertheless, slow to change the way Europeans viewed the world. A French description of the world that went through five editions between 1539 and 1560 completely ignored America.[43] Most Europeans, including men of learning, probably knew very little about the world across

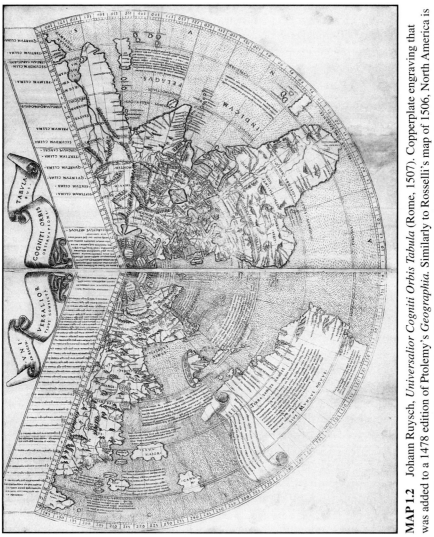

MAP 1.2 Johann Ruysch, *Universalior Cogniti Orbis Tabula* (Rome, 1507). Copperplate engraving that was added to a 1478 edition of Ptolemy's *Geographia*. Similarly to Rosselli's map of 1506, North America is presented here as an easterly protrusion of Asia. *Courtesy of the Osher Map Library, University of Southern Maine.*

the Atlantic Ocean, and what they knew was often wrong. As they came to realize that America was not mentioned in the Scriptures, intellectuals faced some challenging historical questions: did the biblical Flood reach America; what was the origin of the Indians; do all human races have a single ancestor?[44]

Beginning with the discovery of the Canary Islands (probably shortly before 1339),[45] the encounter with natives of newly-discovered lands induced Europeans to formulate new criteria for civility. The old dichotomy between Christians and others was replaced by concepts that contrasted sophisticated civilizations with primitive, savage peoples.[46] Although the Ottoman empire and the civilizations of Japan and China followed erroneous beliefs, they were clearly superior to the natives of Brazil and the hunters and gatherers whom Columbus had found in the West Indies. These were considered irrational beings, not far removed from animals. They lived, according to a French commentator, "sans roi, sans loi, sans foi" (without king, without law, without faith). Even the Aztecs and Incas, despite their advanced civilizations, were sometimes placed in the same category. The definition of civility came to include literacy and education; personal self-discipline; respect for the law; settlement in communities, especially in towns; and the use of money.[47] It has even been suggested that the sudden popularity of the beard in sixteenth century Europe, after many centuries in which facial hair had distinguished Muslim and Jewish males from Christians, was a deliberate attempt to set the Old World apart from the New, where the natives lacked a growth of beard.[48]

"Primitive" natives continued to occupy the minds of learned Europeans in subsequent centuries. Whereas the Europeans had passed through several stages of development, the "savages" were thought to be stuck in pre-history. Enlightenment thinkers assumed that the natives of Africa and America lived through their senses, whereas civilized men had acquired skills that enabled them to think in abstractions.[49] Conversely, other intellectuals were fascinated by these "others" and saw them as noble savages living in a Golden Age, a world of simplicity and innocence.[50] Some European authors compared the more elevated Indian societies, the Incas, the Mayas, and the Aztecs, to Classical Antiquity. Similarities between architecture, deities, and burial customs, among other things, were frequently stressed.[51] In the process, Europeans began to gild their opinions of their own past. Whereas they had previously portrayed their ancestors as coarse and childish, the Middle Ages and Antiquity now came to be viewed as pristine eras. If Indians had formerly been seen as barbarians, barbarians were now perceived as Indians.[52] Michel de Montaigne advanced the most balanced and intelligent view in the late sixteenth century. The French thinker painted the world as an amalgam of different nations, all with their own customs and beliefs. Differences, he thought, were relative, based on the observer's perceptions and biases.

The historian James Lockhart has argued that the Europeans and the more developed American societies judged one another using criteria dictated by their own cultural frameworks. The many similarities between their respective societies in terms of agriculture, religious organization, taxation, and social hierarchy fooled them into believing that principles and practices on either side were essentially identical. This process allowed both parties to hold on to their traditional values and conceptions, their dialogue of the deaf avoiding a close examination of each other.[53]

The extent to which Old World concerns conditioned European views of natives is shown in Benjamin Schmidt's essay *The Purpose of Pirates, or Assimilating New Worlds in the Renaissance* in the present collection. His focus is on the Dutch Republic, which was born around the time that descriptions of other lands, and especially America, became fashionable. The Dutch identified with the Indians, enemies of their own enemy—Habsburg Spain—who supposedly suffered under a similar yoke. However, after the Dutch had started their own settlements in the New World and the first bloody encounters with natives had occurred, compassion with the Indian plight rapidly evaporated.

Even the power of such biased concepts was, however, limited. European intellectuals, merchants, travelers, and missionaries found much they could not understand. This puzzlement led to the notion of "wonders" and "marvels" in exotic lands.[54] European collectors assembled a wide variety of items in an attempt to grasp the workings of the universe. The more obscure the objects that made up the "wonder-cabinets," the higher they were valued. The public theater at the University of Leiden, for example, displayed shoes and sandals from Russia and Siam, Egyptian mummies, and a hammer used by North American Indians.[55]

Medieval myths, derived from Classical authors, often provided inspiring and novel "insights" into the new worlds. Among the "monstrous races" that were said to roam the earth were the *Amazons* (warlike women who lived without men), *Anthropophagi* ("man-eaters"), *Antipodes* (people living on the opposite side of the globe), *Blemmyae* (men with faces on their chests), and *Cynocephali* ("dog-heads").[56] As they mingled "the horrible with the bizarre, the admirable with the repugnant,"[57] many Europeans were likely to believe the assertion of a captive man from Guinea in a contemporary Venetian travel narrative who claimed that unicorns existed in his native country.[58]

Myths about cities of dazzling wealth, such as the Seven Cities of Cibola and El Dorado, motivated European explorers. Seven Catholic bishops fleeing Spain during the Moorish invasion in the eighth century reputedly established the Seven Cities. The Frenchman Jacques Cartier searched for Cibola along the St. Lawrence River in the 1530s, but failed in his mission, as did Jean Ribault, who led an expedition to present-day South Carolina. Later in the sixteenth century Spaniards would seek the cities in New Mexico. Even more exciting were the stories of El Dorado, believed by some to be a native king who covered himself in gold dust, somewhere in northern South America. In the early 1540s, the first Spanish expeditions were sent to find his kingdom. The Spanish discovery of the mines of Potosí (Upper Peru) in 1545 and Zacatecas (Mexico) in 1548 only seemed to prove the existence of infinite riches in the interior. Englishmen and Dutchmen continued the search for El Dorado well into the next century, founding settlements in Guiana, where, according to English adventurer Walter Raleigh, more gold was to be found than in any other part of Peru. The Spaniards, for their part, never abandoned the quest for El Dorado. In Venezuela, in the late eighteenth century, black slaves were still sent on scouting expeditions.[59] Throughout the centuries, the myth of El Dorado thus served as a stimulus to continue the work of exploration and conquest.[60]

The legend of King Solomon's mines, allegedly located in Ophir, inspired explorers in both Africa and the Americas. Although Ophir's riches—gold, silver, ivory, and apes (I Kings 10:22)—seem to suggest an African site, Columbus convinced himself, after discovering an abundance of gold, that Hispaniola was actually Ophir. In the early seventeenth century, a Portuguese author identified Ophir as the Brazilian port city of São Jorge, adding that the Brazilian Indians descended from the ancient Jews, as could be proven by the many words, names, and customs that had been passed down.[61]

Gregorio García, a Dominican friar from Spain who lived in Mexico for nine years, also recognized Hebrew words in native languages. In a book he published in 1607, he tried to prove that the Native Americans were the descendants of the Ten Lost Tribes of Israel.[62] Jews often readily accepted such stories, especially when they pointed to the existence of a sovereign Jewish kingdom somewhere on the face of the earth. That might, after all, be a sign of the imminent messianic era.[63] In Amsterdam in 1644 a Portuguese crypto-Jew named Antonio de Montezinos claimed he had met Hebrew-speaking Jews, descendants of the Ten Lost Tribes, in northern South America. Amsterdam Rabbi Menasseh ben Israel accepted his account as evidence of the coming of the Messiah, since the precondition of Jewish scattering all over the globe seemed in the process of being fulfilled. To accelerate this dispersal, Menasseh started planning new Jewish settlements in the Americas.[64]

The history of the Americas led to serious debate among European intellectuals in the eighteenth century, as Jorge Cañizares-Esguerra demonstrates in his chapter in this volume titled *Whose Centers and Peripheries? Eighteenth-Century Intellectual History in Atlantic Perspective.* Dismissing both native sources and the accounts of European travelers, officials, and clerics, some sailed across the Atlantic to gain first-hand knowledge, while others preferred to write conjectural histories. Skeptical of the ability of European travelers to grasp the American past, given their gullibility and their ignorance of native languages, Americans themselves also began to write the history of the New World. Their works are among the most sophisticated historical works produced at the time.

THE WESTERN EUROPEAN CHALLENGE

Early in the era of transatlantic discovery, Western Europeans contested the division of the New World between Spain and Portugal. Explorers and privateers led the way in their efforts to challenge Iberian hegemony. During his three voyages in the service of the English king between 1496–1498, Venetian-born Giovanni Cabot found land, probably Newfoundland, and may have ventured as far south as New England. With permission from the French monarch another Italian, Giovanni da Verrazano, explored the eastern seaboard from Cape Cod and the mouth of the Hudson River before proceeding to Florida. Before long, French ships started raiding Spanish vessels and trading with Brazilian natives. In the 1560s, English privateers took over. Their hero, Francis Drake, named "El Draque" in the Spanish colonies, seized three Peruvian mule trains laden with silver (1572) and occupied Santo Domingo and Cartagena (1585). In the long term, however, his actions created little more than fear. Drake died in a battle with the Spanish in the Caribbean in 1596. Thereafter, the Dutch became the main scourge of the Iberians, as they took their rebellion against

Habsburg domination of the Netherlands to the West Indies. The merchants of the Low Countries soon discovered the commercial potential of the New World.

After 1621, Dutch activities in the Atlantic were coordinated by the West India Company, which embodied the spirit of innovation that became a hallmark of the Dutch economy in the seventeenth century. The West India Company was more than a joint-stock company, as the United Provinces (of the Northern Netherlands) granted the Company the rights to have an army, wage war, and make peace with distant rulers. Such privileges enabled the Dutch to intensify their struggle with Spain. The Dutch strategy was to strike at Spain's rich overseas colonies, and thus reduce the Hapsburgs' ability to finance their war in the Low Countries.

The most spectacular victory of the Dutch against their enemy was the capture, by Admiral Piet Heyn, of the Spanish silver fleet as it sailed from Veracruz to Seville in 1628. The cargo included more than four million pesos of silver and other colonial products. As mass celebrations took place in the Netherlands, the Spanish king fainted dead away.[65] The conflict assumed global proportions, as the Dutch seized Java, Sumatra, and the Spice Islands in the East Indies, and established outposts in many other parts of the Indian Ocean. The Dutch also successfully invaded Brazil (1630), assuming full control of the sugar business. In order to provide slaves to work the sugar cane fields in Brazil, the Dutch seized the Portuguese slaving station at São Jorge da Mina on Africa's Gold Coast, as well as the coast of Angola. Dutch forces expanded the Brazilian territory under their control until a local rebellion of Portuguese landowners broke out in 1645, which created a momentum for the anti-Dutch parties. This rebellion was never suppressed, and nine years later the last Dutch soldiers abandoned Brazil.

Although the Dutch were driven from Brazil, this venture did considerable damage to the Habsburg treasury. Furthermore, the diversion of Habsburg naval power to the waters off Brazil left the Caribbean open to colonization by European nations, big and small. Such incursions stopped almost entirely after Portugal gained its independence in 1640, relieving Spain of the task defending Brazil.

MIGRATIONS

Given the vastness of the Americas, European governments, lacking the resources to colonize the new regions, often encouraged private individuals to do the work. This was as much true for Spain and Portugal as it was for the English, Dutch, and French. The authorities' incapacity to colonize was often due to the extraordinary cost of European wars which drained their treasuries, ships, and manpower. So it came to pass that Frenchmen established colonies in the Antilles of which the French crown was hardly aware.[66]

The European proprietors in America soon discovered that their lands lacked an essential ingredient. Some were devoid of people, and where the whites encountered sizable Indian populations they faced resistance or at least refusal to adapt to European ways. The need arose, therefore, to recruit large numbers of European settlers.[67] While Pennsylvania and New Jersey drew large numbers of colonists, Maryland and the Carolinas struggled to lure people from across the ocean. Similarly,

New France and Louisiana remained unpopular destinations, whereas the Caribbean islands of Guadeloupe and Martinique attracted a steady stream of immigrants. Although migration to the Dutch colony in North America, New Netherland, was relatively modest, it did increase in the decade before the English takeover of 1664.

During the Thirty Years War in Europe (1618–1648), Czech theologian and educator Jan Amos Comenius foresaw the rise of America: "Once the eastern parts, Assyria, Egypt, the Jewish lands, flourished; they excelled in the arts of war and letters. Both [arts] then passed to Europe; barbarians overran everything there. Now again in Europe everything is rebelling, crumbling, raving, approaching a general downfall. The New World by contrast is beginning to flower."[68] Nevertheless, it is not easy to explain why so many Europeans decided to move to America instead of settling elsewhere on their own continent. To many emigrants, the attractions of the New World were greater than those of the Old. Among the Northwest Europeans, this was especially true for the English. French and Dutch emigration numbers pale in comparison to those of their neighbors across the Channel. The English were involved in a Great Migration, a term that is traditionally preserved for the settling of New England in the years 1630–1641. The label is in bad need of revision, however, since it involved 'only' 21,000 people. Larger numbers of migrants went elsewhere. As Meaghan Duff indicates in her chapter in this volume, *Adventurers Across the Atlantic: English Migration to the New World, 1580–1780,* no more than 44,500 of Britain's transatlantic migrants (one in eight) moved to the northern and middle colonies in the entire seventeenth century, compared to 200,000 (more than half) who settled in the Caribbean and 120,000 (one-third) who went to the Chesapeake.

The Great Migration brought many religious refugees to the New World. They included religious separatists and people who feared the gradual introduction of Catholic elements in the Church of England.[69] Some settled in the newly-founded town of Boston, whose residents realized that in terms of wealth and usefulness to the empire, their port city was no match for the English plantations in the Chesapeake and the West Indies. As Mark Peterson writes in *Life on the Margins: Boston's Anxieties of Influence in the Atlantic World* in this collection, they hoped at the same time to create a society that was morally superior to that of their southern counterparts. Peterson goes on to reveal the ambivalent relationship Boston would have with the Atlantic world, marked by involvement as well as withdrawal.

Some migrants who left England for New England hoped they might return to their mother country once the turmoil caused by religious persecution and, later, civil war had subsided. Some did indeed cross the Atlantic once more, either because the situation in England seemed safe again, or because homesickness, family duties, or other personal reasons forced them.[70] Religious dissenters also formed an integral part of French colonialism. Huguenots (French Protestants) were present in the short-lived colony at Rio de Janeiro (1555–1558) and monopolized the French settlement in Florida, which Spanish forces destroyed in 1565. Three thousand French Protestants moved to English North America after Louis XIV ended their protection in France by revoking the Edict of Nantes in 1685.[71]

Dutch America, likewise, was a haven for religious minorities. Although Calvinism was the official religion, private worship of other religions or denominations was allowed in New Netherland (the Dutch colony in North America), despite the protests of local Dutch ministers. Lutherans, Puritans, Anabaptists, Quakers, Mennonites, and Catholics were found in New Amsterdam about 1650. Their multiple backgrounds created a veritable Tower of Babel—a French priest who visited Manhattan observed that the four or five hundred inhabitants spoke eighteen different languages.[72]

Nevertheless, in the Dutch as well as the French colonies, it was generally the church (Calvinist or Catholic) that played a key role in the transmission of metropolitan culture. In New Netherland, the Dutch Reformed Church "guarded the language and cultural heritage, defended European values, and fostered the community spirit."[73] In other respects, there was cultural continuity too, as suggested by the names New England, New France, New Netherland, and New Sweden (the Swedish colony in Delaware, 1638–1655). In matters of language, food, stories, songs, festivals, and holidays, the colonies resembled the metropolis. These traditions were maintained in a world that was, at the same time, alien. Settlers had to cope with often radically-new natural and social environments, as they exchanged familiar urban regions for isolated settlements. Women were always a small minority among the immigrants, and, unlike men, rarely single.[74]

Most Europeans who migrated across the Atlantic came for economic, not religious reasons. There was ample opportunity for craftsmen throughout the Atlantic world. Peasants were another sizeable group of migrants. Lured by the prospect of owning land, landless Portuguese rural laborers left for Madeira, the Azores, or Brazil. Younger sons of Spanish and Portuguese noble families, facing an uncertain future at home, embarked to improve their social standing. They occupied senior overseas military or administrative positions.[75] A remarkable case of upward mobility involved the serfs in the domains of Duke James of the Baltic principality of Courland. The Duke encouraged them to migrate to the island of Tobago, his prized possession in the Caribbean, where they not only received the status of freemen, but became slave owners as well.[76]

In her contribution to the present volume in her essay *Searching for Prosperity: German Migration to the British American Colonies, 1680–1780,* Rosalind Beiler argues that books and pamphlets were an important instrument to promote migration. Colonial proprietors circulated promotional pamphlets that held out the promise of abundant, cheap, and fertile land. Much was also made of religious toleration and the light tax burden awaiting settlers.

How did migrants pay for the transatlantic voyage? There were plenty of them, either soldiers or sailors, who did not pay at all. One in five sailors on board the Spanish Indies fleets deserted in an American port.[77] Other Spanish émigrés received loans or donations from relatives in Spain or the New World. Legal migrants paid half of the passage costs in Seville and the rest within a month of arrival.[78] Before 1700, a majority of the white settlers of British America, and a substantial percentage of the settlers of the French colonies, signed some form of contract before embarkation.[79] The signing of a contract made them "indentured" workers. The contract bound them for a specified amount of time to a master, commonly a planter. The cost of the voyage to the New World was advanced to the worker, who had to repay the amount during his or her indenture. Crucial in their recruitment were merchants who operated as go-betweens. Other servants sailed without written indentures and were sold on arrival. Local legislation dealt with the "custom of the country" regarding these servants. A third group promised to pay their fare within a week or two after arrival. If they failed to do so, the ship's captain sold them into servitude.

Because they were drawn from a larger pool of laborers, indentured servants in the American colonies outnumbered the "customary" servants, who were able to pay their own way. To agree to indentured servitude for a given time was thus a useful way of financing migration.[80] Most of these indentured servants, though, were "underemployed, frustrated, fearful, but still enterprising young artisans, journeymen, and casually employed workers." On the other hand, free tenants lured by land speculators were relatively affluent and usually arrived in families.[81]

For many émigrés, America was not the promised land they had imagined. Early migrants sometimes faced precarious subsistence levels. Famine and disease, for instance, took the lives of 350 of the 530 settlers arriving in the French colony on St. Christopher in 1627. Others did not even make it to the New World. Disease took the lives of eighty of the 350 passengers on board an overcrowded English ship bound for Barbados in 1638. As many as two thousand German migrants to North America may have died at sea in 1749, while on one ship in 1752 only nineteen out of two hundred survived the transatlantic voyage.[82] Once ashore, the brutal working conditions decimated the ranks of the servants. A royal official estimated in 1681 that of six hundred *engagés* (as the French servants were called) that had arrived in the French West Indies in recent years, fewer than fifty had survived their three-year tenure. Indentured servants in early French and English America were in some ways treated like African slaves. Masters could dispose of them at will, and generally behaved cruelly toward retrieved runaways. A servant might be won or lost in a card game, and his diet was hardly superior to the typical slave menu. In other ways, the servants were better off. They had recourse, for instance, to the courts, where their rights were often upheld.[83]

Migration is a phenomenon that frequently feeds on itself. Most of the 975 Spanish migrants who embarked for New Andalusia (in eastern Venezuela) in 1569 were recruited from parts of the country with significant internal migration, which suggests that the last to arrive were the first to seize the opportunity to sign up for the Americas. Similarly, large numbers of indentured servants who ended up in British North America, in particular the Chesapeake, had first left their home town or village for London. For those who could not make a proper living, yearned for more adventure, or simply abhorred life in the English capital, London served as a springboard to the New World. Amsterdam had the same function in Dutch migration, not just for residents of the United Provinces, but for immigrant Germans and Scandinavians as well.[84]

Why would an inhabitant of one of the numerous German states want to move to the New World? Travel conditions were hard, and during the many international wars from the mid-eighteenth century through the Napoleonic era, the entry to America was completely cut off. Seven out of eight migrants from Southwest Germany moved not to the New World, but rather to Prussia, Russia, and the Habsburg empire. Still, the same region sent no less than 100,000 people to British North America in the period 1683–1783, about as many as the number of English settlers that arrived there.[85] Such a westward flow of Germans suggests that the Atlantic world "formed a single vast labor market."[86]

JEWS AND THE INQUISITION

Jews formed yet another group of migrants. To them, 1492 was a sad milestone, the year in which Queen Isabella and King Ferdinand ordered their wholesale expulsion from Spain. The Catholic rulers thus attempted to transform Spain into a homogeneous Christian country a few months after the last Muslim kingdom in the Iberian peninsula had been defeated. Jews who remained would automatically incur the death penalty. An estimated 30,000 Jewish families left the country, while some 10,000 families remained behind. They were obliged to become "New Christians," often converting only outwardly. The vast majority of the exiles crossed the border into Portugal. Within five years, however, the Portuguese king had all Jews in his country forcibly converted, prompting another exodus.

The loss of so many men and women cost Spain dearly. The exiled subsequently enriched Spain's rivals and enemies, the Ottoman Empire first and foremost, with their talents and expertise. It is true that various groups of Genoese, Flemings, and Germans filled the void of Jewish financiers, but these were foreigners, not prone to take the Spanish interest to heart.[87] The subsequent diaspora brought Sephardic Jews and New Christians to various parts of Europe, as well as the wider world. A few escaping New Christians may have been the first Europeans in interior Africa,[88] while others managed to sail to the Americas, sometimes disguised as soldiers or priests. After several unsuccessful royal decrees issued to thwart Jewish immigration, Inquisition courts were established in the Indies to root out heresy. In 1570, a tribunal was opened in Mexico City, whose jurisdiction extended to the far north (New Mexico), across Central America, and even to the Philippines. The tribunals of Lima (erected in 1571) and Cartagena de Indias (1620) prosecuted heretics in South America. Although the Inquisition could formally only try Christians for their heresies, Jews might be punished if they were to consult the devil, if they possessed the Talmud or other prohibited Jewish books, and if they maintained that Jesus Christ were a mere man, and his mother not a virgin.

The Inquisition was aware that a worrisome number of (crypto-)Jews arrived in Mexico, where they were rapidly integrated into social and economic life, working as physicians, lawyers, cobblers, traders, or shopkeepers. The heads of clans often paid for the passage of a nephew or cousin. In several towns, they would have access to a secret synagogue, which was simply a room in a private house or a space in a store. Under the circumstances, women became the repositories of Jewish culture, maintaining customs and traditions that had originated in Iberia. Because they were illiterate and had no access to education, Judaism was stripped of much of its theological sophistication and largely reduced to customs and rituals.[89]

Portugal founded its own Inquisition in 1536 and soon (1558) opened a tribunal in Goa (India), whose jurisdiction extended from East Africa across all of Asia. No Atlantic counterpart arose, but the Lisbon tribunal monitored Brazil and West Africa. This did not prevent numerous New Christians, attracted by Brazil's prosperity, from settling there in the last quarter of the sixteenth century. This era coincided with Habsburg's control of both Spain and Portugal (1580–1640), which enabled many New Christians to cross into Spain and its colonies to escape the Portuguese Inquisition, which was more active than its Spanish counterpart. The *conversos* settled in the southern cone of South America, where they often engaged in illicit commerce. Others moved to Lima, whose local Inquisition court alleged in 1636 that the New Christian dominance of local commerce was almost complete;[90] Cartagena de Indias, where the male Portuguese residents frequently gathered in the house of two of their own to discuss business deals and keep religious services; and Angola, where they were active in the African slave trade.[91]

Their almost-carefree lives ended in the 1630s, when the Spanish Inquisition's South American tribunals acted decisively, seizing property and punishing New Christians. An elaborate *auto-da-fé* took place in Lima in 1639. One year later, Portugal achieved its independence from Spain and joined an anti-Spanish alliance. Now it was the turn of the Holy Office's Mexican court to take measures. All Portuguese settlers of New Spain were branded "enemy aliens," and several of them died in *autos-da-fé*.

Another serious blow dealt to Sephardic Jewry was the fall of Dutch Brazil. In the 1590s, New Christians had started moving from Portugal to Amsterdam, where they formed a closely-knit group, as their sons and daughters usually intermarried. Most reverted to their ancestral beliefs. Lured by the promise of religious tolerance, hundreds, rich and poor, went to Dutch Brazil, a colony started in 1630. By 1641, they constituted the single most important group of immigrants.[92] Conditions were so favorable that the first synagogue in the western hemisphere was inaugurated in Recife, the main city of Dutch Brazil. The defeat of the Dutch spelled the end of the Jews' sojourn. By 1654, all Jews had left, most for Amsterdam, although two dozen of them made it to New Amsterdam (present-day New York City), where they formed the first Jewish community on North American soil.

The mid-seventeenth century was a period of readjustment for the American Jews. Before long they would abandon Spanish America almost entirely, while the New Christians of New Spain and Peru assimilated into the society of the Old Christians. The major New World destinations for Jews became the Caribbean colonies of England and the Netherlands. Jewish merchants on the Dutch-held island of Curaçao, where Jews constituted one-third of the white population, and English Jamaica and Barbados, successfully used their family networks across the Atlantic, with various relatives acting as business associates. By 1679, the Jews made up two percent of Barbados' population, but owned one-fifth of the island's urban wealth, despite several legal barriers.[93] Mercantile and financial activities also predominated in the rapidly-growing colonies along North America's eastern seaboard. In Dutch Suriname, on the southern shore of the Caribbean basin, agriculture was more important. Until the mid-eighteenth century, Jews ran scores of plantations in Jodensavanne, the most autonomous of all Jewish communities in the world.

CATHOLIC MISSIONS

Spain's rightful ownership of its new colonies in the Americas was derived from papal bulls issued by Pope Alexander VI, a Spaniard. The bulls conceded the right and duty to the Catholic rulers Ferdinand and Isabella to convert the heathen in the New World. This power, sometimes known as the royal *patronato,* gave the rulers extraordinary rights in Church affairs, and thus intertwined religious authority and political power. It was the king who designated the most suitable candidates for the bishop in the American provinces. Although he was still ultimately appointed by the Pope, the bishop was in all other respects a Spanish state employee. The Crown also assumed a large measure of control over the monastic orders. It paid for the monks' clothes, books, and travel costs.[94]

In the papal bulls of 1455 and 1456, well before Vasco da Gama had found the route to India or Columbus had discovered America, the Order of Christ was granted the sole right of converting—on behalf of the Portuguese Crown—natives in all islands and countries from Cape Bojador, via Guinea, to the Indies. Consequently, in many African coastal regions, Christianity blossomed.[95] The Christian mission was most successful in Congo, whose rulers adopted the new religion voluntarily. In sharp contrast to their early counterparts in the New World, Catholic missionaries in Congo adopted an inclusive concept of Christianity.[96] Thus, prior to their forced shipment to the Americas, quite a number of Africans became Christians. Some of them served as catechists in towns and plantations in the New World, fostering an African form of Christianity.

In Brazil, Portugal's colonial efforts began quite slowly. In 1500, Franciscans aboard the Portuguese fleet that discovered Brazil offered the first Mass in that country. It was not until 1551 that a papal bull empowered the Portuguese King to create the first Brazilian diocese—and until 1677 the only one—in Salvador (Bahia).[97] Shortly after the start of the Mexican conquest, Franciscans joined the conquistador Hernán Cortés, assuring him that God had chosen him to establish a new Church in this uncorrupted land. The Franciscans felt that the millennium, the period of a thousand years during which Christ was to reign on earth, was imminent, and that a conversion of the world was a necessary prelude to the second coming of Christ. Among the innocent peoples of America, they could build a Church resembling that of Christ and the early apostles.

This utopian Catholic ideal was incompatible with the military character of the Conquest. Fear of punishment from the invaders prompted numerous Indians to convert to a religion which they scarcely understood. Civil authorities questioned the spectacular missionary successes of conquistadors such as Pedrarias Dávila, who claimed to have baptized 400,000 natives in the year 1525 alone. A Peruvian governor told an assembly of provincials of the religious orders that, according to his information, "out of more than three hundred thousand men (Indians) who are baptized, no more than forty are truly Christian and as many idolatries exist here as before."[98]

Even where idolatry was seemingly unknown, as in parts of Brazil, the missionary effort was by no means an easy one. The Jesuits sent to the Portuguese colony were dismayed to find that the native Brazilians had no concept of God, marriage, or sin.[99] What compounded the problem was that the Jesuits did not understand the native language, Tupi. This led to the training of seasoned Portuguese settlers and orphan boys from Lisbon to act as interpreters. The penitent told his sins to the go-between, who related them to the Jesuit and then came back with the priest's reply.[100] Mutual understanding benefited tremendously from the arrival in 1553 of a nineteen-year-old Basque, Father José de Anchieta. Within six months of his arrival he had composed a rough draft of the grammar of the Tupi language.[101]

The Jesuits achieved their most spectacular success in the forested region between Brazil and Paraguay, where, from the late sixteenth century, they created a network of as many as thirty communities with perhaps 100,000 inhabitants. In the villages the Jesuits taught farming techniques and provided religious instruction. These communities caused—and still cause—intense debate. Spanish colonists in Asunción and Buenos Aires regarded the communities, which produced tea and cotton, as economic competitors. They accused the Jesuits of hoarding a valuable labor supply. Both Portuguese and Spanish authorities saw the missions, which they referred to as the "Jesuit Republic," as a threat to their riverine network between Brazil and modern Argentina. To ward off Spanish slave raiders and their counterparts from São Paulo, the *bandeirantes,* Indian males, were armed and trained. This step protected the mission for almost a century.[102]

To intellectuals then and now, the Jesuit Republic has been a source of considerable controversy. Some see it as a utopian experiment, removed from the corrupting grasp of Europe. Others have argued that it was a Jesuit slave state, in which Indians were exploited and their lives directed to the tiniest detail. These arguments were rendered moot when, in 1767, the Spanish Crown, concerned by rumors that Jesuits were conspiring against the King in Spain, decided to crush the entire order. Their expulsion from Spain and its colonies followed the earlier exile from Portugal and Brazil (1759) and the declaration that made them illegal in France (1764).

Missionaries in America usually tried, with mixed results, to extirpate pre-Columbian religions. In Mexico, Cortés' forces destroyed Indian religious sites, cleaned them with lime, and replaced images of Quetzalcoatl and other Indian gods with images of Christ and the Virgin Mary. However, in a process of religious syncretism, pre-Columbian and European religions became mixed, as priests constructed churches out of the stones of destroyed temples, and religious saints like the Aztec's Tonantzin and the Virgin Mary became intermingled, creating a new national symbol, the Virgin of Guadalupe. This process also occurred in Africa in 1658 when the king of Allada sent envoys to Spain in an attempt to obtain baptism. Capuchin monks, in conjunction with the Spanish Inquisition, drew up a catechism that mentioned the two elements of which the local godhead was composed, Vodu and Lisa, but identified them as God and Jesus Christ.[103]

The question of the extent to which religious syncretism was consciously guided by the Church, or whether it was largely a spontaneous development, remains a thorny issue. Catholicism appealed to Africans and Indians precisely because of the similarities with their own religions. Baptism and a Christian life, for instance, seemed to guarantee a reunion with loved ones after death.[104] It has been argued that Christianization did not mean that Africans suddenly accepted an entirely new world view. African conversions took place in a process in which Christian revelations were accepted, while Europeans approved of certain revelations of African mediums and diviners. Not until such an exchange was conducted could local deities merge with Catholic saints and angels.[105]

Syncretism is a term that conceals more than it reveals. It would be incorrect to assume that native religions, after the encounter with Europeans, developed into neatly compartmentalized sets of "traditional" and Christian beliefs. Rather, old and new religions were interwoven in various ways. Andean healers, for instance, mediating between the supernatural world and people's needs and concerns, adopted Christian concepts and prayers into their rituals. In doing so, they expanded their sources of sacred power.[106]

Objects supplied by Christians also fulfilled an important function. The Abenaki of New England enhanced their spiritual power by bartering for specific objects such as beads and mirrors. Europeans sneered at such trifles, but the spiritual dimension was of far greater significance to the Abenaki than the material side. Spiritual power was a better guarantee for them to survive inclement winters than gold.[107]

THE WORLD OF TRADE AND PRODUCTION

While gold was a decisive motive for Portugal's expansion in West Africa, precious metals were also on the minds of Spain's conquistadors. Just as King Ferdinand had dreamed about establishing lines of communication between the Canary Islands and "the mines of Ethiopia" (Africa),[108] the search for precious metals, as well as spices, motivated Columbus' first expedition.[109]

However, except for the earliest years, it was silver, not gold, that was discovered and exploited in Spanish America. Silver was needed as a medium of exchange in Europe as the continent's economies embarked on a period of new growth after 1450. Silver mines in Alsace, the Tyrol, Saxony, Bohemia, and Silesia were subsequently exploited again. As New World mines started operating, silver revolutionized European commerce. Silver, sometimes sequestered from private merchants in Seville, was increasingly used to finance Spain's numerous European wars and foreign trade imbalances. In this way, silver was diffused to Genoa and other Italian states, the Atlantic coast of France, and Spanish troops in Germany and the Low Countries. The flow of American silver facilitated the shift of Europe's economic axis in the sixteenth century from the Mediterranean to the Atlantic.[110] By the eighteenth century, about seventy percent of all precious metals was exported to Spain and Western Europe. Thereafter, these metals were re-exported to the Baltic, the Levant, and the Far East.[111] Thanks to the Manila Galleon, which sailed from Acapulco to Manila 1573–1811, Mexican silver also became an important means of exchange in China.

To guard the flow of silver against pirates and privateers, Spanish officials reorganized the country's transatlantic trading system, the *carrera de Indias*.[112] The architects of the *carrera de Indias* wanted two annual fleets to sail from Spain. The *flota,* the first fleet, left around July 1 for Veracruz in New Spain, where it arrived in September. After hibernating, the fleet would sail back at the end of May or in early June, stop in Havana, and reach Spain by the end of the summer. In the sixteenth century this fleet was made up of dozens of ships escorted by two galleons, vessels of over 500 and up to 800 tons, square-rigged and well-armed. The second convoy, the Tierra Firme fleet, was also called the *galeones,* because it was escorted by six to twelve armed galleons. It was of similar size and left Seville in May or June, arriving via Cartagena de Indias on the Isthmus of Panama around August. This fleet also returned the following summer.[113]

The famed silver mountain of Potosí, source of Spanish wealth. From *Il Gazzettiere Americano contenente un distinto ragguaglio di tutte le parti del Nuovo Mundo* (3 vols., Livorno, 1763), vol. III. *Courtesy of the Osher Map Library, University of Southern Maine.*

The location of silver mines determined the routes of these fleets. The fleets to Veracruz serviced the Mexican silver market, while those to Nombre de Dios on the Isthmus of Panama served the great silver mines of Potosí (in modern Bolivia). Veracruz was a city of local traders, innkeepers, and customs and treasury officers. Six hundred slaves were employed as cargo porters. Other exports included hides, wool, dyewood, indigo, and cochineal. Imports from Spain included wine, textiles, grain, paper, candles for the Church, ironware, and mercury, which was necessary to refine silver.[114]

In 1570 Nombre de Dios was a backwater with less than two hundred houses, but when the fleet arrived, "tent cities and temporary canvas warehouses would spring up on nearby beaches, and roaring commercial and social interaction would give these places the appearance of frenzied, round-the-clock activity."[115] Such a *feria* (trade fair) could last for several weeks. Just as in Veracruz, European commodities were exchanged here for American products, especially silver.[116]

Nature proved to be an even greater enemy to the treasure fleets than foreign interlopers. In the year 1563 alone, seven ships were driven ashore at Nombre de Dios, five were lost in the Gulf of Campeche, and fifteen wrecked in the harbor of Cádiz.[117] Passages between the Old World and the New remained hazardous, but the convoy system succeeded in protecting virtually all merchantmen crossing the Atlantic. From an economic point of view, the convoy system was flawed by the slow and unwieldy way in which goods were transported. In Spain, merchants sometimes urged postponing the sailing date because their goods were not ready. Postponements meant lengthy gaps between colonial demand and Spanish supply. There were delays on the colonial side as well. The transport of silver from the highlands of Potosí to the coast, thence by ship to Panama City, and across the Isthmus by mule trains to Portobelo was a complex affair. The fleet's own schedule was dependent on winds and the anxiety to avoid the hurricane season.[118]

As the sixteenth century advanced and Spain's territorial expansion in the New World continued, it was not unusual for conquistadors and merchants who had gone to the New World to come home to Seville, where they invested in the transatlantic trade. They had large real estate holdings in America and huge investments in New World sugar production, mining, herding, and pearl fishing.[119] For example, the conqueror of Mexico, Hernán Cortés, became the Marquis del Valle, lord of the rich valley of Central Mexico. He was the master of 115,000 *encomienda* Indians, at least according to his own estimate, and the first to plant sugar cane in Mexico. Many would follow, or try to follow, in his wake.

In Spain, thanks to the actions of its powerful merchant guild, Seville, despite its inconvenient location more than fifty miles up the Guadalquivir river, became the headquarters for Spain's transatlantic trade. The official receiving point for bullion, the Torre del Oro, was located there. The New World riches acted as a magnet on many foreigners—merchants, sailors, speculators—who settled in the port city.[120]

In the viceregal capital cities of Mexico City and Lima, an increasing number of merchants specialized in selling *feria* products. Many of them were engaged in both silver production and export, and created an alternative circuit alongside the official one.[121] With business operations expanding, the Lima merchants began to bypass the *ferias* in the late sixteenth century sending employees to Seville and Cádiz to do direct business. By the 1620s, these *peruleros* did an extensive trade in Andalusia, especially with foreign business houses, and ended up practically controlling both wholesale and retail markets.[122] However, by the second half of the seventeenth century, foreign smuggling had undercut the *peruleros* and forced them out of the market.

Price battles between the merchants of Spain and their American colleagues figured largely in the history of the fleet system. The Americans would postpone most purchases to the very end of the *feria,* when the departure date was made public and the Spanish merchants, anxious to sell their goods, lowered their prices. *Flota* ships would be anchored for weeks or months in Veracruz and San Juan de Ulúa. During this period Spanish merchants were living in Mexico City and paying rent.[123]

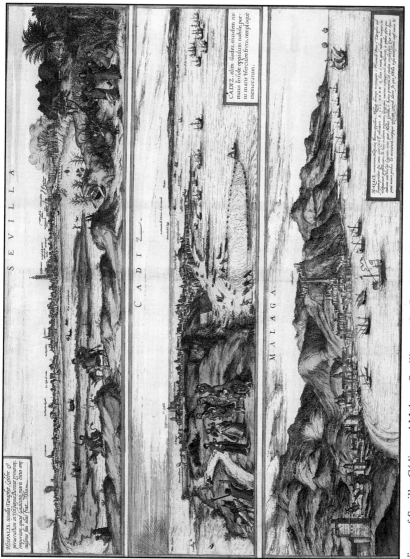

Views of Seville, Cádiz, and Malaga. Seville was the first hub of Spain's transatlantic trade, officially succeeded by Cádiz in 1717, when the Guadalquivir River was silted up, blocking Seville's access to the Atlantic. From: George Braun and Frans Hogenberg, *Civitates Orbis Terrarum* (1574-82). *Courtesy of the Osher Map Library, University of Southern Maine.*

Although the seventeenth century is sometimes called the age of Spain's decline, silver imports from its colonies did not diminish. On the contrary, silver production more than doubled compared to the previous century. It would double again in the eighteenth century. The relative weight of the production areas shifted; whereas Upper Peru (Bolivia) accounted for almost half the production before 1700, its share fell dramatically in the next one hundred years, and Mexico became America's chief silver producer.[124]

It has been argued that "beyond the Line," that is, in the Caribbean and South Atlantic, there was rarely peace of any kind.[125] Nonetheless, despite the growing naval power of its enemies, Spain was able to hold on to its major mainland and insular possessions. It was only peripheral areas, such as the Guianas and certain of the smaller Caribbean islands that fell under the sway of Northwest Europeans.

Unable to beat Spain, Northwest Europeans decided to collaborate with the Iberians. Foreigners soon dominated the *carrera de Indias.* They had the necessary capital and products that the New World wanted. At the close of the century, much of the silver arriving from America was no longer brought ashore, but collected directly by foreign ships in Cádiz, which had succeeded Seville as the hub of the Indies trade. French, Genoese, Flemish, English, and Dutch traders all had a stake in the *carrera,* while the share of Spanish-produced goods aboard the fleets leaving Cádiz dropped to a mere five percent in 1691.[126]

On the other side of the Atlantic, Northwest Europeans exploited the numerous problems inherent in *carrera de Indias,* including the weakness of Spain's textile industry and the high costs involved in the convoy system. From their new bases in the Caribbean, Dutch, French, and English traders illegally provided the inhabitants of Spanish colonies with contraband textiles, hardware, and spices in return for bullion and locally produced crops. This trade began to take business away from Spanish merchants, repeatedly wrecking the trade fairs. At the same time, the fairs were hit by the Far East trade via Acapulco, which brought Chinese cloth, gold, and chinaware to New Spain in exchange for bullion, cacao, and cochineal.[127]

Likewise, thanks to the Treaty of Utrecht of 1713, British ships were allowed to enter Spanish American ports by virtue of an agreement between the Spanish state and the South Sea Company. These so-called Annual Ships were involved in large-scale illicit transactions. This hurt the Mexican and Peruvian traders who had invested in the cargoes of *flotas* and *galeones,* and strongly resented the trade of the Annual Ships.[128]

Portugal also tried to protect its transatlantic commerce, particularly after the fiasco of 1647–1648, when Dutch privateers captured three-quarters of Lisbon's trade with Brazil. Unfortunately, the plan to send fleets every year from Lisbon to Rio de Janeiro, Recife, Salvador, and Maranhão was unfeasible. Sugar and tobacco planters paid the price for the lack of shipping; they were often hit twice in a row, since the fleet arriving the next year would carry two harvests, thereby driving prices down. The Spanish trade system made less sense in the case of the Portuguese Atlantic, since the transports involved a much larger proportion of perishable goods.[129]

A feature Portugal shared with Spain's transatlantic trade was the infiltration of foreign merchants. By virtue of Anglo-Portuguese treaties signed in 1654 and 1703,

English merchants came to dominate Portugal's transatlantic trade. They benefitted from Brazil's gold and diamond boom, obtaining two-thirds of Brazil's gold in exchange for their supplies of cloth and other commodities. Throughout the eighteenth century, gold was the most important product that the Portuguese fleets brought to Lisbon.[130] Timothy Walker argues in his chapter in this collection, *Lisbon as a Strategic Haven in the Atlantic World,* that bullion imports were so massive that they enabled the Portuguese to rebuild their capital city after a powerful earthquake in 1755. The Marquis de Pombal, Portugal's chief minister 1756–1777, introduced comprehensive plans aimed at retaining precious metals within the empire and emancipating Portugal's Atlantic trade from its dependence on foreigners. Like Spain, however, Portugal, never developed a national merchant class, one with sufficient capital, intelligence, and market savvy to take advantage of the bullion that flowed through Lisbon on the way to more energetic European entrepreneurs.[131]

TOBACCO AND SUGAR

While Europeans never gave up their dreams of new Eldorados, as time passed other sources of wealth, such as tobacco and sugar, became increasingly important. The Spanish began to cultivate tobacco in Hispaniola and some Caribbean islands, and seed from Trinidad probably found its way to the English colonists of Virginia, where in 1612 John Rolfe, the husband of Pocahontas, took up cultivation of *Nicotiana tabacum.* Spanish growing, harvesting, and curing methods, more complex than Indian practices and responsible for a better tasting product, were adopted in Bermuda and the Lesser Antilles and Chesapeake. As a cash crop, tobacco was vital to the survival of the early non-Spanish settlements in the Antilles because it could be produced by smallholders with relatively modest amounts of capital and manpower. Before 1680, indentured servants not only produced the tobacco of Virginia and Maryland, many of them turned planter after the terms of their contracts had been fulfilled.[132] Consumption spread to the Old World, and so did tobacco production, which was established in England, Wales, France, Brandenburg, the Palatinate, and the United Provinces, the main area of European cultivation.[133]

The South Atlantic had its own tobacco trade. In the last quarter of the seventeenth century a regular link was forged between the tobacco region near Brazil's capital, Bahia, and several African destinations. Brazil's tobacco planters produced three annual harvests, only one of which found a market in Lisbon. Planters prepared the other two grades for sale in Africa, giving this tobacco a particular taste and aroma. Portugal's African colonies of Angola, São Tomé, Principe, and Benguela were among the importers, but the main customer was the Gold Coast. In ever larger numbers, Bahian vessels exchanged their tobacco shipments for African slaves.[134]

The middle decades of the seventeenth century saw the transition from tobacco to sugar in the English and French Caribbean. Tobacco floundered, because productivity was lower than the competition in the Chesapeake, and the quality inferior.[135] The war against the Dutch in Brazil distracted Hapsburg defenses in the Caribbean, facilitating the settlement of French and English in the Windward

Islands. As the war hampered Brazil's sugar production, prices skyrocketed, providing an opportunity for the English and French settlers in the West Indies to adopt sugar as a new crop.[136]

The "sugar revolution" in the Caribbean was labor-intensive and demanded large-scale operations to be profitable. Since Europeans were too small in number, and unwilling to perform the brutal stoop labor required in planting and cutting cane, large numbers of workers would have to come from Africa. Thus, sugar and slavery came to be bonded in the Caribbean. As the Cuban sociologist Fernando Ortiz has observed, tobacco, grown by small farmers, was a democratic crop, while sugar, requiring vast plantations and slave labor, was not.[137]

The "sugar revolution" was propelled by a "consumer revolution" in Europe, in which, thanks to the rise of incomes and aspirations, sugar and other tropical commodities came increasingly into the hands of ordinary consumers. While none of the goods had previously been in large demand, their subsequent per capita consumption rose steadily. Sugar enjoyed the most spectacular expansion, overtaking grain in the mid-eighteenth century as the most valuable commodity on the world market. In 1792 crowds gathered in revolutionary Paris to protest the rising price not of bread, but sugar.[138]

Sugar had proved to be a bonanza in Brazil, which remains the world's largest producer of cane sugar to this day. Its production had a multiplier effect, as it required the investment of capital in sugar mills and African slaves.[139] Once it moved to Barbados and other Caribbean islands, including Cuba in the eighteenth century, sugar was responsible for one of the most dramatic regional transformations in the history of the western hemisphere. Spain had taken up West Indian sugar cultivation a century earlier, using Canarian processing techniques, but without lasting success. In the hands of the English and French, sugar was enthroned as the premier cash crop. From a backwater, the area became an economic laboratory, where the reign of capitalism went unchallenged. The tobacco planter was ousted by the entrepreneur who operated a factory-type business that required massive investments: "He needed one or two mills to extract juice from the harvested cane, a boiling house to clarify and evaporate the cane juice into sugar crystals, a curing house for drying the sugar and draining out the molasses, a distillery for converting the molasses into rum, and a storehouse in the nearest port for keeping his barreled sugar" until it could be shipped to Europe.[140]

A new demographic *milieu* was created in the process, as the coexistence of small groups of Europeans and natives gave way to a population dominated by slaves imported from Africa. The environment also suffered, as forests were cut down to provide fields and fuel for sugar cane operators.[141]

IMPERIAL AND TRANS-IMPERIAL TRADE

A common feature of the Spanish and British empires in the Atlantic was the relative insignificance of colonial markets for domestic industries. The interests of manufacturers who wanted to find colonial outlets for their commodities were usually subordinated to those of businessmen involved in growing colonial crops for the European markets. The explanation is simple: Spain and, for a long time, Britain, sent goods mostly to the colonies that had originated elsewhere in Europe. Industrial products (textiles and hardware) dominated supplies to certain areas (New Spain, Buenos Aires, the Thirteen Colonies), while agricultural products and foodstuffs were preferred in other places (Caracas, the British West Indies).[142] As the eighteenth century advanced, however, the North American market increased in importance for England. By 1772–1774, the mainland colonies took 47 percent of all English manufacture exports (woollen cloth, linens, silk, cottons, and hardware), which helped the English offset the decline of their exports to Europe.[143]

In other respects, Spanish and British trades across the Atlantic had little in common. For example, Britain's well-studied tobacco trade with the Chesapeake—which provided the British with their most lucrative commercial North American connection[144]—was fundamentally different from Spain's bullion trade. Much of the tobacco was shipped under the so-called consignment system. British merchants loaded tools, furniture, clothing, and other items intended for the planters on their ships for the westbound voyage, and arranged for warehousing and marketing in Britain. The planter, who owned the tobacco until it was sold, took care of the risks and all expenses made prior to the sale. These arrangements were not necessarily advantageous to the planter, who found himself in a permanent state of indebtedness. The merchant granted him credit against the security of his next tobacco crop, and the planter hoped that the next harvest would make good the debt. Frequently, it did not.[145]

The sugar business of the French and British did not deviate substantially from the tobacco model, insofar as it was managed and financed from Europe, while the crop was produced for the metropolis, where it was either consumed or re-exported.[146] Historian David Hancock has revealed another model, in which the management and distribution is not located in the metropolis. He shows how the traders in Madeira wine responded to specific tastes and opportunities from Boston to Bahia and Copenhagen to Canton, thus creating a highly customized product. This decentralized principle may also have been operative in the Carolina rice trade after 1731.[147]

The triangular trade, which brought manufactured goods from England to Africa and slaves from Africa to the Caribbean, and thence sugar and rum back to England, although often cited in textbooks, was not the most common form of Atlantic trade. Rather it was the shuttle, or round trip voyage, that predominated. Round trip voyages produced experienced captains and increased the chance of a punctual delivery and a landing around the time that colonial crops were available. While not exceptional, multilateral voyages were the domain of risk-takers. These voyages might be necessary when a dependable home market for certain commodities was lacking.[148] Atlantic trade could be minimal if an area produced little in the way of marketable goods. Canada received no more than a dozen French ships per year in 1713–1743, whereas the number of vessels sailing from France to the small sugar- and coffee-producing French islands in the Caribbean rose from 101 in 1674 to 392 around 1750.[149]

While planters, especially in the French Caribbean colonies, always found a ready market for sugar, they had more difficulty in selling sugar's by-products, rum and molasses. Despite the British Molasses Act (1733), which imposed a heavy tax on products from foreign Caribbean colonies imported into British America, a regular rum trade developed between the French islands and New England. Authorities on both sides legalized or connived at the transactions.[150] Illicit exports from European countries to British America were not very common, because the quality of British woollens was higher and the price lower. There was a market, however, for tea. Estimates are that more than half, perhaps even ninety percent, of tea drunk in the Thirteen Colonies had been smuggled in.[151]

Smugglers were generally foreigners or traders in league with other empires. Contraband trade with foreign ships was especially widespread in some parts of Spanish America, as the smaller colonies were not served by the "annual" convoys. Thus, English merchants sailing from Jamaica discovered markets in Cuba and New Granada, Dutchmen from Curaçao sold to Venezuela, and Portuguese traders from Brazil did business with Buenos Aires.[152] The infiltration of Portuguese merchants into the Río de la Plata, which began in the 1580s, was made possible by the Crown union between the two Iberian countries, the proximity of Brazil, the competence of Portuguese seamen, and the Portuguese monopoly (until 1640) of slave supplies to Spanish America. Regular complaints of rival Peruvian traders and Spanish functionaries point to the presence of scores of Portuguese in Buenos Aires and its hinterland, securing silver from Potosí.[153]

Not even warfare could halt friendly inter-imperial relations. The wars of the mid-eighteenth century saw the frequent involvement of so-called flags of truce, ships sailing under a peace flag, in smuggling. Prisoners of war were returned to colonies of their own nation. The ships fitted out for such missions enjoyed an immunity that was shamelessly abused to conduct illicit trade. The ownership titles for these vessels were even for sale on some Caribbean islands. Contraband trade challenged the central notion of colonialism: the mercantilist philosophy that the commerce of a nation's colonies existed exclusively for the benefit of the metropolis. Exports to colonies of rival nations were absolutely forbidden, while colonial imports could only come from the metropolis. This policy was often impossible to enforce, as individuals from different empires wove webs of mutual dependence across the Atlantic world. For example, Portuguese ships (legally or legally) arriving from Angola in Buenos Aires in the 1630s sold their slaves for silver and gold, which they then frequently exchanged for sugar in Brazilian ports, before leaving for Spain, Portugal, Angola, or the Canaries.[154]

Such commercial contacts across imperial boundaries fostered the development of multiple personal and cultural relations in the Caribbean. The architecture of Bridgetown, Barbados, acquired a distinctly Dutch flavor, while the predominantly Catholic population of Dutch Curaçao often listened to a Spanish priest in church on Sundays.[155] The leaders of a revolt in Martinique in 1717, for their part, called for a local government of two chambers in accordance with the English model.[156] Finally, communication networks not only linked traders, but also enslaved blacks. Slave uprisings in Jamaica and nearby Cuba may have influenced one another in the 1730s, while later in the century, even before the outbreak of the great rebellion in St. Domingue, rumors forecasting the end of slavery spread across national and linguistic boundaries.[157]

SLAVERY AND THE SLAVE TRADE

Slaves in the Americas were controlled and coerced by the use of brutal methods. An Italian Jesuit in the sugar region of Bahia in Brazil witnessed slaves being burned with hot wax, branded on the face or chest, and tortured with hot irons. Others had their ears or noses lopped off. The author asked Brazil's slave owners: is such behavior rational or humane?[158] Treated with disdain everywhere, Africans' labor, religion, and culture would nonetheless transform the Americas.

Slavery has been part of the human experience since time immemorial. Slaves made up around one-third of the population of both ancient Athens and Italy during the heyday of the Roman Republic. Slavery receded in the wake of Rome's fall in 476, and it was not until the tenth century that Christian Europeans became involved again in the slave trade. Merchants from Genoa and Venice dealt especially in enslaved people from Greece and the Slavic world. In the Italian colonies founded in Palestine after the First Crusade, slaves were used in agriculture, industry, and as domestic servants.[159]

In the late Middle Ages, Spanish Muslims and Christians raided each other's lands, enslaving and selling their war prisoners. Through trade with Arab merchants, Christian Europe also obtained slaves from pagan sub-Saharan Africa. Lisbon had ten thousand bonded Africans in the mid-sixteenth century, while by 1565 there were over 6,000 in Seville, or one in fourteen inhabitants. Domestic slaves commonly lived in their masters' households, but some both worked and lived outside the masters' homes, living apart in Seville's poorer districts. The first black slaves introduced into the New World came from Seville, and some of them had been born in the city.[160]

The slave trade from Africa to Iberia diminished after the discovery of the New World,[161] but even after the end of the *reconquista,* Muslim seamen from North Africa were seized and sold as far north as London.[162] Muslim privateers from Africa's Barbary states were a match for their Christian counterparts, enslaving thousands and perhaps tens of thousands of Catholic and Protestant sailors. In 1575, Moorish privateers captured Miguel de Cervantes, the author of *Don Quixote,* and did not release him until 1580. The captives were used as oarsmen in galleys, and gardeners and domestics in the households of rich Muslims in Algiers, Tunis, and Tripoli. Freedom could only be obtained through ransom or conversion to Islam.[163]

When the Portuguese reached Guinea, "the land of the blacks," in the late 1440s, they soon entered the slave trade.[164] Slavery in Africa by Africans was a time-honored institution. Since land in Africa belonged to the extended family, the only remaining way of investing capital was to buy slaves. In this sense, the position and treatment of slaves was more akin to that of Europe's free tenants and hired hands.[165] Slaves in Europe and the Americas were usually employed in work shunned by free workers. In the Americas this often meant the dangerous work of cutting sugar cane which involved stoop labor under a blazing sun, danger from self-injury by machetes, and the risk of snake bite and being blinded by the needle-sharp shards of sugar cane.

Ironically, the Portuguese first took part in the African slave trade not to satisfy European, but African demand. Their customers included Akan entrepreneurs who were extending the area for local crop cultivation and needed workers. Lured by the prospect of exchanging slaves for gold, the Portuguese used their maritime expertise to import slaves from more eastern parts of the African coast. After 1515, they developed the islands of São Tomé and Principe, just off Africa, as slave depots, and slave markets also opened on islands like Madeira and the Canaries.[166]

Sugar, originally an Asian crop, had made its way into Europe from Palestine, where it was cultivated on Christian estates in the twelfth century. From there, sugar moved westward from Cyprus and Crete to Sicily and thence to the coast of Islamic Spain. In the late fifteenth century, Christian Castile started sugarcane production in the recently-conquered Canary Islands, where sugar became so important that it was adopted as an alternative currency. In the early sixteenth century, as enslaved islanders in Madeira and the Canaries began to die from European diseases, African slaves were imported. While sugar production in the Canaries declined, in the Madeira islands, where native Canarians (Guanches) were put to work side-by-side with Africans, sugar thrived. As it found a market in northern Europe, production was expanded. As early as 1493, the islands had eighty master sugar manufacturers. Producing solely for export, and worked by African slaves, the Madeira sugar estate was the prototype of later colonial plantations in America.[167]

In Africa, the Portuguese, and the Europeans who came after them, did not establish "settler colonies," as on the Atlantic islands and in the New World. Due to malaria and other tropical diseases, West Africa was deadly for Europeans. The region had the highest morbidity and mortality rates for outsiders anywhere in the world. It was only in the middle decades of the nineteenth century that European death rates declined, due to improved ventilation, clean water, sewage disposal, and the habit of moving to higher altitudes.[168]

Thus, plans to colonize Africa in the seventeenth and eighteenth centuries were extremely rare. Africa's reputation as an insalubrious place caused Portuguese officials and traders to leave their families behind.[169] Still, a lone French schemer in 1688 designed a comprehensive plan to make Senegal into a settler colony. He anticipated the migration of men and women from France, who would cultivate rice and grain on land that was to be occupied despite the possibility of tensions with natives.[170] The plan never materialized.

A coastal fort, housing a governor, a garrison of soldiers, and a few merchants who rarely ventured far outside, made up the typical European establishment in Africa. This "factory" was fortified, not so much against native encroachment, but to fend off European rivals. The Europeans also counted on naval power to protect their national interests. Philip Curtin has described how a game of musical trading posts evolved in Senegambia, where the "style of warfare among Europeans . . . involved a dominant defender and an aggressive challenger at each stage. In the first half of the seventeenth century, the Portuguese defended against the Dutch, while France and England watched, more or less inactive, on the sidelines. Then as the Dutch became supreme in the 1660s and 1670s, English and French acted together to dislodge them, just as Holland and England were to act together against the French from the 1690s to the 1710s."[171]

As trading partners, Europeans and Africans did not attack each other. As it was, they merely tried to maintain themselves, which meant adjusting to local circumstances. The famous English pirate and privateer John Hawkins, for example, was only able to acquire slaves in Sierra Leone in 1568 by participating in an internal war, engaging himself and his men as mercenaries.[172] Few Europeans before or after Hawkins engaged in battle, however, in their attempt to procure slaves.

While it never extinguished the Islamic trade in black Africans to North Africa and the Middle East, the Atlantic slave trade did become more important as New World demand increased. By 1650, the number of African slaves imported by Christians to America outstripped the number purchased by Muslims in the Middle East.[173] The European side obtained permission to trade by presenting an assortment of goods. Dutch cargoes generally included Dutch and German textiles, East Indian cotton fabric, and loincloth from Benin. The goods the Europeans offered were of high value in the local economies. Indian cotton cloth could be made into clothes, and iron into tools, and both could be used as a form of money.[174]

Most African slaves did not come from the coast, but from the interior. These slaves were used to carry trading goods to the coast. Men carried up to twenty-five kilo each, females up to fifteen.[175] The slaves' backgrounds varied widely. Those sold in Allada around 1670 included "prisoners of war, slaves contributed in tribute by neighbouring kingdoms, people born into slavery within the country, and others enslaved for criminal offences (including the families of those executed for state crimes) and for non-payment of debts."[176] The sale of Africans by fellow Africans was routine because African merchants had no sense of shared ethnic or regional identity with their captives.[177]

The European purchase of slaves could take a long time. The slave ship spent several months sailing up and down the coast until the ship's hold was filled,[178] and then the slaves had to be examined. English captain Thomas Phillips reported in 1693 that "The king's slaves, if he had any, were the first to be offered for sale. . . . [we] observed they were generally the worst slaves in the trunk, and we paid more for them . . . then the *cappasheirs* [headmen] each brought out his slaves according to his degree and quality, the greatest first, and our surgeon examin'ed them well in all kinds, to see that they were sound, wind and limb, making them jump, stretch out their arms swiftly, looking in their mouths to judge of their age; for the *cappasheirs* are so cunning, that they shave them all close before we see them, so that let them never be so old we can see no grey hairs on their heads or beards; and then having liquor'd them well and sleeked with palm oil, 'tis no easy matter to know an old one from a middle-aged one, but by the teeths decay. But our greatest care of all is to buy none that are pox'd, lest they should infect the rest aboard . . . and that distemper which they call the yaws,* is very common here."[179]

Slaves shipped to Spanish America were *piezas de Indias*. A *pieza* was an adult slave in the prime of his or her life (from 15 to 35 years of age), of a certain height and without considerable physical defects. Children and adults with bad teeth, poor eyesight, or a disease were counted as fractions of the ideal slave. Slaves from "nations" in Africa known for rebellion or laziness were anathema. Slaves were like any other commodity: a lack of consumer satisfaction led to a fall in demand.[180]

---

*A chronic infectious disease characterized by bumps on the skin.

The voyage to the New World must have seem to the slaves like a descent into hell, if they had such a concept. Two Jesuits who regularly ministered to the sick and dying aboard slave ships arriving from Africa in Cartagena de Indias invariably found the stench unbearable. They often discovered corpses that were still fettered, flies flying in and out of their open mouths.[181] Gastrointestinal disorders and fevers accounted for most fatalities. The death rate did decline over time, from twenty percent around 1600 to less than ten percent in the late eighteenth century, as slave diets came to include lime juice to prevent scurvy, as well as more African foods and condiments.[182] There were doctors on board tending to the slaves, but they were helpless in the face of rapidly-spreading diseases, which had usually originated in the port of embarkation.[183]

Recent research has shown that the slave business was not as lucrative as once thought. The cost entering the trade, the long time spent purchasing slaves, and especially the long wait for the recovery of all profits, made it hard to run a profitable slaving firm. Only highly capitalized companies were successful. At the end of the day, only a few merchants, brokers, and insurers, as well as some shipyards and transshipment companies, were the beneficiaries of the slave business.[184]

By the 1560s, Europeans were legitimizing some of their slave operations by claiming that they were rescuing natives who might otherwise be killed by enemy nations, but one Spanish writer of that era argued that the Iberians in fact helped to inspire tribal warfare by buying the resulting prisoners.[185] The European presence and demand for slaves did, indeed, change the dynamics. Kidnapping of outsiders increased and some communities began selling their own members, as enslavement replaced other forms of punishment, such as payment, exile, or beatings.[186]

Although the Atlantic slave trade thus accounted for a loss of African population through slave exports, warfare, and displacement, African export revenue and import purchasing power were greatly enhanced. From 1680–1870, profits from the slave trade were used by African slavers to import increasing amounts of goods from Europe.[187] In this way, African production and consumption increased, and the commercialization of the economies was accelerated.[188]

Table 1.1 reveals how the destinations of the Atlantic slave trade shifted over time. While Europe and the Atlantic islands were the main receiving regions before 1600, Brazil took over after that date, ultimately becoming the leading overall importer of Africans during the entire slave era. From 1651 to 1800, the Caribbean, however, was the main slave destination, importing 45.3 percent of all slaves in the second half of the seventeenth century and 54.5 percent in the eighteenth century. North America was statistically insignificant before 1700, and of only slight importance afterwards.[189]

These percentages, however, mask the dramatic growth of the slave trade in the seventeenth and eighteenth centuries. The annual arrivals of African slaves in transatlantic destinations increased in the following way: 1,700 (1476–1500); 3,800 (1576–1600); 24,100 (1676–1700); 68,800 (1761–1800). In the nineteenth century, abolitionism reduced the volume from 57,950 (1801–1830) to 37,500 (1831–1860), before it finally dropping to 3,800 (1861–1870).[190]

Africans were imported to the New World to work on sugar, tobacco, coffee, and cotton plantations and wherever else their labor was needed. Several Spanish colonies had a large native work force, but entrepreneurs still valued African laborers, since they were totally mobile. Indians could only be temporarily removed from

TABLE 1.1 The Transatlantic Slave Trade: Sending and Receiving Regions

Sending Region	1662–1699	1700–1799	1800–1867	Overall
Senegambia	6.5[1]	5.2	7.5	
Sierra Leone		10.9	2.9[2]	21.1[3]
Gold Coast	12.9	9.9		
Bight of Benin	43.6	19.0	15.1	19.6
Bight of Biafra	18.2	18.0	14.4	17.4
W.C. Africa	17.4	37.0	48.4	41.2
S.E. Africa	1.2		11.7	4.1

Receiving Region	1451–1600	1601–1700	1701–1800	1801–1867	Overall
Europe	17.8	0.1			0.5
Atlantic Islands	36.8	1.8			1.2
Spanish America	27.3	21.8	8.9	27.0	16.2
Brazil	18.2	41.8	29.7	59.3	39.3
British WI		19.7	21.9	4.0	16.0
French WI		11.6	25.0	3.9	16.6
Dutch WI		3.0	6.9		4.3
Danish WI		0.3	0.7	0.1	0.5
British NA/USA			6.8	5.7	5.5

Calculated on the basis of Herbert S. Klein, *The Atlantic Slave Trade* (Cambridge: Cambridge University Press, 1999): 208-211.

[1]Includes slaves sent from Sierra Leone
[2]Includes slaves sent from the Gold Coast
[3]Includes slaves from Senegambia and the Gold Coast

their lands. The small size of the respective Indian populations and the aversion of European immigrants, no matter how poor, to the typically long, monotonous, and degrading labor, made the planters' choice of Africans an obvious one.[191]

The two contradictory dominant views which Europeans had of Indians, whom they portrayed as either barbarians or noble savages, were also conspicuous in European depictions of Africans. Perceived African cruelty and brutality served to legitimize enslavement, but as the years passed, and the abolitionist movement gained pace, a growing number of Europeans saw blacks as noble savages. Prior to the anti-slavery movement, blacks in America were equated with animals in various ways. They were bought at markets, branded, and given brutal punishments, and many whites emphasized their beastlike nature.[192] Slave labor was often unskilled, but not always. Many Africans arrived with experience in iron-working, rice production, or animal husbandry, skills that had usually been passed down from generation to generation, and were put to good use in the New World.[193]

An arriving slave lost his or her membership in an extended or lineage family, and along with it, arranged marriages, dowries, and ancestral shrines vanished. As the slaves adapted to new economic and demographic environments, the nuclear slave family emerged as the norm. Marital bonds were stronger than in Africa, where the role of the extended family was more prominent.[194] By no means did blacks mechanically adopt new, American, ways. Rather, their African identities were partially transformed on the other side of the Atlantic. Many Africans were no longer identified as members of a certain nation because they had been born there, but because they behaved like them and spoke their language.[195]

Africans, like Europeans, also brought their religious beliefs, concepts, and practices to the Americas. Their songs, games, dances, and cuisine were all based on African models. Either single nations or entire black communities, from New England to New Granada and from Mexico to Brazil, annually chose their own kings and queens, followed by parades and festivities.[196]

Belief in the spirits of dead kinfolk remained strong in the Americas. The African spirit world "was densely peopled and constantly served individuals in the course of daily activities, by households, religious specialists, village and society-wide celebrations with sacrifices, music, dance and feasting. People sought in particular good health and crops, large families and protection from misfortune. The power of the spirit world was manifested in innumerable ways: through dreams and signs, through direct communication by mediums, through messages interpreted by diviners."[197] For several generations after their arrival, blacks believed that their spirits would return to Africa to join their ancestors after they died. At the same time, slaves adopted elements of their Christian surroundings. African religions, with their numerous gods, some of whom personified destiny or forces of nature, and their spirits of deceased ancestors, were congruent more with Roman Catholic cosmology, in which Mary and a vast array of saints mediated between the believer and the Christian God, than with Protestantism.[198]

Paul Lovejoy, in his essay *Trans-Atlantic Transformations: The Origins and Identity of Africans in the Americas,* maintains that both religion and ethnicity helped enslaved Africans in the Americas to form communities. Many Africans used ethnic identification as a strategy to resist their ascribed identity as racially-inferior slaves. They did not simply fall back upon African practices, but established new identities by forging pan-ethnic groups. Muslims of different ethnic backgrounds, however, identified on the basis of religion. Both factors have to be considered together to get a full understanding of their impact.

Enslaved Africans did not resign themselves to their plight. In his chapter in the present collection, *Identity and Migration: The Atlantic in Comparative*

Perspective, David Eltis reveals the significance of shipboard resistance. The disproportionate number of revolts among Africans who had embarked in Upper Guinea probably forced European slavers to avoid this region, despite its proximity to Europe and the American plantations. Eltis emphasizes African agency, arguing that by revolting, Africans influenced the pattern of transatlantic migration.

Once at work in the New World, Africans tried to escape their bleak existence. Some absented themselves individually for a few days or even weeks, while others ran away, alone or in groups, with no intention of returning. Planters in the French colonies distinguished between these two phenomena as *petit marronage* and *grand marronage,* respectively.[199] Runaway slaves, or maroons, emerged all over America in often impressive numbers. In Venezuela in 1810, for every four African slaves there was at least one runaway.[200] Here and there, maroon settlements became permanent villages, especially where mountains or forests provided safe hideouts. The maroons' strength in Suriname and Jamaica was such that the colonial authorities signed peace treaties with the fugitives.

Protest sometimes took the form of outright rebellion. Many slave plots and revolts had failed or were betrayed at the eleventh hour. One of the most successful slave uprisings in history occured in 1791 in St. Domingue. This French colony, probably the world's largest sugar and coffee producer at the time, had half a million slaves within its borders, predominantly recent arrivals. The rebellion, which elite slaves on some 200 plantations had plotted in utmost secrecy, swept through the colony. Within a month, about 1,000 of the 8,000 plantations were burned.[201]

The French colonial government in St. Domingue had been expecting trouble, but not from black slaves. Rather, they were concerned that the call of the French Revolution in 1789 for liberty had led "free coloreds," some of whom were slaveholders, to seek equal rights for themselves. Although the National Assembly in Paris granted free coloreds full equality on May 15, 1791, the whites in the colony refused to accept it. The free people of color then began to take up arms. At this junction, the slave revolt broke out in August 1791.

Ironically, the slaves did not fight in the name of the Revolution of 1789. Believing that the French king had granted them freedom, they battled to defend Church and King. Their fight was also influenced by African political concepts.[202] In Paris, the leaders of the Revolution valued economic imperatives over humanitarian ideals, as they sent an army to the colony to crush the rebellion. The official proclamation of the end of slavery by the French Revolution's representatives in St. Domingue in August 1793 came too late. The colonial revolution had by then struck out on a course of its own, irrespective of the events in Paris.

A complex war ensued, in which blacks and mulattoes, as well as British, Irish, French, Spanish, German, and even Polish[203] soldiers, participated. Whereas the encounter between Europe and America had been marked by the disastrous effects of Old World diseases on Indians, it was now the Europeans who fell victim, by the thousands, to disease, most notably yellow fever. In comparison, relatively few died in battle.[204] Slavery would not return to St. Domingue, which declared itself independent in 1804. Its new name was Haiti, and it was the world's first independent black state.

FREEDOM AND REVOLUTION

The craving for freedom had motivated some Europeans, including Puritans, Quakers, New Christians, and Jews, to settle in America. While in their mother countries Europeans lived in a straitjacket of rules and regulations, in the colonies metropolitan norms were often not rigorously applied.[205] Court decisions in New England regarding premarital sex were, for instance, remarkably lenient, influenced as they were by a popular secular morality, which contrasted with Old England, where the church and clergy acted as moral guardians.[206] Elsewhere in the Americas, the scope for piracy, corruption, and—as we have seen—smuggling, was much wider than in Europe.

It remains to be seen whether this divergence between European and American practices played a role in the pursuit of political liberty and economic opportunity that marked the Atlantic revolutions in the half-century after 1775. In its broadest sense, political freedom in the Americas meant the demolition of the European colonial system which had dominated the region since the early sixteenth century. Thus, the American revolutionary war against its English masters (1775–1783) inaugurated a period that has been called "the Age of Democratic Revolutions," marked by political upheaval on both sides of the Atlantic.

In North America, the Thirteen Colonies were transformed into the United States of America, informed by an Enlightenment ideology of rationalism, secularism, and democracy which had long been cultivated in Europe, particularly by French intellectuals who despised the decadent aristocracies of Europe. The United States came to serve as a model nation, due to its youth, vast space, and exemption from Old World injustice.[207] The Founding Fathers, on their part, applauded the French Revolution. Whereas John Adams' response may have been to "rejoice with trembling," Thomas Jefferson unambiguously sided with the French revolutionaries, even when they became increasingly radical.[208] He was an exception, however. The terror of 1793–1794 alienated France's American supporters. Likewise, once their Revolution was underway, the French no longer needed foreign models.

The "Age of Democratic Revolutions" did not end with the birth of Haiti in 1804. German author Heinrich Heine wrote in 1823: "What is the great task of our time? Emancipation. Not merely the Irish, the Greeks, the Jews of Frankfurt, the West Indian Negroes and other oppressed peoples in various parts of the world, but emancipation of the whole world (. . . .)"[209] When Heine committed this thought to paper, Mexico had declared its independence from Spain, and Brazil had severed its connection with Portugal. In 1824, the Spanish provinces in South America won their last battle against troops from the mother country, forcing Spain to abandon mainland America altogether.

The revolutionary struggles in the Atlantic world can only be understood in an international context. The North American uprising against Britain would probably not have succeeded without the help of expeditionary forces and cash from Britain's French and Spanish enemies, and military supplies from the French and Dutch West Indies. France also played a key role in the outbreak of the wars in Latin America in the early nineteenth century. Napoleon's invasion of Portugal in 1807 led to the move of the Portuguese court from Lisbon to Rio de Janeiro. The flight to Brazil of the Portuguese king and 10,000 of his supporters caused a remarkable change. Now Portugal became the colony, Brazil the metropolis. It was only a matter of time before Brazil would be independent. One year after he invaded Portugal, Napoleon imprisoned the Spanish king, Ferdinand VII, and his father, Charles IV, and ordered his own brother to fill the vacant throne. The seizure of power set in motion a long chain of unprecedented events on the other side of the Atlantic. Refusing to be ruled by a Frenchman, Spain's colonies first declared their autonomy, and then, one by one, their independence. After Napoleon's defeat and first exile in 1814, Ferdinand returned to the Spanish throne and immediately sent a large army to reclaim his rebellious American colonies. Nine years of warfare ensued, in which the creole insurgents looked to Great Britain as an ally. The British government, however, refrained from sending troops, as it put its own interests in Europe before those of the independence fighters. Until 1814, British soldiers fought alongside Spaniards against the French in Spain's Peninsular War, and after Napoleon's defeat at Waterloo (1815), Britain still needed Spain to assure a balance of power in Europe.[210]

The appeal of the French Revolution was limited in Spanish America, since it had spawned the Jacobin terror and the Haitian Revolution, which was associated with anarchy and violence. Conversely, Great Britain and its constitution were held in great admiration. The separation of executive, legislative, and judicial powers, and the mixture of monarchy, aristocracy (the role of the nobility in the House of Lords), and democracy (embedded in the House of Commons) were considered guarantees of stability and freedom.[211] Still, some "rebels," who had become staunch republicans during the wars with Ferdinand's Spain, considered the monarchical element to be a major defect of the British constitution. In his address to the constituent assembly of Venezuela (1819), the great liberator Simón Bolívar argued: "When I speak about the British Constitution, I only refer to its republican sides. Can one actually call a system in which the sovereignty of the people, the division and balance of powers, civil liberty, freedom of conscience and freedom of the press are recognized, a pure monarchy? Could there be more freedom in a republic . . .?"[212]

The notion of freedom, as defined by the Founding Fathers, was also of extraordinary importance in the newly-emerged United States. The influence of the U.S. model is evident in numerous documents and institutions in newly-liberated Latin America. The Chilean law of 1811 begins with the words: "All men have certain inalienable rights which the Creator has given them in order to ensure their happiness, prosperity, and well-being." Likewise, the constitutions of Argentina (1819), Colombia (1821) and Mexico (1824) adopted the North American model of separation of powers.[213] While certain aspects of the U.S. model were admired, others were greeted with anxiety. Most politicians in Spanish America were hesitant about introducing elements of the U.S. constitution, simply because they were not homegrown. The common belief was that institutions had to match the national character. Federalism, for example, might have had beneficial effects in North America, but was seen as less appropriate for nations that required a strong central government.[214]

The creoles (Americans of Spanish descent) who guided the new states were aware of the dangers of fragmentation in states which were, in many respects, artificial constructs. They also worried about class warfare. The revolutions were, after all, about more than the drive for independence. This had also been true of the revolt in the Thirteen Colonies, where urban riots in the 1760s and 1770s brought various disenfranchised groups who condemned wealth and social inequities to the fore. Similarly, Indians in Colombia in the 1810s used the prevalent anti-Spanish rhetoric to ask the government to undo all the injustices they had suffered in colonial days.[215] It is no surprise, therefore, that in new states like Venezuela, the creole elite was not willing to extend political liberties to all classes in society. They feared that such measures might energize the oppressed slave population and turn the country into a second Haiti.[216]

This mentality also helps explain why the era of revolutions did not end in the independence of the entire western hemisphere. Half of the British colonies remained in the empire, as did a few Spanish. With the exception of Canada, all of them were located in the Caribbean, where the slave-based plantation sector was more economically productive than most of mainland America. The elites in these slave-based islands kept aloof from revolution. If some planters in Cuba favored independence from Spain, the horror stories of the 30,000 French refugees who had arrived from Haiti reminded them of the dangers of revolution. Planters in the British Caribbean, for their part, needed the army, and at times, the Royal Navy, to maintain domestic order. Furthermore, since the British islands enjoyed a monopoly for tropical products in England, they never questioned the ties with the mother country.[217]

ABOLITION AND THE INDUSTRIAL REVOLUTION

Eric Williams, historian and President of Trinidad from 1961 until his death in 1981, connected slavery and the slave trade to the rise of industrialism in Great Britain. The debate he unleashed continues to this day. Williams argued that the triangular trade gave a triple stimulus to British industry. In Africa, blacks were purchased with British manufactures. They were shipped to plantations, where they produced tropical products that were processed in England, giving rise to new industries. Finally, supplying the slaves and their owners to the plantations created a market for British industry, New England agriculture, and the Newfoundland fisheries.[218]

The participants in the debate of the "Williams Thesis" agree that British trade did increase strongly in the late eighteenth century, around the same time that the Industrial Revolution began,[219] but what was the relationship to the slave trade and the "plantation complex"? One answer is that the slave trade and slavery in themselves were not motors of commercial and industrial growth. Rather, it was the rise in consumer demand in Britain for sugar and other colonial products that the slave system had facilitated, which in turn created export opportunities for British textile manufacturers in Africa and the colonies. Slavery is certainly part of the picture, but not the whole story.[220] David Eltis has even argued that, in economic terms, this trade was insignificant. Circa 1800, he argues, it accounted for less than 1.5 percent of British ships and less than three percent of British shipping tonnage.[221]

Williams suggested a direct link between the capital accumulated in the slave trade of Liverpool, Britain's largest slave-trading port, and the emergence of manufactures in Manchester. Up to 1770, one-third of Manchester's textile exports went via Liverpool to the African coast, and one-half to the American and West Indian colonies. Capital accumulated from the Caribbean trade financed James Watt and his steam engine. Likewise, the founders of Liverpool's Heywood Bank had African interests, while at least three men associated with England's first great railway project were involved in the triangular trade.[222] Later historians have pointed to the importance of markets in the slave trade for manufacturers from Manchester and other industrializing English towns, and to the long-term credits from Manchester manufacturers that were used to finance Liverpool's trade.[223] Yet despite such evidence, historians have so far failed to establish the share of industrial development that can be linked directly to the slave trade.

The idea, suggested by some, that the development of capitalism dictated the abolition of slavery, is also problematic. It seems that slavery remained viable throughout the eighty-year struggle for emancipation (1808–1888), perhaps because the industrialization of agriculture did not acquire major force until the end of the nineteenth century. This means that slave-powered colonies in the New World could have survived. A less cynical explanation for emancipation emphasizes changing ideas about fellow humans, ideas expressed in the Scottish and French Enlightenment as well as in contemporary theological debates, and disseminated first by the Quakers and English politicians such as William Wilberforce and Thomas Clarkson.[224]

Once Britain had made the first move, outlawing the slave trade to (1807), and slavery in its own colonies (1833), other countries followed suit, frequently under pressure by the Royal Navy. Slaves in the French and Danish colonies were emancipated in 1848, and those in the Dutch Caribbean had to wait until 1863. In Spanish America, abolitionism grew out of the wars of independence (1810–1824) and the need for black soldiers. It took a while, however, for all slaves to be freed: Chile led the way (1823), followed by Central America (1825), Mexico (1829), Uruguay (1846), Colombia (1850), Argentina (1853), Peru (1854), Venezuela (1854), and finally Paraguay (1870). Spain formally banned the slave trade in 1820, but for obvious economic reasons tolerated illegal trade to its Caribbean colonies of Puerto Rico until the 1850s and to Cuba until 1865. Abolition came in Puerto Rico in 1873, and in Cuba in 1886.

What about Brazil? In the 1810s, British Foreign Minister George Canning hoped to use the prospect of British recognition of Brazil's independence from Portugal as an inducement to abolish the slave trade. Economic interests prevented Brazil from immediately accepting such a settlement, but Emperor Dom Pedro I continued to entertain the idea, which led to his abdication in 1831. The slave trade continued, however, and slavery was only abolished in 1888, when the last remaining half a million slaves were freed. At least officially, slavery was henceforth banned from the western hemisphere.

The end of slavery and the crumbling of the European empires in the Americas closed an era in Atlantic history. What came undone from the late eighteenth century onward were the multiple linkages that held together the Atlantic world. Beginning in the thirteenth century, these linkages had impacted a growing number of areas, far beyond the Atlantic coastlines of Africa, Europe, and the Americas. The silver mines of Potosí in Upper Peru and Zacatecas in Mexico were very much part of it, as was the Palatinate, which sent so many Germans across the ocean. Equally important were the various regins of interior Africa where the New World's enslaved laborers originated.

Migration from the Old World to the New did not diminish after the abolition of the slave trade. The flow of Africans largely stopped, but Europeans started arriving in increasing numbers. The demise of Europe's empires in the Americas did not extend to Africa, where European colonialism grew rapidly after 1870. In Latin America an informal kind of economic imperialism by the great powers remained, which in turn was supplanted by the growing economic and political influence of the United States. These were fundamentally new enterprises, though, characteristic of a new Atlantic world.

1

PERSPECTIVES

Although they were very disparate towns, Boston and Lisbon, linked by the great circular movement of Atlantic winds and currents, were sister cities in the making of the Atlantic world. Lisbon was a cosmopolitan and multi-cultural society molded by millennia of interchange with the ancient Mediterranean, the capital of a far flung Asian empire, a city skilled in surviving in a turbulent world. Boston, by contrast, was newborn; without history. Boston harbored the utopian dream of being a new kind of Atlantic city, a model of humanity unsullied by the nastier side of human nature; an anti-Portugal.

In the seventeenth century, the Boston of Mark Peterson's "Life on the Margins: Boston's Anxieties of Influence in the Atlantic World" was scarcely more than a small town, a colony on the northern flank of the British Empire in America. Even so, its early history was marked by an extraordinary struggle between utopian isolationists who wanted to reject the Atlantic world or at least to moralize it, and realists who sought full participation in Atlantic markets. The tension between utopian and realistic drives, between moral reform and economic profit, led Bostonians to be called Yankee hypocrites, who simultaneously practiced sharp trading and ostentatious piety. It grew to be a major seaport, thanks in part to engagement in the slave trade. Boston rejected racial and cultural mixing, the multi-culturalism which Peterson sees as the very essence of the Atlantic world.

Timothy Walker's Lisbon ["Portuguese Paradox: Lisbon as a Strategic Haven in the Atlantic World"] portrays a maritime crossroads city whose location near the intersection of the Mediterranean and the Atlantic had, over three millennia, attracted the sailing ships of Phoenician merchants, Muslim invaders, Portuguese colonizers, and the warships of the Royal Navy. Despite its frequent dependence on foreign champions for survival, Lisbon was the base for Portugal's remarkable maritime achievements: the exploration of the African coast and the discovery of a route to Asia which led, in turn, to a Portuguese empire in the Indian Ocean, and the discovery and colonization of Brazil. Lisbon was remarkably skilled in the arts of survival, a true chameleon of a city, shifting its relations from neutrality to join alliances constantly in order to survive. Its plethora of trading partners from around the globe led some to think of it as an Asian city; others thought it the most African city in Europe.

Life on the Margins: Boston's Anxieties of Influence in the Atlantic World

Mark A. Peterson

In his fondest dreams, John Winthrop imagined that Boston would be "as a Citty vpon a Hill," a community knit together in brotherly affection, a beacon of justice and mercy, an exemplar to his fellow Puritans in England, and a model for future English colonies throughout the Atlantic world: "[H]ee shall make vs a prayse and glory, that men shall say of succeeding plantacions: the lord make it like that of New England."[1] Twenty-five years after the founding of Boston, Winthrop's fellow Puritan, Oliver Cromwell, had his own words to describe the city and the colony of which it was already the hub: he called it "a poor, cold, and useless place."[2] When the Lord Protector of England's thoughts turned to a "Western Design" for expanding England's global power, he imagined rich, warm, and useful places such as Jamaica and Hispaniola, places where England might "gain an interest in that part of the West Indies in possession of the Spaniard."[3] To that end, Cromwell ardently encouraged New Englanders to abandon their poor, cold colonies and migrate to Jamaica, where they could be of use to England's greater glory.[4]

Cromwell was not alone in thinking that Boston was a remote and unpromising outpost of Britain's Atlantic Empire. In their heart of hearts, Bostonians knew that their city was not, or at least was not yet, the hub of the solar system. The island colonies to the south were warmer, richer, and more useful than their own to the empires—British, French, Spanish, Portuguese, or Dutch—that established them. Yet Bostonians were also aware of the insufferable climates, the soaring death rates, the vicious profiteering, the human exploitation, squalid living conditions, and sinful ways of life that characterized these competing plantations. They hoped and prayed that their own experiment would be a place where, in Winthrop's words, "the riche and mighty should not eate vpp the poore, nor the poore, and dispised rise vpp against theire superiors . . .".[5]

This was early Boston's dilemma, and the source of much anxiety through its first two centuries. The city's founders and their successors were ambitious. They aspired to be the brightest star in Britain's imperial firmament, to have an exemplary and beneficial influence throughout the rapidly expanding Atlantic world. Yet at the same time, they feared and mistrusted the propulsive forces that were bringing that world into being, and looked with trepidation upon the chaotic societies emerging as old worlds melded into strange hybrid new ones. If John Winthrop sometimes imagined Boston as a "city upon a hill," he also looked to New England's remote landscape as a refuge, "a shelter and a hidinge place," an escape from the corruption and degradation of England's churches and society, and from the warfare and exploitation that characterized the relationships among Europe's imperial powers.[6] Bostonians wanted to shape the larger Atlantic community without being shaped by it—to prosper within it without catching its contagions. By exploring this tension between the utopian aspirations for purity, for removal from the rough and rude conditions of a grasping world of greed and desire, and the powerful ambitions for influence and significance within that larger world, we can begin to assess Boston's distinctive place in the Atlantic community of the early modern period. For it was not simply in the dreams of its principal founder, but in the longer trajectory of the city's early history, and in virtually every aspect of its development, that this tension can be seen.

We can, for the sake of argument, think of the evolution of the Atlantic community in three stages or aspects.[7] First, contact and conquest, as European imperial powers explored the far reaches of the Atlantic basin, laid claim to the rich resources it found, used force to uphold those claims, and incidentally created new trans-Atlantic and cis-Atlantic linkages among previously remote and isolated locations.[8] Second is the process by which these new linkages were solidified in economic terms, where exploitable resources of the Atlantic world were knit together in stable patterns—the commercial trade in staple crops, the evolving labor market, especially in slaves, and the commoditization of land that characterized the Atlantic economy.[9] Finally, we can think of the emergence of Atlantic cultures, syncretic blends of the various "old world" societies of Europe, Africa, and the Americas that met and interacted in these zones of contact.[10] These stages need not be thought of as strictly chronological; they were all aspects of a broad process of development, taking place at different rates over diverse regions of the Atlantic world. This essay explores the tensions Bostonians felt between aspiration and anxiety in each of these three aspects of development, these three main ligatures of Atlantic society: the realm of imperial affairs, the conquest and dominance of territories; the realm of economic development, trade, and commerce, including, most significantly, the slave trade; and the realm of culture.

In 1630, when Boston was founded, England's imperial ambition, its interest in pursuing Atlantic expansion, was at low ebb. The Stuart monarchs had offered only weak support for the Protestant cause on the European continent during the Thirty Years' War, with miserable consequences. Part of what drove Winthrop and his fellow Puritans from England was their fear that the Catholic successes in Europe would soon sweep England as well.[11] Furthermore the unofficial Elizabethan strategy of preying on Spanish shipping in the Caribbean, and looking to Atlantic colonies as potential staging grounds for launching the Sea Dogs' raids, had faded from view, replaced by the Stuarts' desire for a Spanish alliance.[12] Boston's founders did not see themselves as partaking in a grand English expansionist project, but fleeing from a foundering nation to a safe haven. And for its first half-century, in part as a matter of policy, in part through geographical accident, Boston and its interests were indeed extremely remote from the centers of imperial conflict in the Atlantic world.

As the northernmost English New World colony, Boston was far from threatening the Spanish Main, and even the sea lanes that brought Caribbean traffic back to Europe veered away from the North American continent far to the south of the New England coast. Sensibly enough, Spain never contested the English presence in

Massachusetts Bay—why bother?[13] More immediately, Boston's location placed it roughly midway between the Dutch outpost at New Amsterdam and France's expansive but thinly settled colony along the St. Lawrence. Yet here, too, Boston posed little threat and saw little conflict with either of these potential enemies in the first half-century of settlement. The Hudson and the St. Lawrence, not the Charles and the Mystic, were clearly the routes to the lucrative fur trade of the North American interior that the French and Dutch both sought. Early Boston was mainly a somewhat suspicious trading partner, rather than a threat, to its nearest imperial neighbors. Even at the moment of English conquest over Dutch New Amsterdam, Boston and New England neither took part in nor gained much advantage from an operation directed by the metropolis.[14]

Similarly remote in the early years was the possibility of extensive conflict with powerful native American confederations. The coastal regions of Massachusetts had been decimated before the New England settlement by waves of smallpox and other diseases, so that the immediate area around Boston was much depopulated.[15] The more powerful Indian confederations in the interior, the Abenakis to the north and the Iroquois to the west, were sufficiently distant as to have little to do with the new settlements around Massachusetts Bay. It would not be until 1675 that Boston was drawn into a major imperial conflict, King Philip's War. The war, in part the result of Iroquois, specifically Mohawk, expansion into western Massachusetts, put increasing pressure on English-Indian relations that were already collapsing under the pressure of New England's growing settler population.[16] Even this bloody two-year war never spilled over into other imperial relationships: New France did not join the conflict, and New England fought the war on its own, without assistance from the metropolis.[17]

In short, then, it can be said that for its first half-century, Boston hewed closely to its initial goal to be a refuge and a hiding place for the godly, remote from the imperial conflicts that characterized so much of the early Atlantic world. Even during the protectorship of the more-or-less sympathetic Puritan, Oliver Cromwell, Boston remained largely aloof from his "Western Design." Although a few Bostonians helped to plan the expedition, few New Englanders heeded Cromwell's advice and moved to the Caribbean to fight the Spanish.[18] Unlike many Atlantic port cities, early Boston never heard the pounding of enemy cannons or the march of occupying soldiers in its streets. The sole exception to this claim in fact proves the rule. The only time Boston was occupied by enemy forces and placed under martial law was when England itself tried to end Boston's long-standing commitment to independent self-governing isolation. When James II revoked the Massachusetts charter in 1685 and lumped New England with New York under a single over-arching royal government, English troops and a military governor tried, but failed, to convince Bostonians to conform to the larger imperial project. The rebellion of 1689, in which Edmund Andros, the military governor, was arrested and deported, demonstrated conclusively that two generations after its founding, Bostonians held fast to their commitment to avoid entanglement in imperial ambitions.[19]

The nearly simultaneous rebellion in Britain against Andros's patron, King James II, and the subsequent installation of a Dutch Protestant on England's throne in the so-called "Glorious Revolution" of 1688–1689, utterly transformed Bostonians' view of their place in the imperial contest for Atlantic power. Unlike the hated crypto-Catholic Stuart monarchs, William of Orange took an active interest in forming Protestant alliances and advancing the Protestant cause in Europe and across the Atlantic as well.[20] His efforts, and those of his successors, the Hanoverians, to reorganize and consolidate Britain's overseas possessions were designed to increase their potential for military and economic gains against Catholic, and especially French, competition.

This sudden alteration in Britain's imperial agenda and the ideology that underlay it brought about an instantaneous change in the nature of Boston's participation in the imperial and military affairs of the Atlantic world. The isolationism of the charter period gave way to steadily increasing involvement in, and enthusiasm for, Britain's wars for empire. From 1689–1697, Bostonians engaged in a series of dismal expeditions against French Canada, and fought to keep France's Abenaki allies from destroying its straggling settlements in the district of Maine, in what amounted to a minor sidelight to King William's War against Louis XIV.[21] Despite these feeble beginnings, Boston's contribution grew larger with each successive imperial conflict, reaching an initial plateau in 1745, with the surprising capture by Sir William Pepperell and his New England troops of the French fortress at Louisbourg during the War of the Austrian Succession ("Extraordinary Events, the Doings of God," one Boston clergyman called it).[22] Then came an even more remarkable triumph in the later stages of the Seven Years War. With an enormous percentage of New England's sons and Boston's resources given over to the cause, the war culminated in General James Wolfe's victory on the Plains of Abraham and the expulsion of France from North America.[23] "Auspicious Day!" Thomas Barnard called it in his election sermon in Boston in 1763, "when Britain, the special Care of Heaven, blessed with a patriot-Sovereign, served by wise and faithful Councellors, brave Commanders, successful Fleets and Armies, seconded in her Efforts by all her Children, and by none more zealously than by those of New England, . . . has it in her Power to demand Peace of the most Powerful Enemies, on Terms, just and equal, safe, highly advantageous and glorious. . . ."[24]

But just as suddenly as Boston's enthusiasm for imperial conquest had emerged with the Glorious Revolution, it evaporated with this glorious victory over the Gallic foe. The conquest of New France, in Bostonians' eyes, muddied the ideological clarity of the preceding seventy-five years. Now, with the acquisition of French Canada, Spanish Florida, and the vastly bewildering native American interior, and with the sudden absence of a formidable enemy, Britain's empire was a far more complex and confusing structure within which to align Boston's provincial and archaic interests. When pressed for further contributions to an imperial cause that no longer seemed quite so compelling, Boston's old isolationist instincts returned in the form of protest and violent resistance. Five years after Thomas Barnard's rousing encomium, Boston would see an occupying army for the second time, as once again royal troops arrived to insist on the city's full participation in the empire. Seven years after that, Bostonians would finally hear the sound of heavy artillery, as Royal Navy ships swinging at anchor in the harbor poured shells onto the New England volunteer soldiers trying to retake their own capital city from the hands of their patriot-Sovereign and his wise Councellors, brave Commanders, and successful Fleets and Armies.[25]

Early Boston's attitude toward imperial and military affairs in the Atlantic world could swing suddenly and dramatically from remote isolation to active participation, but tended to remain stable at one pole or the other for long stretches of time. When we turn to consider Boston's part in the evolving Atlantic economy, the tension between polar opposites is present as well. Here, however the anxieties of influence played themselves out not in sudden transformations after generations of continuity, but steadily, persistently, on a yearly, daily, even hourly basis. The conflict between the potential for prosperity in the Atlantic economy and the fear of corruption and confusion that commerce could bring in its wake was played out again and again in the daily lives and consciences of Bostonians from one generation to the next.

A brief look at Boston's economic and commercial relations makes it easy to see why the city was never attacked by foreign powers. Unlike many Atlantic port cities, Boston was no plum—it did not stand as gateway to a rich hinterland of valuable commodities, nor was it a depot for the transshipment of treasure. Portobelo, on the isthmus of Panama, held the key to the riches of Peru, and Veracruz did the same for Mexico. Havana provided a strategic stronghold in Caribbean navigation, while the fortress and settlement at Louisbourg on Cape Breton guaranteed access to the riches of the St. Lawrence Valley and the Great Lakes.[26] Possession of Charleston offered control of the Carolina rice and indigo plantations. Philadelphia and New York were gateways to the fur trade of the Susquehanna and Hudson valleys, where lucrative markets in Iroquoia and fertile farmlands for settlers lay in wait.[27] By contrast, Boston and the Charles River provided access only to the truck farms of Watertown and Dedham. It is true that Bostonians did have a valuable export commodity, the codfish of the Grand Banks, still enshrined as the "sacred cod" in the legislative chambers of the Massachusetts State House, but the city's location gave it

View of the harbor and town of Boston in 1723. From George Francis Dow and John Henry Edmonds, *The Pirates of the New England Coast 1630–1730* (Salem, Mass., 1923).

no exclusive access to the fisheries—Basque fisherman from the Iberian peninsula had been working the banks for centuries before Boston was founded.[28] Still, New England's rocky farms, in conjunction with the fisheries and whatever other odd commodities could be scraped together, provided Boston's merchants with the means to enter the Atlantic commercial system in a potentially lucrative but highly anxiety-provoking way.

The anxiety was a product of the conflict between the ambitions and the social ethics of the city's founders and their successors. John Winthrop articulated a vision of benevolent economic interdependence, a "model of Christian charity" built around the Golden Rule, a vision that retained a great deal of its power for Boston's first two centuries.[29] In its first decade, the city's magistrates censured one of their own, the merchant Robert Keayne, for selling imported nails at an inflated market rate rather than a fair customary price.[30] Nearly a century later, the poor of Boston rioted when a merchant named Andrew Belcher chose to export grain for profit at a time of local shortage—his ship was boarded and scuttled. The judge in the case, a fellow merchant and church member, justified the rioters, not the merchant, and the city soon built a granary to keep reserves on hand against such future conflicts.[31]

These and similar strenuous efforts to defend the ideal of communal interdependence within Boston were made all the more significant by the city's constantly-increasing engagement in the Atlantic commercial system, in which the basic premise of competition, buying low and selling high at every opportunity, ran counter to Winthrop's "model." As a result, Boston's Puritan merchants developed an extraordinary reputation for hypocrisy. The ostentatiously pious but sharp-trading Yankee became a comic stereotype in the wider Atlantic world, and that stereotype was grounded in reality. The correspondence of John Hull, merchant and mintmaster of seventeenth-century Boston, contains a series of letters in which he defends himself against charges of duplicity by overseas trading partners.[32] Yet within Boston and greater Massachusetts, Hull could indeed be a model of Christian charity, a founder of churches, overseer of missionary activities, public servant, and friend to the poor. Even in the early nineteenth century, when Boston's Francis Lowell pulled off one of history's greatest feats of industrial espionage, committing to memory the workings of English textile mills in Manchester and replicating them along the banks of the Charles, the profits from what was arguably industrial piracy were turned steadily toward local, but only local, charitable causes.[33] Hard trading, sharp dealing, and the seeking after advantage were justifiable in the competitive world of the Atlantic economy, but at home, charity and the golden rule should prevail. As Winthrop put it, quoting Galatians, "doe good to all [but] especially to the household of faith."[34]

Given this concern with fairness and charity at home, one feature of early Boston's commercial life stands out as entirely anomalous and requires a bit of explanation, a feature that was rare if not unique among Atlantic port cities. Boston lacked a regulated public market. That is, for the internal trade in the ordinary commodities of daily consumption, foodstuffs, bread, produce, livestock, household goods, clothing, small handicraft articles, and the like, Boston had no regular market day on which buying and selling was regulated by public officials, and no established marketplace where the watchful eye of authority could ensure the fairness of transactions. Instead, trade took place all over town; in streets, alleys, and yards, and at all hours of the day or night, save of course on the Puritan Sabbath. Regulated markets had been commonplace in Europe since medieval times, yet whenever Boston's merchants and civic leaders attempted to establish them, and there were several such attempts, popular opposition was so great that the public markets were never used. At one point in the 1730s, when the town meeting voted to set up three market stalls for this purpose, rioters disguised themselves in the robes of Puritan clergymen and destroyed the market structures in the night.[35] When the Huguenot merchant Peter Faneuil offered to donate a large, handsome Georgian building to the town free of charge, the town meeting quite nearly refused the offer for fear that the structure would be used to house a regulated public market. Only by forswearing any such intention did Faneuil gain the approval, by the slimmest of majorities, to give the city the hall that bears his name.[36]

Bostonians' persistent and vehement opposition to this otherwise commonplace feature of early modern urban life has long been a puzzle to historians, and has usually been described, unconvincingly, as an odd product of local politics and religious custom. The most plausible explanation of the puzzle emerges only by considering the Atlantic context of the problem. In most Atlantic port cities, the local markets in daily necessities were quite distinct from the trade in staple commodities produced by the region. Sugar, tobacco, coffee, and rice were often handled by large trading factors, usually based in metropolitan centers. In Boston, by contrast, the trade in local commodities merged seamlessly with the overseas mercantile trade. Without a single reliable staple commodity (save fish), the overseas merchants of

Faneuil Hall in 1789, named for Peter Faneuil, who gave the building to the city of Boston along with a market house. From Walter Muir Whitehill, *Boston: A Topographical History* (Cambridge, Mass., 1959).

Boston competed with local consumers for access to goods that both groups demanded—that was Andrew Belcher's problem when he tried to ship grain out of the city. The popular opposition to public markets always expressed the fear that a regulated market would be dominated by large-scale merchants who could manipulate prices and quantities of available goods, that it would give the overseas merchants too much control, too easy access, to the commodities consumers needed in their daily lives. Ordinary Bostonians consistently preferred to put their faith in the fair dealing of their fellow citizens, rather than run the risk of having local markets dominated by the impersonal forces and amoral ethics of the Atlantic market economy. The rioters in clergymen's gowns who tore down Boston's market stalls were, in their way, inarticulate precursors of recent protest movements against globalization.[37]

Nowhere was the conflict between the ethics of the local community and the values of the Atlantic market more pressing than in Boston's relationship to slavery and the slave trade. Winthrop's model of Christian charity encouraged Bostonians to avoid treating human needs and desires as impersonal commodities, to resist measuring the cash value of the human predicament. Nonetheless, this ethical principle was severely challenged by the burgeoning Atlantic slave trade, in which human beings were themselves the commodities. This dramatic disjunction was pointed out starkly by Samuel Sewall, devout Puritan and successful Atlantic merchant, whose early published protest against the slave trade put it this way: "There is no proportion between Twenty Pieces of Silver, and LIBERTY. The Commodity it self is the Claimer."[38] Even those Bostonians willing to engage directly in the slave trade and import unfree Africans were sensible of the climate of opinion in the city and sought to avoid popular opprobrium. A revealing series of letters between a group of prominent Boston merchants and their ship captain in 1681 shows that the merchants instructed the captain to land his cargo of slaves not in Boston, but in Rhode Island, or if that proved difficult, to unload them at Nantasket under cover of darkness, rather than risk bringing them directly into Boston.[39]

By Atlantic standards, Boston's ostensible involvement in slavery and the slave trade seemed relatively light. At its height in the colonial period, African slaves in Boston numbered around 1,000, no more than about 7 percent of the total population.[40] Boston merchants were not even the leading slave traders in New England, a dubious distinction that belonged to Newport, Rhode Island.[41] Considered more carefully, however, Boston's economic success was entirely predicated on the existence of a thriving slave trade and slave-based economies. In 1645, when struggling to find a solution to the economic depression brought on by the sudden end of the Great Migration to New England, Emmanuel Downing, John Winthrop's brother-in-law and fellow landed gentleman, argued that the only hope for prosperity lay in importing large numbers of slaves ("Moors," he called them) to produce crops more cheaply than English labor, exchanging unruly Indian captives for seasoned African slaves. Winthrop opposed this cynical but all too accurate understanding of the market in human commodities, but Winthrop and Downing's more mercantile colleagues soon discovered an alternative.[42] Boston's merchants, and the city as a whole, would grow rich by supplying the West Indian colonies with New England fish, livestock, barrel staves, shingles—anything, save for slaves at first, that the monocultures of the sugar islands demanded but failed to produce for themselves. Over time, as the New England rum industry prospered from the availability of West Indian sugar, Boston merchants shipped rum to West Africa in ever greater volumes, where they purchased slaves for sale in the West Indies. They then brought more sugar back home, intensifying the cycle of production, commerce, and human exploitation.[43]

This dependence on and contribution to slave economies—from the seventeenth-century merchants' need for the markets of the sugar islands to the cotton supplies that Boston's nineteenth-century "Lords of the Loom" demanded from the "Lords of the Lash" in the Cotton Kingdom—was the dirty secret of Boston's economic success for most of its first two centuries. As such, it helps to explain Bostonians' peculiar ambivalence about slavery and race. On the one hand, Bostonians from Samuel Sewall to William Lloyd Garrison took leading parts among North Americans in opposing the institutional basis of slavery and the slave trade. Yet the charges of hypocrisy that challenged the righteousness of Yankee merchants in their business dealings found an analogy with respect to slavery. The desire to avoid the taint of the slave trade, or at least the appearance of involvement in slavery, did not necessarily translate into Christian charity toward Africans or their descendants in Boston. Samuel Sewall's early argument against *The Selling of Joseph* was premised in part on Biblical principle, but also maintained that Africans could never become fully integrated into Boston's community: "they can never embody with us, and grow up into orderly Families, to the Peopling of the Land: but still remain in our Body Politick as a kind of extravasat Blood."[44] In other words, when Bostonians expressed opposition to the institution of slavery, they were not necessarily expressing their solidarity with the enslaved. In their eyes, Africans were never likely to be knit together with English in one body of Christian fellowship. Indeed, one recent historian has linked the post-revolutionary movement for gradual emancipation in New England with a parallel desire to suppress or disown the presence of blacks and the history of slave-owning in the region altogether.[45]

If an unusual desire for racial purity was one uncomfortable aspect of Boston's relationship with the larger Atlantic culture, it was a desire that was at least consistent with other ways in which Bostonians aligned themselves within the Atlantic world's cultural milieu. For if it can be said that the Atlantic world produced a common culture (a dubious proposition at best), then the hallmark of Atlantic culture was mixture, the blending of peoples, languages, cultures, customs, currencies, religions, and rituals into previously unknown hybrid forms. The sheer linguistic creativity that arose to describe racial and ethnic interchange is evidence of this: words like *métis, mestizo, maroon, cimarron, mulatto, quadroon,* and so forth met the need to catalogue the mixing of Atlantic peoples. Pidgin languages, native to no one but essential to facilitating trade and political negotiations, came into being as provisional solutions to the "New World Babel."[46] Historians have similarly groped for terminology to describe the shadowy worlds, the borderlands, marchlands, margins, or "middle grounds" produced by these exchanges, zones of contact where old boundaries "melted at the edges and merged."[47] One of the more provocative interpretations of "circum-Atlantic culture" argues that "substitution" is its chief characteristic. As cultural contact killed off people and destroyed economies, belief systems, and rituals in any given place around the Atlantic rim, the substitution of new elements for old and the consequent melding of formerly alien traditions was the source of tremendous cultural creativity.[48]

Early Bostonians would have none of it. New England was, ethnically speaking, the most homogeneous of all of Britain's overseas possessions (Map 2.1). After the Great Migration of 1630–1642, in which virtually all the migrants were English (and many of those came from a relatively small range of origins within England), most of the region's settler population grew as the result of natural increase.[49] The British Empire's polyglot emigrants of the eighteenth century mostly avoided the area east of the Hudson. The Puritan founders of New England were initially overjoyed that there were few Indians left in the first places where they settled. In their eventual contact with the native population, and especially in later missionary efforts, Boston's leadership developed plans diametrically opposite from those of the French and Spanish. If New England's Indians were to be converted, it would have to be on Puritan terms, with Indians living in English-style towns, adopting English farming, English manners, and English forms of government, under the expectation that they would become literate. John Eliot's heroic efforts to learn, preach, and write in the Massachusett language was not for the purpose of forging a hybrid middle ground, a melding of the two cultures into something new, but to bring an unmediated Protestant religious experience to Indians in all its purity and completeness. His Indian Bible, the first, and for decades the only Bible published in Boston, and the English devotional tracts he translated into a language spoken by few and read by almost no one, did exactly that.[50]

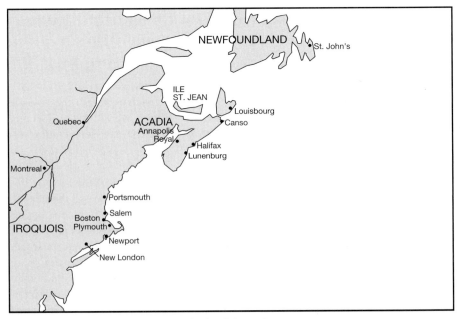

MAP 2.1 Boston and New England in the eighteenth century.

Melding with the Indian population was anathema in New England, and even converting Indians to English ways was ultimately secondary to Boston's larger cultural purpose, which was to maintain truly reformed churches, a culture of godliness, to use their term, that seemed impossible to attain amid the corruptions of Stuart England. The Puritan movement was grounded in the refusal to accept the hybrid, half-Roman, half-Reformed Church of England, with its noxious mixture of the godly and the profane in its parish churches, and its lack of will and discipline to exclude visible sinners. Once established in Massachusetts, and especially in Boston, the Puritan congregations guarded their purity jealously, expelling even their fellow religious radicals, Baptists, Quakers, and antinomians, who might have been allies in England but were now beyond the pale, and in so doing alienating even their fellow Puritans across the Atlantic. Where Winthrop insisted on exclusion, Cromwell chose toleration.[51]

Even in their attempts to shape the daily life of the city, Bostonians resisted the tendencies of Atlantic culture. Boston may also have been unique in the Atlantic world for its complete prohibition on theatrical entertainments of any kind, a ban that lasted from 1630 through the 1790s. Theater was, metaphorically, everything that Atlantic culture was, a place where persons and bodies could freely be substituted one for another, where identities were blurred, mixed, and confused. Visual communication—gestures and actions—trumped language, for the language of theater was notoriously slippery. Actors said words not their own, words that were lies, fictions, misrepresentations of reality. The stage itself was a kind of middle ground, a liminal space where the common rules of ordinary life no longer applied.[52] Boston's Puritan leaders, with their fondness for the "plain style," for the transparency and purity of the word, loathed the theater. A proposal to stage a "scenical divertisement" in the Town House met with a withering response: "Our Town House was built at great Cost and charge for the sake of very serious and important Business; . . . let it not be abused, . . . let not Christian Boston goe beyond Heathen Rome in the practice of shamefull Vanities."[53] It was not until 1792 that the legislative ban on theater was finally lifted.[54]

Yet, even in the realm of culture, where the desire for purity and refuge from a corrupt world seemed so strong, early Bostonians also had their ambitions for influence and engagement with the larger Atlantic community. In one sense, such engagement was unavoidable, no matter how distasteful. As New England's metropolis, its center of government and commerce, Boston was the chief point of contact with the outside world. By comparison with the rest of New England, Boston's population was more transient and more diverse than anywhere else in the region. Boston was the place where new products, new ideas, new forms of dress, manners, and speech entered the culture. So long as Bostonians could engage the greater Atlantic world on its own terms, in highly selective ways, these forms of contact could be enormously rewarding without undermining the more utopian aspects of Boston's ambitions.

An extraordinary example of this selective outreach occurred in the early decades of the eighteenth century. As Bostonians realigned themselves within the British Empire's newly aggressive and militant Protestant foreign policy, leading Bostonians, from clergymen such as Increase and Cotton Mather to merchant princes such as Jonathan Belcher, son of Andrew, discovered European continental pietism. They engaged in a remarkable transatlantic correspondence with their counterparts in farflung outposts, from Saxony to India to Georgia and back again to Boston. Within this network of conversation, this pietistic colony of the Republic of Letters, they traded ideas on the promotion of piety, charity, education, and missionary efforts, the reform of commerce, opposition to the slave trade, aid to Protestant refugees from Catholic persecution, and the construction of universal languages and principles for the elimination of divisions among the Protestant confessions.[55] It was in this era that the French Huguenot refugee population was silently absorbed into the city's culture, when Faneuils and Reveres became English.[56] This was, in other words, a rare moment when Bostonians found it possible to align their parochial interests with larger forces and trends in the Atlantic world, with little risk of sacrificing their purity or integrity.

In the long run, such opportunities were few and far between, and more often than not, involvement in the Atlantic world meant dealing with the threatening and unpredictable forces of that world as they came up. No matter how well Bostonians could chart the currents of the Atlantic, read and predict its political, commercial, and cultural weather in light of their own best interests, the potential was always there for a hurricane, a force that could wreak havoc with their ambitions and upend their traditional values. In 1721, one such metaphorical hurricane inundated the city in the form of a smallpox epidemic.[57]

The nature of smallpox as a disease, and the response of Bostonians to its dangers, seemed almost peculiarly designed to expose the city's anxious and conflicted relationship with the larger Atlantic world. One of the most infectious and gruesome of all communicable diseases, smallpox killed and maimed its victims at an alarming rate, but left its survivors immune for life from further infection. Starting in 1630, the disease had struck Boston in epidemic fashion with great regularity, recurring every twelve years. Then in 1714, the regularity was broken, perhaps because a measles epidemic the year before had killed many children, leaving few susceptible victims in the city for smallpox to take. The 1721 epidemic, therefore, was both long anticipated but something of a surprise as well. It arrived, of course, as a consequence of Boston's commercial traffic in the Atlantic. A ship called the *Seahorse*, owned by a local merchant, returned from the Caribbean island of Salt Tortuga in April, 1721, and rumor spread that it carried infected passengers. The selectmen voted to have a local doctor inspect the ship, but the results were inconclusive, and apparently several people on board, including one African, had already entered the city and soon came down with the first signs of the disease. One of smallpox's deadly features within the context of the early modern Atlantic was its relatively slow incubation period. An exposed person could make it through one leg of an Atlantic circuit without showing symptoms.

The traditional response to the disease, and the one which the Boston selectmen immediately took, was consistent with the isolationist, refuge-seeking, "Puritan" strain in Boston's history—quarantine. The ship itself was sequestered on Spectacle Island in Boston Harbor, to prevent further spread of the disease. The infected African was quarantined in the house where he was staying, and the selectmen began a house-to-house search, looking for further signs of epidemic danger. Families began shutting their children in at home, or, if they could afford it, sending them out of the compact, crowded, dirty city, away from the docks and wharves that brought danger, into the safety of the countryside. This last solution was ruinous to the town's economic life, and potentially disastrous to its public health as well. A strict quarantine could shut down trade, making commercial life impossible and endangering the city's food and fuel supplies, as country people became reluctant to bring goods to a festering city with empty markets.[58]

Circulating through the Atlantic world in the years before 1721 was an alternative approach to treating the disease, diametrically opposed to quarantine and flight. Several prominent Bostonians were willing to try this approach staking their reputations, the lives of their families, and their hopes for notoriety in the larger Atlantic community. Variolation, also known as inoculation, had long been practiced in Africa and the Near East as a means to fight smallpox. Samples of the disease would be extracted from the pustules of an infected but still relatively healthy person and "kept warm in the bosom of the Person that carries it," while small cuts or pinpricks were made in the arm of an uninfected person, and a drop of the infected matter or "variole" was then mixed into the blood. Ideally, the inoculated person would break out in only a few small and non-scarring poxes or pustules, and then make a full recovery while gaining lifelong immunity.[59] In other words, inoculation offered salvation from smallpox, not by refuge or isolation, but by fully embracing the disease, taking it in to one's home and body, or, as the perfectly apt commercial metaphor of the time described it, "buying" the disease. However, in this as in all commercial transactions, *caveat emptor* was the rule—a bad inoculation could kill as readily as the real disease.

Information about this practice reached Boston and came to the attention of Cotton Mather, the city's leading Puritan minister, along two different Atlantic circuits. One source was the Royal Society in London, of which Mather was one of the few colonial members. In 1714 and 1716, the Royal Society *Transactions* printed accounts by two different doctors who had observed the practice, Emanuel Timonius in Constantinople and Jacob Pylarinus, a Venetian physician who had seen it performed in Smyrna.[60] Mather read these accounts and discussed them at the time with friends, but he also had an independent and personal source of his own. A decade earlier, Mather's North End congregation had presented him with the gift of a slave by the name of Onesimus, who had described for his owner a virtually identical practice in his native North Africa, and showed off the scars on his own arm as proof of his immunity. Other Africans in Boston confirmed for Mather the reports of his own slave. Taken together, these varied informants convinced Mather of inoculation's value, and he was determined to introduce the practice when smallpox next struck Boston.[61]

In June 1721, as the number of reported cases grew from one to three to eight to dozens and fear struck the city, Mather circulated a manuscript among the medical practitioners of the town in which he described and recommended the use of inoculation. The manuscript itself was an odd combination, summarizing the accounts in the Royal Society *Transactions*, one of which was published in the Latin, while also describing Onesimus's account in a labored attempt at rendering his slave's English dialect. His most notable convert was a locally-trained physician and apothecary named Zabdiel Boylston. Before the month was out, Boylston had inoculated a middle-aged African servant, the servant's young son, and Boylston's own six-year-old child as well, and Mather soon joined the cause, inoculating his own children who had not yet had the disease.[62]

News of Mather and Boylston's experiments had an incendiary effect on the town. That these two amateur physicians were deliberately spreading a deadly disease brought enraged protest from many quarters. The *New England Courant*, Boston's new irreverent and cosmopolitan newspaper founded by Benjamin Franklin's older brother, and publisher of the latest in European literary fashions, openly ridiculed Mather. In its pages and in other local newspapers, the only Boston physician with a medical degree from a European university, William Douglass of Edinburgh, took Mather to task for his scientific naivete and his willingness to believe the testimony of slaves.[63] By late September nearly 3,000 people, a quarter of Boston's population, were infected, but Mather and Boylston persisted, and by the end of November they had inoculated nearly 200 volunteers. The extremity of the disease brought on extreme reactions—on November 14th, a "grenado," an iron bomb filled with gunpowder and turpentine and a lighted fuse, was thrown through Mather's bedroom window. The assassination attempt failed, for in passing through the window, the fuse fell out. Attached to the unexploded bomb was a note: "COTTON MATHER, you dog, Dam you; I'l inoculate you with this, with a Pox to you."[64]

Part of the reason for the violent local response to inoculation was surely a matter of fear of the unknown at a time of great peril. The reaction was also a product of the strange inversion of Boston's customary relationship to Atlantic world forces. For now William Douglass, the international authority figure with formal training and university credentials, and the *New England Courant*, the brazen and satirical critic of Boston's Puritan ethos, were the advocates for tradition, for isolation, for quarantine. On the other hand, Cotton Mather, the Boston homebody, self-trained amateur physician, and scion of the most conservative Puritan family in the city was embracing the most cosmopolitan, the most innovative, the most dangerous, the most Atlantic of solutions. He was actively reaching out for assistance from fallible human beings; Catholics, infidels, foreigners, and slaves, rather than standing still and waiting on salvation from New England's god.

Castigated at home, Mather found vindication overseas. London was experiencing its own severe smallpox epidemic in 1721. Its newspapers reported on Boston's inoculation controversy and in November, the same month he escaped the "grenado," Mather wrote the first of three reports on his experiments with Boylston, which were published by the Royal Society in 1722.[65] Mather's reports were quickly appended to the influential publications of Dr. Charles Maitland, a leading London physician and promoter of inoculations, and, although this may have been entirely coincidental, the British royal family embraced inoculation immediately after the appearance of Mather's second report.[66]

Through this strange set of inversions, the smallpox crisis of 1721 stands as a curious emblem of the promise and the risk, the hopes for influence and the anxieties over purity, that characterized Boston's first two centuries as a city on the margins of the Atlantic world. The city's successful entry into the Atlantic commercial economy, the fact that its wharves were constantly in use by ocean-going merchant ships, made it much more likely that deadly epidemics would enter the city as well. In traditional terms, the only way to reduce the risk was to avoid the traffic, close the city, and pray for divine relief. Luckily, the evolving Atlantic culture and the new forms of knowledge and practice brought together by Europeans and Africans offered a new and characteristically Atlantic solution to the problem. For most Bostonians, the risk was too high—the great majority refused to "buy" inoculation in 1721. It seems fitting that the man with the courage to promote inoculation, to risk infecting his family and friends for the greater good of the beloved community, even at the cost of marginalization within that community, was grounded in Boston's Puritan past and committed to the integrity of its traditional culture, and yet was also receptive to the varied voices of the Atlantic world and found his greatest vindication in that expansive arena as well.

➡ FOCUS QUESTIONS

1. Discuss the tensions between Boston's desire to be a world model of purity and humanity, "a city on a hill," and the lure of participating in the "Atlantic World" with all of its morally disagreeable but frequently attractive commercial possibilities.
2. How was the nature of the city's conflicting tendencies reflected in the incident in which a nail bomb came flying through Cotton Mather's bedroom window?
3. How did Boston, once scorned by Oliver Cromwell as a "useless place," come to play a significant role in Atlantic history?

Lisbon as a Strategic Haven in the Atlantic World

Timothy Walker

Portugal faces west toward the Atlantic. The nation's 737-kilometer (458-mile) Atlantic coastline, with its dozens of snug harbors, forms the southwest corner of Europe. Lisbon, the Portuguese capital, shelters behind a windward line of hills on the northern bank of the Tagus River;[1] the city overlooks a perfect natural harbor where the Tagus opens into the sea. Seafaring peoples have used this site at the mouth of the Iberian Peninsula's longest navigable waterway for well over three thousand years. Phoenicians, Greeks, Romans, Visigoths, Moors, and Christians all have found safe anchorage for their vessels in the Tagus estuary.[2] Whether for purposes of seaborne commerce, colonization, or warfare, Lisbon is the best deepwater harbor in southwest Europe.

Sailing ships, of course, are beholden to natural elements for their power; in the early modern world, oceanic and atmospheric forces dictated potential sea routes and destinations. Prevailing wind and current patterns in the north Atlantic form a giant, clockwise-rotating weather cycle, which in turn determined the patterns of trans-Atlantic navigation. From Lisbon, steady currents flow south along the Portuguese coast, eventually picking up the westward-flowing Canaries Current off the coast of North Africa near Madeira. Strong, near-constant easterly winds, the Northeast Trades, blow in the autumn out of North Africa to carry vessels southwest past the Cape Verde Islands and on toward the Caribbean and northeast coast of Brazil. From the Cape Verde Islands, mariners could either sail south to find the Guinea Current, which would carry them southeast along the African coast, or they could ride the North Equatorial Current westward toward the Caribbean. Once in the West Indies, sailing vessels could pick up the Antilles Current near Puerto Rico, which flows northwest toward Florida. From there, the powerful Gulf Stream swept ships northeast along the North American seaboard, then eastward past the Azores Islands and on toward Britain or the Bay of Biscay. Strong westerly winds, too, blow steadily out of North America to carry vessels eastward across the north Atlantic. Off the Iberian Peninsula, other Atlantic currents turn south to flow along the Portuguese coastline, thus completing the circuit.[3]

Lisbon, the westernmost capital in Europe, sits neatly on the eastern edge of this hemispheric weather system. Medieval and early modern navigators voyaging from northern Europe, the Mediterranean, or the Americas, therefore, were often obliged to include Lisbon in their itineraries. Atlantic wind and current patterns facilitated the flow of commerce through Lisbon harbor. They also helped to determine, and then maintain, Portugal's colonial holdings throughout the Atlantic World.

Two seventeenth-century engravings of Lisbon: Hessel Gerritsz, *Typvs Hispaniae* (Amsterdam, 1617) and John Seller, *A Chart of Spaine* (London, ca. 1671). *Courtesy of the Osher Map Library, University of Southern Maine.*

Geography, climate, technology, and politics thus combined to place Lisbon at a wind-driven maritime communications nexus.

Due to its geographic position, Lisbon developed into an important maritime way station between southwest Europe and several distant destinations. The city's convenient locale, as well as its status after 1500 as a distribution point for numerous rare commodities from Portuguese holdings in Africa, Asia, and South America, made Lisbon a logical stopover on commercial and military voyages originating at almost any point in Europe or the Mediterranean. Ships outbound from northern Europe were obliged to sail by Lisbon to get to virtually anywhere else in the world. Whether traveling between northern Europe and the Mediterranean; between Europe

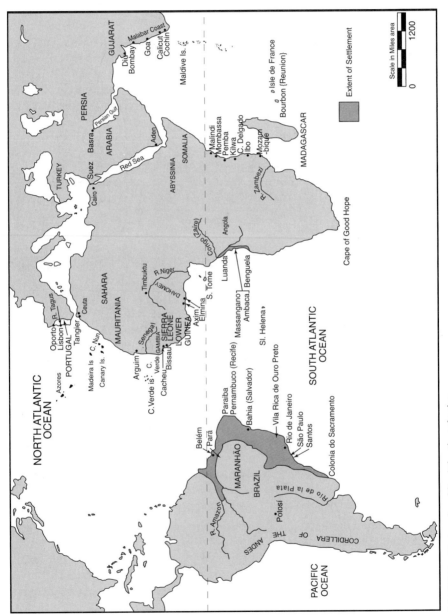

MAP 3.1 Portugal and its Atlantic colonies

NORTH ATLANTIC OCEAN

SOUTH ATLANTIC OCEAN

PACIFIC OCEAN

Azores
PORTUGAL
Oporto
Lisbon
R. Tagus
Tangier
Ceuta
Madeira Is
Canary Is.
C. Nun
SAHARA
MAURITANIA
Arguim
C. Verde is.
Senegal
C. Verde
Bissau
Cacheu
GAMBIA
SIERRA LEONE
LOWER GUINEA
Timbuktu
R. Niger
DAHOMEY
Axim
Elmina
S. Tomé
GUINEA

TURKEY
PERSIA
GUJARAT
Diu
Bombay
Goa
Calicut
Cochin
Malabar Coast
ARABIA
Basra
Persian Gulf
Aden
PERSIA
Suez
Cairo
Red Sea
ABYSSINIA
SOMALIA
Maldive Is.
Malindi
Mombassa
Pemba
Kilwa
C. Delgado
Ibo
Mozam-bique
Isle de France
Bourbon (Reunion)
MADAGASCAR

Congo (Zaïre)
Angola
Luanda
Massangano
Ambaca
Benguela
St. Helena
Cape of Good Hope
Zambezi

R. Amazon
Belém
Pará
MARANHÃO
BRAZIL
Paraiba
Pernambuco (Recife)
Bahia (Salvador)
Vila Rica de Ouro Preto
Rio de Janeiro
São Paulo
Santos
Colonia do Sacramento
Rio de la Plata
Potosi
CORDILLERA OF THE ANDES

Cape of Good Hope

Extent of Settlement

Scale in Miles area

0   1200

and West Africa or the Americas, north or south; or between Europe and the Far East or South Pacific via the Cape of Good Hope or Cape Horn, all voyages could put into Portugal's principal port. Hence, Lisbon during the early modern period became a maritime crossroads, a point of connection for cultures and commerce in the Atlantic Ocean and beyond.

This section will outline Lisbon's strategic significance in the Atlantic World. I will consider that significance as it applies to several spheres of human endeavor. I will start by considering Lisbon as a strategic haven in the military sense; a port that, time and again, proved pivotal in European conflicts, often with global implications. This will be followed by a discussion of Lisbon's strategic significance as the administrative hub for worldwide Portuguese colonial interests, and the paradoxical power relationship that placed the diminutive Portugal at the center of a rich sprawling empire. I will next assess Lisbon's strategic significance in economic terms, principally as a redistribution point for wealth brought to Europe from Asia and Brazil.

LISBON AS A STRATEGIC PORT

From the earliest times of European coastwise navigation, all seagoing powers came to appreciate Lisbon's great practical worth as a harbor. The very name for the land that Lisbon rules refers to the region's importance as a place of maritime activity and refuge: "Portugal" is derived from the Latin *Portus Cale*, or "port of entry (or gateway) to *Cale* (a warm country)."[4] In time, Europe's naval commanders came to understand that, during times of general conflict on the continent, access to Lisbon harbor was crucial for the safety and re-supplying of their fleets. Ships from many nations put in to the Tagus for victuals or to refit.

The British in particular, until the mid-twentieth century, made frequent use of the Tagus estuary for martial and mercantile ends. Not only was Lisbon's wealthiest and most powerful resident community of foreign merchants known as the "English factory," but trade with Britain usually accounted for half, and at times nearly seventy percent, of Portugal's annual foreign commerce during the eighteenth century.[5] Celebrated as Europe's "oldest alliance," the Anglo-Portuguese relationship of reciprocal trade and military support traces its roots to the Treaty of Windsor (1386); Oliver Cromwell reinforced this bond with a diplomatic alliance in 1654. After the restoration of the Stuart monarchy in England, Anglo-Portuguese relations were cemented anew in 1662 by the marriage of Charles II with Catarina of Bragança, daughter of Portuguese monarch João IV. The bride's extraordinary dowry included Tangier and Bombay (strategic ports in their own right). During the long eighteenth century and throughout the Napoleonic wars, the British fleet demanded and usually received access to the Portuguese royal arsenal on Lisbon's waterfront. There, British Royal Navy commanders requisitioned guns, powder, shot, and other essential ships' stores, even during times of declared Portuguese neutrality.

Long before the British achieved their favored status, however, Lisbon's walled town and waterfront had often provided the stage for historic maritime events. For example, in 1147, a Christian army under self-proclaimed Portuguese king Dom Afonso

Henriques took Lisbon by storm, ousting the region's longtime North African Muslim rulers. Lisbon's fall, however, was accomplished with significant help from a combined Anglo-Norman, Flemish, and German army of Crusaders *en route* to the Holy Land. This victory confirmed Dom Afonso's rule and allowed him to continue his reconquest of western Iberia. By the middle of the thirteenth century, the heirs of Afonso Henriques had expanded their realm and consolidated power within the nation's modern perimeters.

During the fifteenth century, in the little cove of Restelo in Belém (a suburb ten kilometers west of Lisbon), Portuguese expeditionary fleets under the command of such explorers as Bartolomeu Dias, Vasco da Gama, and Pedro Álvares Cabral weighed anchor, bound for India around the Cape of Good Hope. Today, Belém is the site of the magnificent *Jerónimos* monastery, built during the first quarter of the sixteenth century in the distinctive Portuguese Manueline style. Carved stone anchors, coiled ropes, coral, armillary spheres, and other maritime motifs grace the monastery's façade. Manueline architecture takes its name, of course, from the contemporary monarch, Dom Manuel the Fortunate, who reigned over Portugal's most celebrated period of seaborne achievement. As wealth from the India and China trades began to flow into Lisbon, the king ordered that *Jerónimos* be built to commemorate the opening of the sea route to Asia in 1498, and the discovery of Brazil in 1500.

Lisbon also holds a place in the story of transatlantic maritime discovery. In 1493, the Portuguese capital was the first port to which Christopher Columbus returned, storm-tossed and separated from his other remaining ship, following his pathfinding voyage to the Caribbean. His small vessel and diminished crew had taken a terrible beating on the homeward voyage; thus, Columbus maintained that putting in to Lisbon for repairs, rest, and supplies was unavoidable. Still, using Lisbon as a first port of call, no matter how necessary, created an instant scandal in Spain; Ferdinand and Isabella understandably suspected that Columbus had provided information to their neighbor, a traditional rival.

The Spanish need not have worried about Columbus' loyalty. Although Dom João II, the Portuguese monarch, received Columbus with courtesy—the Italian explorer was, after all, a former subject, having sailed in the Portuguese service and married into one of the leading noble families of the realm—his triumphant account of his discoveries met with skepticism in Lisbon. Portuguese mariners and court advisors did not believe Columbus' assertion that he had found a simple, rapid westward sea route to Asia. Seventy years of Atlantic exploration in quest of an eastward passage to India around Africa had led the Portuguese to conclude that Columbus' claims could not be true. While confident that he had not reached Asia, the Portuguese did realize that Columbus had clearly found something, and so they hastened to safeguard their hard-won claims through careful negotiations at Tordesillas (Map 3.2). In that obscure Castilian-ruled town, chosen for its proximity to the Luso-Spanish border, they concluded the 1494 treaty that divided the world with Spain. Three years later, Vasco da Gama's small fleet cleared Lisbon harbor for India; the success of his voyage forced a *de facto* settlement in the matter of trading rights in the East, if only temporarily.

Less than a century later, however, Spanish and Portuguese state endeavors had been joined under the crown of Spain's Philip II (known as Felipe I in Portugal).

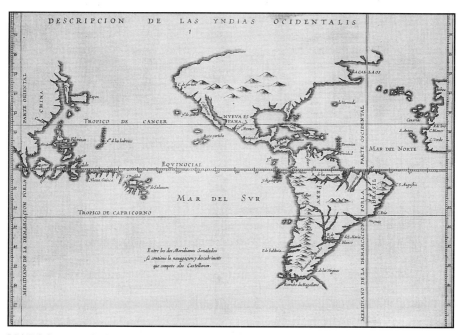

MAP 3.2   Map depicting the line of demarcation that divides the world into Spanish and Portuguese spheres, as agreed upon in Tordesillas in 1494. Antonio de Herrera, *Descripcion de las Yndias Ocidentalis* [sic] (Amsterdam, 1622). *Courtesy of the Osher Map Library, University of Southern Maine.*

Beginning in 1580, after the young Portuguese monarch, Dom Sebastião, perished without heir during an ill-conceived military expedition to Morocco, Portugal had been subsumed under the Spanish Habsburg crown. During this time of "Spanish captivity," which lasted until 1640, Lisbon became, in the words of one Portuguese historian, Spain's "veranda on the Atlantic." Portuguese ports (principally Lisbon) served as a base of operations for Spanish military and commercial expeditions in Europe, but also supported Spanish colonial operations in the Americas.[6]

In 1588, the Spanish Armada—more than one hundred twenty vessels—fitted out in Lisbon harbor before sallying to invade England. The Portuguese supplied half of the fleet's largest and most heavily armed warships. These galleons, designed for convoy service in the *Carreira da Índia* (Portugal's trade with India and the Far East by way of the Cape of Good Hope), formed the core of the Armada's fighting strength. In addition, Lisbon's environs and hinterland provided personnel and cargo ships to carry the Armada's abundant supplies.

Sixty years of Spanish control over all Iberia had serious implications for Portuguese possessions overseas, particularly in the Far East. Unsuccessful Spanish attempts to quash independence aspirations in the Habsburg Netherlands resulted in a protracted struggle with global consequences: because of their affiliation with the Habsburg crown, Portuguese trading enclaves in Asia and the Atlantic became free game for Dutch raiders. Between 1600–1640, armed merchant forces of the Dutch

East India Company, the V.O.C., snapped up nearly a dozen key Portuguese commercial possessions in the *Estado da Índia* (Portugal's empire in Asia). English expeditions, too, used the Iberian unification as an excuse to strike at Portuguese trade and attack homeward-bound ships of the India fleet. One such incident, the capture of the richly-laden Lisbon-bound carrack *Madre de Deus* off the Azores in 1598, brought enough prize cargo to London to double the value of the Royal Exchequer.

The Portuguese found these setbacks frustrating; subordination to Spanish rule was limiting their ability to defend their overseas empire. Even though the two Iberian overseas empires remained, ostensibly, administratively separate, the Portuguese saw their meager military resources repeatedly commandeered for use with Spanish missions, thus leaving Portugal's own enclaves vulnerable.

In 1640, with Spanish military attention overburdened by engagements elsewhere, disaffected Portuguese elites seized their chance for the restoration of the Portuguese monarchy. British sea power and Lisbon harbor played important roles in securing the throne for the new king, Dom João IV. The Portuguese War of Independence lasted twenty-eight years. Control of Lisbon was, of course, fundamental to the Portuguese struggle, since the port provided access to supplies and trade that sustained the long-embattled monarchy. A treaty signed with Oliver Cromwell in 1654 provided military aid, but put the Portuguese at a disadvantage; Cromwell extracted commercial concessions that created the foundations of the powerful English merchant community in Lisbon. The consequences of the treaty were many. Lisbon played host to a strong (indeed, often overbearing) English presence for three centuries. Subsequent events in Britain strengthened the Portuguese military position against Spain. A key treaty signed with the newly-restored Charles II in 1661 gave Portugal further seaborne assistance from Britain: ships, arms, men, and money, all the fruit of expanded British trade in Lisbon. However, ceding Bombay and Tangier to England as part of Catarina of Bragança's dowry further eroded Portuguese imperial integrity. Perhaps one outcome was worth the price: in 1668, with the Treaty of Lisbon, the Spanish finally recognized Portuguese sovereignty.

Europe's incessant wars over succession, commerce, and empires during the late seventeenth and eighteenth centuries provided the Portuguese with numerous opportunities to restore their sovereign interests through entangling alliances. However, given its relative weakness, Portugal found that sitting on the sidelines was the wiser option when the Great Powers clashed.

During the War of Spanish Succession, begun in 1701, a "Grand Alliance" composed of England, the Netherlands, and Habsburg Austria fought against the combined forces of Spain and France. Portugal, courted by both sides, entered the war in May 1703 alongside the British. Access to Lisbon and other ports along the Portuguese coast proved decisive for the Grand Alliance. Archduke Charles of Austria, the Anglo-Austrian candidate for the Spanish throne, owed his success and coronation as Charles III to Lisbon harbor, which became his main base of operations for campaigns in Estremadura and León. However, with allied reversals in the field, and at the negotiations that led to the Treaty of Utrecht (1713), Portugal's interests were compromised when the Grand Alliance did not compel the Spanish to return Portuguese border territories occupied during the hostilities. Years of warfare had drained the treasury and devastated the countryside; Portugal's military forces, acting alone, were not sufficient to reassert control over the ancient borders.[7] Thereafter, defense of the nation and empire became increasingly a matter of diplomacy rather than arms. To avoid invasion or territorial losses in the colonies, Portuguese rulers learned to maintain a judicious neutrality when Europe's great powers went to war. Forced by the circumstances of their military weakness and consequent vulnerability, both at home in continental Europe and in their imperial enclaves, the Portuguese were forced to walk a diplomatic tightrope and follow a policy of neutrality.[8]

THE PORTUGUESE PARADOX

Why should we think of the Portuguese experience in the early modern Atlantic World as a historical paradox? Given the circumstances surrounding the establishment of the Portuguese seaborne empire, and Lisbon's position in it, in what ways did reality contradict reasonable expectation? Simply stated, given its relative size and power, Portugal was nonetheless able to organize the world's first global maritime commercial and colonial empire, a considerable part of which was on the opposite side of the planet. In an age of wind-powered ships and primitive navigation, such an achievement is paradoxical.

Portugal in the fifteenth and sixteenth centuries was small in population and resources. Around 1450, Portuguese territories were home to just over one million people—a tiny population on which to base a global expansion.[9] Lisbon had approximately 60,000 inhabitants; two hundred years later it had perhaps 150,000. In comparison with other larger European states, the monarchy was not wealthy; per-capita agricultural output was low. Despite these limiting factors, the Portuguese developed their maritime capabilities to such a high state that, beginning in 1415, they could support global expansion and exploration, something no other European kingdom would undertake for generations. The Portuguese were the first Europeans to systematically explore the West African coastline and people the offshore islands they discovered: Madeira, the Azores, and the Cape Verde Islands. By the end of the fifteenth century, they had pushed their explorations around the Cape of Good Hope and on to western India.

Portugal became the first modern European nation-state to establish maritime colonies outside of Europe, thanks to the ruthless application of superior seaborne technology—artillery mounted aboard strongly-built ships. Portugal developed a complex network of rich maritime enclaves on three continents beyond Europe. By the first quarter of the sixteenth century, far-flung Portuguese holdings in all the world's oceans possessed colonial administrations—some entrenched and some precarious—that looked to Lisbon for law, protection, and a cultural standard set in the Iberian metropole. The Portuguese established imperial bases in Morocco, Madeira, the Azores, Guinea, São Tomé, Princípe, Cape Verde, Brazil, Angola, Mozambique, Zanzibar, Mombasa, Hormuz, Diu, Damão, Bassaim, Goa, Cochin, Ceylon, Malacca, Timor, Tidore, Ternate, the Banda Islands, Macao, and Nagasaki. Taken together, these territories represent such an enormous geographical area that holding them together as a coherent, viable overseas empire required a mastery of navigation and logistical strategy.

Portugal's ascendancy in the sixteenth century relied on its web of sea links. Garrisons on land were often small and constantly in danger of loss due to disease or local unrest. Authorities in Lisbon administered and defended this network despite enormous logistical impediments and lack of manpower. This shortage of personnel and material and financial resources meant that the full commercial potential of the Portuguese network was never fully realized. The lack of resources—what the Portuguese called *falta de condicões*—was chronic both at home and throughout the empire; dearth is a constant theme and factor in Portuguese history.

AN ATLANTIC NATION WITH A FOCUS ON THE EAST

Another aspect of the Portuguese paradox is that its imperial aspirations focused on the eastern hemisphere and particularly on India and China for their spices, drugs, textiles, and luxury goods. Asia and the *Estado da Índia* remained the primary focus of Portuguese imperial energy for nearly two centuries, until the 1680s. The cumulative weight of resources invested in the fifteenth century explorations, the tremendous effort and amount of treasure expended to establish bases in Asia, and the heavy emphasis placed on the Treaty of Tordesillas (1494), which gave a Papal sanction and political legitimacy to Portuguese territorial claims in the eastern hemisphere, dictated that this be so. Despite serious setbacks in the seventeenth century, when many *feitorías* (trading stations) fell to the Dutch, the Asia trade remained profitable, on the whole, until the nineteenth century.

Even after substantial losses against the Dutch and, to a lesser extent, the English, the Portuguese restoration monarchy showed a dogged willingness to continue to defend the much-reduced eastern empire. The discovery of gold in Brazil in the 1690s—and later, in 1729, diamonds—motivated imperial authorities to reorient their efforts toward the Atlantic. Once the Portuguese began to appreciate the wealth of the Brazilian interior, Lisbon's merchant class and the ministers serving in the *Conselho Ultramarino* rapidly started to expand links with São Paulo through the port at Rio de Janeiro. In a very short time, Brazil assumed an economic centrality to Portuguese imperial interests. Gold and diamonds from Brazil brought fabulous wealth to Portugal for seventy years and more; it was a fundamental source of state wealth and the mainstay of state solvency.[10]

Until the 1670s, Brazil had been subject to a curious Portuguese version of "salutary neglect." Even the organization of a colonial government in Brazil was done almost as an afterthought in the mid-sixteenth century; for fifty years following discovery in 1500, colonists in Brazil developed their society with little state interference from Lisbon. The Overseas Council did not believe that Brazil's interior had commercial possibilities. Consequently, the royal government resorted to an ancient method of land disposal, dividing Brazil's vast seaboard into quasi-independent districts, called *capitanias* (captaincies or fiefdoms), and virtually abdicated government authority to feudal lords from Portuguese noble families who were charged only with developing the land and protecting royal interests. Towards the end of the sixteenth century, expanding sugar and tobacco production along the Brazilian coast began to change Lisbon's views of its colony. When Brazil's fertility attracted Dutch and French encroachment in the seventeenth century, the Portuguese home government could not spare sufficient military forces to drive out the intruders. After the Dutch invasion of 1630, the *Brasileiros* were left largely to their own devices to recover the colony for the Portuguese empire; in the event, victory was achieved through the use of armed slave soldiers.

Underlying nearly all commercial activities in Brazil was forced labor, first by Amerindians captured locally and later by Africans imported in vast numbers from Angola, Senegal, the Guinea Coast, and Mozambique. Plantation-based production of sugar and tobacco was exceptionally labor-intensive, and the African slave markets that opened first in Salvador de Bahia soon spread to all regions of Brazil. Ranch-based leather production, too, required many hands to work as cattle herdsmen, skinners, and hide tanners. An ever-expanding seaborne slave trade, financed and directed from Lisbon, was essential to maintain Brazil's plantation economy. Brazil absorbed approximately one-third of the entire trans-Atlantic traffic in African slaves between 1540 and 1860. Even so, lucrative plantation commodities remained subordinate to Asian goods in the overall imperial picture.

While other Brazilian products, such as sugar, tobacco, and dyewoods, also contributed significantly to the fortunes of the Portuguese empire, Brazilian gold became a central pillar of the Portuguese domestic economy in the eighteenth century.[11] The influx of gold from Rio de Janeiro began in earnest only in 1699, with the completion of direct roads from São Paulo to the gold fields deep in the Brazilian interior. Production levels soon outstripped anything the Spanish or Portuguese colonial bullion trade had known before. As much gold flowed out of Brazil in the first fifteen years of the boom as had entered Seville from Spanish America between 1493–1660. From 1705–1755, the average amount of gold unloaded and registered at Lisbon amounted to better than 10,000 kilos annually. Seventeen twelve was an early peak year with imports of 14,500 kilos; the all-time high, 25,000 kilos, occurred in 1720. These figures do not take smuggled gold into account, which most authorities at the time estimated conservatively to amount to a further one-third above legal imports.[12]

This golden windfall enabled the Portuguese state to indulge in expenditures that made the court of Dom João V (1706–1750) the envy of Europe. Brazilian gold paid for a royal program of monumental building undertaken during the first half of the century, such as the colossal Baroque monastery at Mafra. Gold paid for grain imports to a nation which could no longer feed itself, and for luxury goods, manufactured items, and machinery that were shipped to Portugal and Brazil from workshops in England, Holland, and Italy. Finally, following the devastating 1755 earthquake, Brazilian gold and diamonds made the reconstruction of Lisbon possible.[13]

Brazil's rise to economic prominence and the simultaneous dramatic shift away from the eastern colonies, of course, points to another aspect of the Portuguese paradox: the economic focus of the empire—that is, the source of Portuguese wealth—was always far from the imperial center. The metropolis maintained its place as the administrative capital, but the home nation was itself of relatively minor significance to the collective fortunes of the empire. In the context of Europe, Portugal remained a small, weak realm—a poor country with a rich and expansive empire.[14]

As early as 1738, the visionary Portuguese royal advisor and diplomat Luis da Cunha had suggested moving the seat of Portugal's empire across the Atlantic from Lisbon to Brazil, leaving a viceroy to run the metropolis, as was done in the *Estado da Índia*.[15] Da Cunha correctly recognized that Brazil was vulnerable to indigenous unrest and foreign incursion, both unfavorable to Portuguese imperial interests. To occupy Brazil with a royal presence, da Cunha argued, would deter hostile invasion, inhibit the growth of an independence movement, and protect the royal family from hostile European rivals. From 1807–1821, the Portuguese metropolis was indeed governed from the empire's most important colony, Brazil, the royal family having fled a French invasion. Da Cunha may have been right in his own day, but by the time the imperial seat moved across the sea, Brazilian seeds of independence had already taken root. Within a year of the crown's return to Lisbon, Brazilians declared themselves separate and free from Portuguese rule.

Lisbon: The Most or Least Atlantic of European Capitals?

It might be argued that Lisbon was Europe's most Atlantic capital. It enjoyed direct, regular communication and interaction with every landmass washed by the Atlantic, just as it does today. From the late Middle Ages, Lisbon's merchants sent ships to navigate Atlantic waters, engaging in commerce with Flanders and the Hanseatic League in northern Europe, while Portuguese fishermen had long sailed far into the North Atlantic in search of codfish and mackerel. Beginning shortly after 1500, Portuguese fishermen established summer bases for drying fish on the coast of North America. As European settlements expanded in the New World, Lisbon's diverse commercial interests extended to the Caribbean, Africa, South America, and the various Atlantic archipelagos.

As the finest port in southwest Europe, Lisbon became a natural *entrepôt* for trans-Atlantic commercial routes. Merchant communities from most European states settled in Lisbon. Principal among them were the English, whose annual trade with Portugal was equal to that of all other nations combined. French, Spanish, Italian, and Flemish merchants also lived in Lisbon at various times, as did commercial representatives from North America and the Hanseatic League. Due to persecution in their homeland, a sizable group of Irish Catholic clerics, too, made their home in Lisbon. Between roughly 1460–1780, this cosmopolitan Atlantic port held a large and diverse population of African slaves (commonly hovering around ten percent of the city's residents), as well as returned colonial residents of Portuguese descent from around the Atlantic basin. Thus, the dynamics of commerce, the fisheries, religious intolerance, slavery, and colonial migration created an Atlantic *demi-monde* within Lisbon's environs.

Lisbon was also the least Atlantic of Europe's major ports. Outwardly, the non-Western connection is apparent: the architectural quilt of the city displays a curious blend of elements from North Africa and the Far East, worked into the general European fabric. Due to Lisbon's centuries-long focus of commercial and colonial activities in India, the spice islands of the Far East, and other parts of Asia, *Lisboetas* were subject to the charge of displaying a distinctly Eastern mentality. In the eighteenth century, foreign observers spoke of Portuguese "Orientalism"; the ways of Lisbon's inhabitants, whether in matters of business, government, socializing, or love, were described as Byzantine, closed and secretive.[16]

Additionally, one must remember that a considerable number of Lisbon's residents were Asians or Portuguese who had lived in port communities beyond the Atlantic sphere. Colonial merchants brought exotic goods to Lisbon from tropical ports in the mystic East and piled them up in the warehouses of this strategic harbor. These valuable cargoes were carried to Lisbon in ships manned by polyglot crews, many of them recruits from the Portuguese colonies, which were far more culturally diverse than the colonial holdings of Spain.[17] Thus, the cosmopolitan population of the capital reflected all the empire.

LISBON AS THE ECONOMIC HUB OF THE PORTUGUESE EMPIRE

The Portuguese Atlantic mercantile sphere was very active and interconnected. From the Brazilian rain forest came exotic woods used both for dyes and construction, as well as indigenous medicinal plants. South America also provided vast quantities of sugar, gold, diamonds, tobacco, hides, and leather. North America contributed codfish, grain, flour, rum, cordage, ships' stores, and products derived from the whaling industry. Ships bound from ports in the Baltic brought cereals, amber, wheat, metal, German-made arms and armor, machinery, and even mercenaries to Lisbon. To feed its population, Portugal imported one-fourth to one-third of its staple grain needs.[18]

Commerce with Britain was especially brisk; imports of woolen cloth, finished wool manufactures, and other textiles were paid for with high volume exports of wine and gold bullion. From the Portuguese Atlantic islands—Madeira and the Azores—Lisbon acquired grain, sugar, wine, grapes, woods, and vegetable dyes. Through Portuguese enclaves in Morocco, Lisbon's merchants shipped barley and wheat, honey, figs and dates, wax, indigo, metals, and textiles. Port cities in the Mediterranean Sea shipped mostly Italian and French luxury goods.[19]

Portugal imported one hundred percent of its dried codfish, an essential element of the popular diet. Trade with Scandinavia consisted mostly of salted codfish and herring; these traditional foodstuffs were usually exchanged for the very salt that kept this cyclical trade going. Salt, of course, was a major strategic Portuguese export commodity, being fundamental throughout the Atlantic world during the early modern period for food preservation. Few European countries could produce enough salt domestically to meet their own demands. Thanks to a hot, arid climate and coastal topography that facilitated the construction of numerous *salinas* (salt pans), Portugal produced a large surplus of salt specifically for export, and exchanged directly for codfish caught by foreign fleets in the North Atlantic. The Grand Banks of Canada and the waters off Cape Cod, Massachusetts, had been valued fishing grounds for the Portuguese since Columbus' time, providing generations of peasants and poorer city dwellers in Catholic Portugal with their Friday repast. Dried and salted in North America or Scandinavia, *bacalhau*, or codfish, was consumed in such enormous quantities in Portugal that it became known in the vernacular as the *amigo fiel*, or faithful friend, of the masses. However, the domestic fishing fleet could not meet national demand; by the 1770s, Portuguese merchants were spending £ 57,000 a year on imported American codfish.[20]

Outbound commerce from continental Portugal to the rest of the Atlantic World originated in Lisbon, principally, from which metropolis trade was monitored, taxed, and controlled. To understand the salient features of this commercial export activity, it is necessary to stress six key points.

First, relatively few of the most valuable and commercially-successful goods exported from Lisbon originated in Portugal. Portugal's domestically-produced export commodities tended to be high-bulk, low-value agricultural items that, while important to the landed aristocracy for earning revenue, were not the primary focus of Lisbon's commercial interests. Domestically-produced export items included salt, various types of wine, olives and olive oil, citrus fruits, and cork. In addition to being sent to consumers in the Portuguese overseas colonies, these goods found markets in northern Europe, North America, the Caribbean, and Africa. However, such commodities often left Portugal in the holds of foreign ships, having been exchanged for manufactured goods or foodstuffs from elsewhere in the Atlantic.

Second, the Portuguese mercantilist system always relied on the re-export of goods from imperial holdings far afield. In terms of value, though, the mainstays of Lisbon's commercial export business came from the royal colonies in Asia and Brazil.

Third, from 1640–1800 Portugal frequently ran a trade deficit, the imbalance of which was made good with payments of sugar, gold, and diamonds, all originating from Brazil and produced or mined with African labor. Portugal commonly imported far more than it exported.[21]

Fourth, customs revenues on trade were vital for Portuguese government solvency. Up to sixty-five percent of all state revenue was collected in the form of customs duties, consular charges, payments on the trade of goods for which the crown held a royal monopoly, and the royal share of one-fifth of all gold entering the metropolis from Brazil.[22]

Fifth, in general, Portugal's Atlantic economy of the sixteenth and seventeenth centuries was based on sugar, tobacco, and salt. The first two commodities came initially from the Atlantic island colonies; later, Brazil became the major producer of both sugar and tobacco, quickly eclipsing Madeira and the Azores. Continental Portugal produced only one product in this fundamental economic triad.[23]

Sixth, in general, the Portuguese imperial Atlantic economy of the eighteenth and nineteenth centuries was based on gold, leather, and wine. Again, continental Portugal produced only one product in this economic triad, but even then Madeira had become a major contributor to wine production in the Atlantic sphere.[24]

By the eighteenth century, extraordinary quantities of Brazilian gold and diamonds were reaching Lisbon. After a powerful earthquake devastated Lisbon in 1755, bullion shipments from Brazil offset the enormous cost of rebuilding the Portuguese capital city. Gold and diamonds also paid for foodstuffs before and after the earthquake to make up for domestic shortfalls. Though Lisbon benefitted from monumental buildings, little of the wealth from abroad went to develop a more healthy national domestic economy—few efforts were made to promote domestic manufacturing or to expand food production. As a result, much of the wealth derived from Brazil did not accumulate within the Portuguese realm, but quickly migrated to other parts of Europe.[25] Payments flowed out from Lisbon as fast as bullion came in, going to various points in Europe to pay for the luxury goods and common manufactures that Portugal did not produce. Much of the benefit of the Brazil trade ultimately accrued to British merchants, or to bankers in the Netherlands. Brazilian bullion permeated the European economy of the eighteenth century to such an extent that it can be said to have stimulated commerce in the same way that Spanish silver did during the sixteenth and seventeenth centuries.[26]

Theoretically, at least, Portugal had a closed colonial mercantilist system; foreign interlopers were not permitted access to Portuguese colonial commerce without special license or treaty agreement. Brazil, for example, was restricted to almost all would-be foreign traders. However, there were always smugglers, buccaneers, and interlopers ready to pounce on any opportunity to engage in Brazil's rich trade. Most were Dutch, English, and French. Encroachment and smuggling were common in Africa, Madeira, and the Azores as well. Portuguese naval might was never sufficient to keep out unlicensed trade.

Major Portuguese trading partners whose ships frequented Lisbon harbor included, in order of number, volume, and importance, the English, French, Dutch, Italian, Spanish, Brazilians, and, after 1776, the Americans. England and the American colonies dominated Portuguese foreign trade in Lisbon in the late seventeenth and eighteenth centuries. Prior to U.S. independence, on average about four hundred Anglo-American ships cleared Lisbon each year. Typically, these British-flagged vessels accounted for three to six times as many ships as the next closest Portuguese trading partner nation. France, the Netherlands, Italy, and Spain represented this important second tier of trade partners.[27] In addition, a handful of trading ships entered Lisbon harbor each year from Denmark, Sweden, Russia, and the German Hanseatic States.

English dominance in the eighteenth century was due in part to the Methuen Treaty of 1703. Negotiated during the War of the Spanish Succession, this accord was essentially a mutually beneficial trade agreement between England and Portugal. The war had denied Britain a principal outlet for domestic woolens and cut off access to French wines. Therefore, envoy John Methuen negotiated in Lisbon to allow the duty-free entrance of English woolens into Portugal, in exchange for which the Portuguese received a favored status for Port wine; these passed through British customs at a rate of taxation one-third less than that of French wines. The Methuen agreement had an impact far outlasting the war; it laid new foundations for Anglo-Portuguese commercial ties that continued, growing ever more complex well into the nineteenth century.[28]

The Port wine trade had been underway since 1678, well before the Methuen Treaty. It is difficult to understate the importance of Port wine to the British wine market. In just over a century, between 1678–1789, the annual average of Port wine exports to Britain from Oporto, on the Douro River in northern Portugal, expanded steadily from under 700 pipes per year to over 40,000 pipes annually. By the latter date, Portuguese wines accounted for nine-tenths of all wines imported to the British Isles.[29]

Meanwhile, the American Colonies developed a particular taste for Madeira wine. The provisions of the British Navigation Acts did not restrict English ships from conducting trade with the Madeira islands, which were not considered part of the European network for purposes of trade. Therefore, wines, fruits, and other products could move freely and directly from Madeira to the colonies in America without first passing through ports in Britain. Unburdened by English duties and handling costs, Madeira wine entered the American market much more cheaply than Port wine, which had to be transshipped through England under the Navigation Acts.[30]

During the course of the eighteenth century, Madeiran wine merchants and American shippers increasingly took advantage of this situation, building up a commerce which nearly eclipsed wine imports from other regions into the English colonies. In America, Madeira wine graced the tables of virtually all wealthier households, where it was consumed in enormous quantities. Even before 1720, Madeiran vineyards were producing about 20,000 pipes of Malmsey and 800 pipes of brandy annually, the great majority of which were destined for markets in the New World. These figures represent a tenfold increase over production in 1650. The annual consumption of Madeira wine in the Americas, which included the West Indies and New England, averaged about 6,500 pipes per year by the late eighteenth century.[31]

Following the conclusion of the American Revolutionary War and the signing of the Luso-American peace and trade treaty in 1786, the final fifteen years of the eighteenth century saw an ever-expanding volume of trade between the U.S. and Lisbon. Tables of ship arrivals to Lisbon harbor, systematically reported in the *Gazeta de Lisboa*, help tell the story: in 1788 the Americans, entering with sixty-five merchantmen, ranked fifth among Portuguese trading partners, following Denmark with sixty-seven, the Dutch with ninety-two, France with 161, and England with 357. Two years later, the Americans ranked a close third with eighty-four ships, just one fewer than the Dutch; the French meanwhile dropped to fourth place with sixty-two ships and the British still dominated with 364. The Americans held a steady share of the Lisbon trade through 1798; with ninety-five ships, they ranked fourth behind the Swedes and the Danes, with 181 and 116 merchant vessels respectively, while the British figure of nearly 500 ships still led by a wide margin.[32]

The French invasions of continental Portugal during the Peninsular War brought the Portuguese Atlantic mercantile system to an end. Having fled the imperial capital, the royal family and court remained in Brazil until 1821. The Anglo-Portuguese treaty of 1810 rewarded the English for Wellington's defense of the metropolis and opened Brazil wide to trade with British merchants. Shortly thereafter, Brazilian independence in 1822 ended the direct colonial relationship with continental Portugal and allowed Brazil to trade with all European and American maritime nations. However, the loss of Portugal's most valuable Atlantic colony did not diminish the importance of Lisbon as a cultural paradigm, a seaport metropolis that set cultural standards for Portuguese-speaking territories on the Atlantic rim and around the world.

In 1826, political reformers in Lisbon and Oporto proclaimed the Portuguese Republic, which launched a turbulent era of constitutional monarchy in continental Portugal. Portuguese preoccupations turned inward, focusing on domestic politics. Maritime exchange through Lisbon continued, of course: yearly ships still arrived from India and slave merchants continued to ply the Atlantic, but, after the loss of Brazil, Portugal's commercial role in the Atlantic world diminished markedly.

Even so, Portugal's reduced empire did not lessen the general utility of Lisbon harbor as a strategic port of call. Merchant vessels and men-of-war alike found Lisbon as inviting an interim destination as ever. Moreover, with the expanded role of the European powers in Africa during the nineteenth century, the Portuguese capital saw a corresponding rise in colonial maritime traffic. Lisbon's importance as a safe haven for Atlantic vessels thus remained unchanged into the twentieth century.

➡ FOCUS QUESTIONS

1. Discuss the unique geographical and climatic situation of Lisbon which led to it becoming a "communications nexus" for Europe since the age of the Phoenicians.
2. Discuss Lisbon's paradoxical relations with England.
3. How could a Portugal of modest agricultural and human resources become the center of a global empire with Lisbon at its epicenter?

2
EUROPEAN MIGRATION

A variety of reasons motivated Englishmen in the seventeenth century to move across the ocean. The push factors, as Meaghan Duff argues, included land enclosures, lowered wages, and rising costs of living. The move to America was not as sudden as it may appear, but occurred in a society where migration was common: the English people were remarkably mobile. Most migrants were indentured servants, and if they survived the passage to the New World and their indenture, they were generally better off than their friends who had stayed behind in England.

Both sending and receiving regions changed significantly in the eighteenth century. Rosalind Beiler shows that, as early as the 1680s, large numbers of migrants from the German-speaking world also settled in the British colonies, lured by books and pamphlets, letters from friends, and enchanted by the prospect of inexpensive, fertile, and abundant land, a light tax burden, and religious toleration. Whereas young males dominated among British migrants, Germans often traveled in extended families and with friends. Conditions aboard deteriorated as increasing numbers of destitute Germans sailed in the eighteenth century. At the same time, it became less attractive for them to settle a world away.

Adventurers Across the Atlantic: English Migration to the New World, 1580-1780

Meaghan N. Duff

INTRODUCTION AND OVERVIEW

In the past generation, professional historians, demographers, and economists have revolutionized the field of migration studies. New computer technologies and more rigorous forms of analysis have changed not only the scale and depth of this research, but also expanded the dimensions of the enquiry and challenged many of the basic assumptions about European expansion overseas from the sixteenth through the eighteenth centuries. Scholars in the 1940s and 1950s imagined that emigrants abandoned a settled Old World in search of better economic and social opportunities in a restless New World.[1] Recent research inverts this assessment: English colonists forsook a mobile and modernizing England for a more stable and traditional existence across the Atlantic.[2] Geographically, Britain's westward expansion now appears, not as several distinct arrows of conquest and penetration west into North America and the Caribbean, but as a great arc of interactive parts sweeping north and west through Scotland, Ireland, Newfoundland, Nova Scotia, mainland North America, and the West Indies.[3] This was a tremendous multi-focal process, one which encompassed the voluntary and coerced transfer of thousands of people, one which ultimately transformed the societies and cultures of European, African, and Indian peoples living everywhere in the Atlantic world.[4]

Social historians have used various interpretive frameworks to account for individuals' migratory impulses. Whether pushed out of Europe by diminishing economic opportunities or pulled to America by the promised easy riches, motivation remains the most elusive question relating to immigration. Some people left England fleeing bad harvests, unemployment, personal tragedy, limited opportunity, and religious or political persecution. Others certainly journeyed to America because of their political ambition, religious fervor, or acquisitiveness. Still more may have abandoned England in a quest for adventure or a simple curiosity about the lands beyond their island home. It is impossible to rank such motivations for the migrants as a collective. Individually, we know that people often left for a variety of reasons— some idealistic, others practical, some quite basic, and others extremely complicated. Despite this complexity of motives, an analysis of the changing numbers of potential migrants over time, the fluctuations in domestic and colonial demands for labor, the opportunities to find and fund transatlantic passage, and the relative attractiveness of competing destinations explains many of the larger trends in English migration to North America in the seventeenth and eighteenth centuries.[5] Before we can appreciate the significance of these trends, however, we must first assess the migration patterns of Europeans before 1500.

THE MEDIEVAL BACKGROUND TO EUROPEAN EXPANSION OVERSEAS

Historians of migration and expansion have long understood that the movement of Europeans beyond the geographic confines of their continent did not begin with the voyages of the Portuguese and of Columbus at the end of the fifteenth century. Rather, Europeans had scattered contacts with other areas of the world as early as the eighth and ninth centuries, and more extensive involvement with the lands of the eastern Mediterranean, large parts of Asia, the coastal regions of northern Africa, and the islands of the northern Atlantic beginning in the eleventh century.[6] These medieval examples of migration *beyond* the boundaries of Europe are important in this context because they anticipated later movements of peoples across the Atlantic. In the Middle Ages, however, they involved only small numbers of people who did not, for the most part, achieve any lasting success as settlers. These early migrations stand in sharp contrast to the widespread population movements which were taking place *within* Europe for much of the medieval period. This process, which is often called internal colonization, occurred extensively in the previously-settled regions of England, France, Germany, and the Low Countries. Sometimes internal colonization involved no actual migration, such as when a village expanded to take in land immediately adjacent to it; on other occasions new settlements were created in order to develop the local economy.[7] Additional forms of medieval population movements included religious pilgrimages, military expeditions, and more routine journeys to trading centers. Where conquest occurred, colonization soon followed. While such settlements typically came at the expense of a country's previous inhabitants, these medieval European experiences provided many precedents for the emigrants who left the British Isles and the Continent in search of a better world after 1500.[8] For most of these individuals, however, their first move carried them across the countryside, not across the Atlantic.

LOCALISM, MOBILITY AND THE PHENOMENON OF ENGLISH INTERNAL MIGRATION

Thousands of relatively small rural communities, interspersed with a moderate number of towns and a handful of great cities, composed early modern English society. Its various subdivisions—the village, the parish, the county, the town—all had their own integrity as social units. Localism was an important element in both the social experience and the mentality of sixteenth and seventeenth-century people, but it was only one element. As historian Keith Wrightson has argued, the myth of the relatively isolated, self-contained, and static rural community is a powerful element in our conception of the past, yet it is at best a half-truth. While Englishmen and women belonged to their villages and parishes, they also moved in a much larger world.[9]

Research reveals that the population of England was surprisingly mobile. One study suggests that the majority (at least 60 per cent) of English adolescents left home to become servants in husbandry.* By their mid-teens, almost all boys and a smaller number of girls entered the service of masters living near their family home. As servants they provided essential labor for farmers whose children were too young to work or who had left home. At the same time, their absence permitted poor families to reduce the number of persons they had to feed and clothe. In general, opportunities for youths to become servants varied with population growth and commodity prices. A rising population glutted the servant market and reduced real wages, encouraging farmers to hire cheap day laborers rather than servants.[10]

From the perspective of overseas emigration, the crucial transition came when dissatisfied servants or unemployed and adventurous youths broke free from this local migration system and moved to cities like Bristol or London. In 1520, only five percent of English men and women lived in towns with a population in excess of 5,000 and only 55,000 people called London home. By the turn of the century 200,000 people lived in England's capital city and its suburbs, while another 300,000 lived in towns with more than 5,000 inhabitants.[11]

Seventeenth-century English cities attracted workers from a vast rural hinterland; migrants to Bristol came from an area within sixty miles of town, and London migrants traveled as many as 125 miles to reach the city. Perhaps half the migrants came directly from the countryside, and most of the rest had worked in small towns. After working in the city for a season or for several years, many of these youthful adventurers (almost all boys or young men) indentured themselves for service in the American colonies.[12]

ENGLISH MIGRATION TO NORTH AMERICA

The Sixteenth and Seventeenth Centuries

Only a small number of Englishmen engaged in overseas activity before the 1580s. The majority were fishermen who mined the seas for cod and whales off Newfoundland's coast. Others included those explorers seeking a route to Asia, either by a northeast passage over Europe or a northwest passage through America. This situation changed after 1580, as the growing conflict between England and Spain enhanced the stature of English privateers at home who successfully raided Spanish shipping in the Atlantic. This conflict also strengthened the hand of English statesmen who favored establishing permanent colonial settlements in North America.[13]

---

*Servants in husbandry were unmarried youths, both males and females, hired by farmers or craftsmen on annual contracts signed by mutual consent. They are distinct from indentured servants, who sold their labor to merchants or planters in exchange for passage to North America.

English efforts to colonize the mainland from 1584–1629 resulted in the mysterious disappearances of settlers at Roanoke, the horrendous suffering of immigrants at Jamestown and Plymouth, and the massive destruction of native communities by European diseases. Despite these inauspicious beginnings, the English eventually established permanent, if not always stable, settlements along the Atlantic seaboard. Significantly, the impulse for English activities in the New World originated in the local communities of the Old World. As one historian has noted, "the history of the seventeenth-century English colonies must be seen as a subordinate part of a greater Britain that encompasses not only England but Wales, Scotland, Ireland, and the North Atlantic basin. Migration to Ireland or Maryland was part of a process that began in the smallest English village. English emigrants did not cease being English . . . just because they crossed the Atlantic; rather, they carried their class relations and culture with them."[14] Thus, the changing character of English emigrants over time, as much as the scale of the exodus from the British Isles, effected the societies and cultures created in colonial America.

After 1629 the history of immigration to the mainland British colonies can be divided into three periods: 1630–1680, 1680–1760, and 1760–1776. The first emigrants landed in the Chesapeake colonies between 1630–1680 and in New England in the 1630s and 1640s. Economic conditions in Britain and the American colonies generally explain the ebb and flow of English migration. The early and mid-seventeenth century was a period of population growth, land enclosures, lowered wages, and rising costs of living for laboring people in England. All of these factors encouraged some English men and women to consider migration as a realistic alternative to life in their native communities, in the adjacent towns, or in the cities of Bristol and London. Of the approximately 500,000 people who left England in the seventeenth century for all transoceanic destinations, more than seventy percent emigrated to America (see table 4.1). Most went to colonies which produced cash crops (tobacco, sugar, and rice) or specialized in colonial trade. Approximately 120,000 emigrants went to the Chesapeake, another 200,000 chose the Caribbean, and the remainder settled in New England, the Middle Colonies, and the Carolinas.[15]

Chesapeake settlers in the seventeenth century came from a broad range of geographic regions and communities in England. Historian James Horn argues that at least half were from urban backgrounds. London lay at the center of colonial trade throughout the century. Thus, the vast majority of emigrants, both wealthy and impoverished, began their long journey—which typically lasted between five and nine weeks—at this city's busy port. At least three-quarters of these English immigrants arrived in the Chesapeake as indentured servants who planned to spend four to five years in the service of a master in exchange for the cost of their passage, room, and board. While most emigrants were unemployed men from London's slums, transatlantic ships also carried many servants in husbandry from southern and central England, as well as a smaller number of semi-skilled men and women domestic servants. Fewer men from skilled trades elected to emigrate, but those who did apparently thought that their economic prospects were better in the colonies. The young age of these migrants—most were between fifteen and twenty-four years of age, with twenty and twenty-one years predominating—suggests their low socioeconomic status. Such Englishmen left home with little money in their pockets, and thus, little to lose besides their lives. Assuming they survived the voyage and the unfamiliar American environment, they stood to gain far more than the landless poverty endured at home.[16]

A smaller number of emigrants paid the cost of their own passage to Virginia and Maryland. Like their indentured shipmates, free emigrants were disproportionately young, unmarried men who came primarily from London and counties in southwestern England.[17] These adventurers were more diverse than their indentured counterparts, however. Before 1640, only a few free emigrants arrived in the New World with little more than the clothes on their backs. The majority carried with them as many of the resources necessary to establish a household in the Chesapeake as possible. At a minimum, new arrivals needed to bring food and animals, clothing, bedding, cookware, and iron tools such as hoes and axes. Transatlantic passage and essential goods typically cost a yeoman couple with children £40.[18] A gentry family might expend twice this amount. A few prosperous emigrants arrived with substantial material resources and—even more important—familial, economic, and political connections on both sides of the Atlantic. Within a generation, many of these wealthier colonists established themselves (and their kin) as the chief merchants, landowners, and governors in England's fledgling colonies. By the middle of the seventeenth century, as the colonial economy developed, immigrants arriving with cash or credit could purchase most of the goods needed to establish a household and plantation in the Chesapeake locally.[19]

Acclimation to an unfamiliar environment, a process which settlers referred to as "seasoning," threatened the lives of new arrivals in the seventeenth century. While demographic statistics are difficult to obtain in the absence of regular colonial censuses, two of every five immigrants may have died in their first few of years in the colonies. English men and women in Virginia and Maryland typically suffered from intestinal disorders and many contracted malaria. Even if an individual survived an initial bout of dysentery or fever, he or she often lived on in a weakened physical state and later died at a relatively young age. The life expectancy in the early Chesapeake remained extremely low for generations, but ironically, the region's high mortality rate created the high demand for labor and lucrative economic environment which drew thousands of immigrants willing to toil for years in American tobacco fields. A man casting his lot in the colonial Chesapeake risked losing his life. If he survived, however, the financial rewards could be substantial precisely because so many others perished prematurely. Thus, high rates of migration from seventeenth-century England to Virginia and Maryland preserved these colonies and dictated, at least in part, their socioeconomic character.[20]

While high mortality rates contributed to the Chesapeake's demand for indentured servants, the low ratio of female to male emigrants impeded the region's natural population growth throughout the seventeenth century. According to Horn, "six times more men than women emigrated in the 1630s, and although greater numbers of females sailed after 1650, men continued to outnumber women by nearly three to one throughout the rest of the century." As a result of this imbalance, fewer marriages occurred and thus fewer children were born. The preponderance of indentured servants in the Chesapeake population further constrained the formation of families. While a shortage of females might have led women to marry at an earlier age, law and custom required that most servants complete their indentures before taking a spouse. The inability of women and men to marry until their mid-twenties lowered the colonial birth rate. Collectively, the Chesapeake region's high mortality rate, skewed sex ratio, and late marriage age all hindered natural population increase. This situation persisted until the end of the seventeenth century.[21]

The migration of English servants to the Chesapeake continued until 1680, with the flow of emigrants largely determined by English wages and colonial tobacco prices. If wages in England decreased or tobacco prices rose, more laborers set sail for Virginia and Maryland. Conversely, rising English wages or falling tobacco prices reduced the flow of indentured servants overseas. In the fourth quarter of the seventeenth century, Chesapeake planters confronted a diminishing supply of English workers and turned to African slaves to supply their labor needs. Thereafter, the majority of English emigrants ventured their fortunes in other regions of colonial North America such as the Carolinas and the Mid-Atlantic colonies.[22]

While large-scale emigration to the Chesapeake lasted for nearly a century, the massive transplantation of peoples to New England occurred in barely a dozen years. Settlers in Massachusetts and the other New England colonies encountered circumstances quite different from those in seventeenth-century Virginia and Maryland. Alone among New World colonies founded in the seventeenth century, Massachusetts Bay naturally reproduced its population from the 1630s onward. From the outset, migrants traveled in family groups with more balanced sex ratios. Of the first seven hundred colonists arriving in Massachusetts Bay, three-quarters traveled in the company of kin and nearly two-fifths were female. During the Great Migration, the period from 1630–1641, approximately 21,000 people left England for New England. Significantly, participants in this transatlantic movement reflected the demography of the English population as a whole more so than any other collection of emigrants leaving for New World colonies.[23] (Map 4.1) When the outbreak of the English Civil War interrupted the departure of new emigrants, the New England colonies relied on low mortality and high birth rates to increase the population sixty-six percent by 1650. These circumstances allowed New England to produce its own labor force virtually from the beginning. Although only about five percent of the emigrants who crossed the Atlantic before 1700 came to New England during the Great Migration, by that year their descendants totaled more than forty percent of the European population in the North American colonies (excluding those who had migrated to New York and East New Jersey).[24]

Most historians now agree that a greater percentage of the migrants to New England were urban artisans, and more recent authors have suggested that the prime motive in determining the towns where particular immigrants settled in New England was economic rather than spiritual. While Puritans were far more likely than other English emigrants to migrate in cohesive communities and extended families, recent research indicates that a higher proportion of men than previously believed made their way to Massachusetts. Religious concerns certainly motivated thousands of men and women to board ships bound for this Puritan colony rather than a Chesapeake or Caribbean destination. Yet in making this choice, many of these individuals—especially the young single men among them—are thought to have been primarily concerned with advancing their material interests rather than ensuring

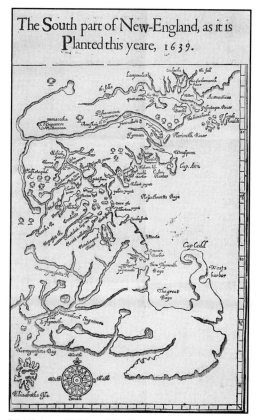

MAP 4.1 William Wood, *Prospect of New England:* The South part of New England, 1639. The Englishman Wood lived in Massachusetts from 1629 until 1633. *Courtesy of the Osher Map Library, University of Southern Maine.*

their religious estate. Regardless of the motives, the scale of English migration to New England was small when considered in an Atlantic content. Its character and demographic significance, however, cannot be measured in the numbers of emigrants alone. When a migration figure of 500,000 English emigrants is compared with the figure of 21,000 people bound for New England, it is immediately apparent that the southern colonies were far more attractive destinations than New England for seventeenth-century English emigrants who crossed the Atlantic. Consequently, scholars have asserted that the demographic experience of English migrants to the Chesapeake, and not New England, was most typical. It was certainly an experience repeated in other high-mortality regions such as the West Indies and South Carolina.[25] (Map 4.2)

By 1640, the English colonists had gained numerical superiority over their European competitors in the Caribbean. The West Indian islands attracted more emigrants

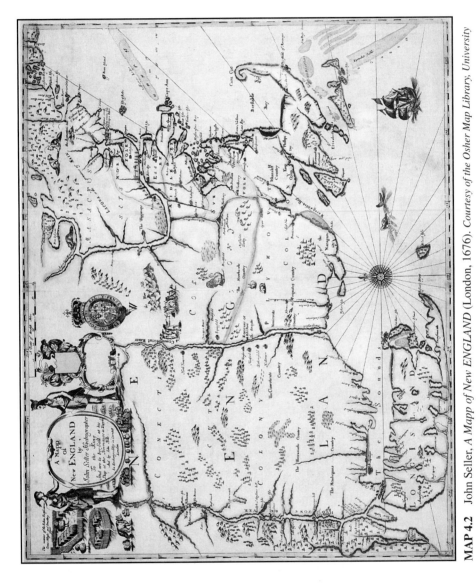

MAP 4.2   John Seller, *A Mapp of New ENGLAND* (London, 1676). *Courtesy of the Osher Map Library, University of Southern Maine.*

than any of the mainland colonies before 1660, suggesting that they were perceived as places offering the greatest economic and social opportunities for young Englishmen. Historians estimate that the white population grew rapidly up to about 1660, when it reached 47,000 and constituted some forty percent of all the whites living in England's transatlantic colonies. Of the total number of white emigrants to America between 1630–1700, about sixty percent went to the colonies in the wider Caribbean.[26]

Emigration to Barbados surpassed all other colonial destinations in the fourth decade of the seventeenth century. The island's white population increased seven-fold from 1635–1639, the result of both successful promotional campaigns and diffi-cult political times in England. Neither the Chesapeake nor New England rivaled Barbados as a destination for settlers during this period. As the colony's population expanded exponentially, so economic investment and trade increased. West Indian planters, who first grew tobacco and cotton and then later converted to large-scale sugar cultivation, initially depended upon English and Irish indentured servants to supply their labor needs. During the seventeenth century almost fifty percent of white emigrants to the English Caribbean colonies arrived with indenture contracts. Jamaica alone attracted more servants than Virginia and Maryland in the 1680s, and this one island drew more settlers than any other English colony up to 1700.[27]

Historians often describe the transition away from tobacco and cotton staple crop production in the English West Indies as the sugar revolution. The large-scale cultivation of sugar required the concentration of capital, land, and labor in the hands of substantial planters. Thus, wealthy freeholders—landowners who enjoyed private property rights, including the ability to grant or sell land and levy taxes—bought out their poorer neighbors, tenants lost their leases, land prices escalated, and the num-ber of small farms declined. English migrants with moderate resources found it in-creasingly difficult to establish a foothold in the Caribbean as tobacco and cotton prices fell and sugar profits rose. By the 1680s, mainland English colonies offered poor emigrants greater economic prospects and better working conditions than the sugar islands.

This economic conversion had considerable implications for the social struc-ture and political life of West Indian society. Sugar meant slaves, and in the English Caribbean it meant African slaves. In 1645, as sugar production took hold, Barba-dian planters possessed only 5,680 slaves. By 1698, these capitalists enslaved 42,000 people. The transformation of the agricultural workforce from white to black occurred even more quickly in other Caribbean colonies. Jamaican planters owned only 1,410 slaves in 1656. At the close of the century, over 41,000 Africans and Caribbean-born blacks labored in this colony.

Mortality among the enslaved was high. Overwork, malnutrition, and resist-ance all contributed to high death rates. As with indentured servant emigration in the Chesapeake, Caribbean planters needed sustained importation of slaves to replenish their dying laborers. In 1688 it was estimated that Barbados needed 4,000 slaves, Jamaica 10,000 slaves, and the Leeward Islands 6,000 slaves to maintain their exist-ing workforces. The combination of sugar cultivation and slave labor represents the dual economic system upon which the Caribbean depended.[28] Ultimately, this sys-tem discouraged English emigration to the West Indies after 1660 and increased the number of migrants choosing colonial destinations on the North American mainland.

The Eighteenth Century

In the second phase of English overseas migration, between roughly 1680–1760, strikingly different patterns of emigration emerged. The first key change was a sharp drop in the number of English men and women moving to North America in contrast to the rise of Scottish, Scots-Irish, and Irish emigration. Settlers arriving from England and Wales declined from more than 350,000 in the seventeenth century to 80,000 in the period from 1700–1780. This decrease in English migration to the mainland colonies coincided with an increase in the migration of peoples from southern Ireland and Ulster. Approximately 45,000 Irish men and women left for America after 1700, while the number of Scots-Irish emigrants rose from at least 20,000 to 115,000 in this same period. The number of Scottish settlers multiplied more than tenfold from 7,000 to 75,000. Even before the rising tide of Irish migration after the American Revolution, seventy percent of all British settlers who arrived in America between 1700–1780 were from Ireland and Scotland. "Whereas seventeenth-century settlement had been mainly English," observes Horn, "eighteenth-century emigration was emphatically British." Significantly, the total number of transatlantic emigrants declined substantially.[29]

The research of historians on migration to and through Pennsylvania is especially important, because Philadelphia became the major port of entry in mainland North America in the eighteenth century. Their findings identify several streams of immigrants passing through Philadelphia after 1700, and they conclude that each group of European emigrants left home for different reasons. Once in America, new arrivals satisfied different demands in the labor markets of the Mid-Atlantic colonies. What is most apparent from the study of this region is that the English element among the immigrants, although economically important, was small in numbers, as compared to the Scots, Irish, and Germans.[30] As historian Ned Landsman has argued, the emergence of the Middle Colonies "represented a distinct phase in British colonial settlement, the time in which disparate English colonial outposts on the North American mainland were drawn together into a contiguous and interdependent line of increasingly British colonies. In the middle was a society in which the aspiration for land to provide for families led to a steady course of extended development."[31] Even though fewer English men and women migrated to North America, and more German speakers arrived, the colonies themselves became more British as the eighteenth century unfolded. Regardless of their ethnicity, the adventurers sailing across the Atlantic still arrived on American shores in search of economic opportunity.

The diversity of the eighteenth-century migration flow to British America is also emphasized by Bernard Bailyn, whose landmark study *Voyagers to the West* treats the passage of peoples to colonial British America during the period from 1760–1776—the third phase of English overseas migration. The principal primary source for his volume is the "Register of Immigrants" compiled by British customs officials during the years 1773–1776, which includes details on the origin, age, status, competence, and intended destination of 9,364 individuals bound as emigrants for North America. Bailyn's most significant finding is that not one but two migration flows are recorded in the customs register. The first group of emigrants had their origins in the southern

TABLE 4.1 Seventeenth-Century English Migration to North America By Destination

Destination	Timing	Scale
West Indies	mostly pre-1660	200,000
Chesapeake	mostly post-1660	120,000
Middle Colonies	entirely post-1660	23,500
New England	1630–1641	21,000
South Carolina	entirely post-1660	3,800
Totals		**368,300**

TABLE 4.2 Emigration from the British Isles to America, 1600–1780

	1601–1700	1701–1780
England and Wales	350,000	80,000
Scotland	7,000	75,000
Ireland: Total	20,000–40,000	115,000
Ireland: Ulster		70,000
Ireland: Southern		45,000
Total	377,000–397,000	270,000

half of England and sailed from the cities of either London or Bristol. These individuals, who were disproportionately young unmarried men, typically worked as artisans. They crossed the Atlantic in small groups and intended to take up skilled employment in the Mid-Atlantic colonies or the Chesapeake. The second group of emigrants came either from Scotland or from northern England. Men and women in this second category were also young, but their skills were primarily agricultural. They typically traveled in larger groups which originated in the same geographic area and sometimes comprised families. After arriving in Philadelphia or New York, these emigrants usually headed west and south in search of inexpensive fertile land. Bailyn found that people in the first group decided to emigrate either because they experienced diminishing demand for their skills at home or because they believed that their skills would command higher wages in the New World. Those in the second group, like their seventeenth-century predecessors, usually abandoned their English homes in pursuit of better standards of living overseas. While economic motivations for emigration predominated in these groups, other reasons for leaving home persisted among individuals and families in the eighteenth century.[32]

Bailyn's research reveals that migrants to the British Atlantic colonies were becoming more highly skilled and specialized in the eighteenth century. Among the emigrants whose occupations are indicated in the register, the largest number described themselves as trained artisans and craftsmen. Most claimed occupations that required skills typically acquired through apprenticeship, some in extremely high-skilled arts and crafts. A wide range of trades appear in the register and a plurality of emigrants had worked in the textile industry. While all the Atlantic destinations so popular in the seventeenth century still drew some people, after 1760 only a fraction went to the Caribbean and even fewer chose the long-established settlements along rivers and tributaries of the Chesapeake Bay. The majority pursued their fortunes in the more metropolitan and commercial areas of the Mid-Atlantic colonies or they established family farms in the southern backcountry. England's overall quantitative contribution to transatlantic migration in this period may have declined, but it remained extremely significant qualitatively.[33]

One exception, though, may be the transportation of English convicts to America from 1718–1775. The leading authority on this subject, historian Roger Ekirch, believes that England transported as many as 36,000 convicts to the British colonies during these years. Over ninety percent of them were bound for Pennsylvania and the Chesapeake region, with the rest sent to labor in the West Indies. The majority of these convicts were English, raising to at least 50,000 the total number of voluntary and involuntary migrants from England to America in the six decades preceding the Revolution.[34]

Taken together, recent analyses suggest that the seventeenth century, rather than the eighteenth, was the crucial century for English migration to colonial British America. By contemporary standards the movement of peoples was tremendous. While the annual exodus from England would be higher in the nineteenth century, the emigration rate relative to domestic population never exceeded that of the period between 1646–1670. The white population in colonial America was overwhelmingly English at the end of the seventeenth century. This situation reversed in the eighteenth century when English settlers, though economically and culturally significant, became the minority of passengers on board transatlantic ships.[35]

SOURCES AND METHOD

The estimates suggested in seventeenth- and eighteenth-century migration scholarship must be used with caution because the surviving sources—and the data they yield—are not evenly distributed across the period. Historians have a wide variety of records available for the study of the transatlantic movement of English peoples in the early modern era. Much recent research has relied upon lists of emigrants departing the English ports of Bristol, London, and Liverpool during several series of years from 1654–1776. Other researchers have exploited ship registers, population estimates compiled by colonial contemporaries, and the first United States census in 1790. In one of the most sophisticated analyses, historians of the seventeenth-century Chesapeake mined the archives for information on the lives of hundreds of settlers in this region, calculated provincial birth and mortality rates, and then constructed tables of life expectancy. From these figures they produced a fairly reliable estimate of the total number of whites who migrated to Virginia and Maryland in the seventeenth century.

As complicated as the quantitative methods employed in analysis of the seventeenth century may seem, they pale in comparison to the difficulties encountered when estimating population changes in the eighteenth century. In the 1700s, the range of destinations, and therefore the demographic experiences of the migrants, were altogether more varied than they had ever been before. Seventeenth-century adventurers interested in America could choose plantations in the Chesapeake or Caribbean over town life in Puritan New England. It was not hard for potential colonists to distinguish among the options. By the eighteenth century, emigrants weighed Philadelphia and New York City against Charleston, compared the Virginia and Carolina backcountries to life along the Georgia frontier. In addition, the increasing movement of peoples from one region to another (particularly southward and westward) further complicates the eighteenth-century data, making it difficult to distinguish between transatlantic migration from Europe and internal migration from other places in colonial America.

EMIGRATION AND CULTURE IN COLONIAL BRITISH AMERICA AND THE ATLANTIC WORLD

The cultural traditions that emigrants carried from the Old World, and the environment that they found in the New, created colonial American cultures. Circumstance at home and abroad influenced this process. Political and economic events in Europe–such as wars, famines, and religious persecutions–changed the sociocultural composition and material resources of emigrants departing for America. Similarly, domestic conditions and developments—such as the availability of inexpensive land, changing Indian relations, and the switch from indentured servitude to African slavery—altered the world which immigrants encountered upon their arrival.

Historians have advanced many explanations for the changing nature of early American cultures. Some argue that Europeans' confrontations with the New World's physical geographies and native peoples most influenced the colonial cultures that developed after 1600. Others maintain that the traditions which emigrants carried across the Atlantic had the greatest impact upon American societies as they evolved from the seventeenth century onward.[36] Whether one subscribes to environment or inheritance theories of cultural diffusion, the changing patterns of European migration to North America certainly altered the formation and perpetuation of cultural patterns over time. Seventeenth-century English men and women settled in every colonial region, and these immigrants, or their descendants, typically dominated the colonial societies which evolved. Though often challenged by disease, weather, and Indian enemies, English immigrants in New England, the Chesapeake, and the West Indies attempted to replicate many of the political institutions, social systems, and cultural traditions they experienced in England. This pattern likely continued into the eighteenth century along frontier areas of colonial America, where immigrants tended to cluster together in religious or ethnic groups.

The relative impact of English and other European immigrants and their cultures upon established colonial societies diminished by the early eighteenth century. In each colony, the proportion of immigrants in the population decreased within several generations of its founding. Especially in the New England and the Mid-Atlantic regions, places with comparatively high birthrates and sustained natural population growth, the migration rates needed to rise substantially in order for immigrants to exert a proportional influence on colonial American cultures. Since such increases did not happen, later immigrants either assimilated into Anglo-American society or found a way to establish separate communities within the broader colonial culture.[37] Thus, the falling rate of English migration to North America, even when accompanied by a rising tide of German and Scots-Irish emigration, did not hinder the Anglicization of colonial cultures in decades preceding the American Revolution.

In conclusion, the initially English, and later broadly European migration of peoples across the Atlantic prevented any part of the colonial world from evolving in isolation. This process helped to integrate the economies, cultures, and to a lesser extent, the politics of the Atlantic world through the seventeenth and eighteenth centuries. Sustained contact with England and with other colonies (through internal migration, re-migration, and trade) connected individuals, families, economies, and cultures on both sides of the ocean. Such interaction between early Americans and their European counterparts ensured that, as historian Alison Games has recently argued, "this new Atlantic world was balanced on a fulcrum between remote colonial outposts and frequent interaction."[38] While England's colonies certainly differed from one another, these variations did not evolve in a vacuum. The annual inflow of immigrants constantly renewed European influences in America, and internal migration expanded regional colonial cultures into new areas. The continual movement of British men and women across the Atlantic was not intended to Anglicize the colonies—England had better political and commercial ways to effect this change. Such a development, moreover, was naturally limited by colonists' encounters with the American environment and its native inhabitants. Yet the ebb and flow of emigrants did foster communications between the New World, the Old World, and the broader Atlantic world which joined them together. The vast expanse of ocean which seemed at first glance to separate men and women in America from their friends and families in England, ultimately became a heavily-traversed passage connecting peoples and cultures, colonies and the kingdom.

➡ FOCUS QUESTIONS

1. What is internal migration and when did it take off?
2. How did migration patterns to British America change after 1680?
3. Why did the influence of newly-arriving immigrants decline in the early eighteenth century?

Searching for Prosperity: German Migration to the British American Colonies, 1680–1780

Rosalind J. Beiler

In May 1717, a young man named Caspar Wistar packed his belongings, collected the money he had saved, and set out from a little Palatine village a few miles south of Heidelberg for the British American colonies. The son of a forester, he had worked as a hunter's apprentice "until the Lord of all Lords inspired" him "to travel to Pennsylvania."[1] The young man's family and friends tried desperately to convince him not to leave, but he was determined to go. So he went to Heidelberg, where he was to meet a ship to take him down the Neckar River to the Rhine River and on to Rotterdam.

When he recalled his journey some twenty-five to thirty years later, Wistar remembered most vividly the difficulty of leaving home. He did not write about the transatlantic voyage, the part of the journey so many other immigrants described. Instead, he told of the many tears that he and his family and friends had shed when he left home. His departure was complicated by the fact that the ship on which he had hoped to travel was delayed in Heidelberg for eight days. Rather than return home and face a second tearful departure, he decided to visit relatives on the other side of the Rhine River. Wistar remembered that he left Heidelberg with a "heavy heart."[2]

When he was about a half an hour outside of the city, he decided to turn around and look back one last time: "There I saw from afar someone running and waving with his hat. I stood there waiting until he came. Who should it be but my father's servant, who said to me that my mother could not find peace until she had seen me once more, and she would be there shortly." The young man waited for his mother and when she arrived, they "embraced each other around the neck and cried with one another." After some time had passed, and they both had stopped crying, she tried to convince him to return home with her, but Wistar refused. He said that if he went home, his "heart was so taken with the new land that I could not stay and because it was so, I pleaded with her sincerely to let me go now in God's name." So he continued on his way. In two short sentences, he states in a matter-of-fact way that he traveled from Bacharach to Rotterdam, from Rotterdam to London, and from there to Philadelphia.[3]

Wistar suggests two sources for his emotional departure: first, he was leaving against the wishes of his parents and friends; and, second, Pennsylvania was not as well known in 1717 as it was in the 1740s. Each of these suggestions, however, raises more questions. Why did he decide to leave home in the first place? What had he heard about Pennsylvania? Why did he choose Pennsylvania over Carolina—the other British colony whose proprietors were actively soliciting German-speaking settlers?

During the earliest years of migration, promotional literature played an important role in recruiting settlers and establishing expectations about the colonies. As the century progressed and the numbers of newcomers increased, letters to friends and family members at home provided additional first-hand accounts of the opportunity and difficulties involved in moving across the Atlantic. In addition, "newlanders," those who had already made the journey and returned to Europe to transact business or recruit additional colonists, gave oral reports about the colonies and assisted immigrants with their transportation arrangements. By the time German migration began to taper off in the 1760s and 1770s, a large flow of people, information, and goods, had crossed the ocean in both directions and created a German presence in the New World that was unimaginable in 1717 when Wistar set off for Philadelphia.

FLOW AND COMPOSITION OF GERMAN-SPEAKING IMMIGRANTS

Wistar was one of 100,000 or more German-speaking immigrants who traveled to the British American colonies between 1680–1780.[4] While these settlers shared a knowledge of the high-German language, they did not necessarily have a common political or cultural background. Germany did not exist as a nation in the eighteenth century. Instead, most of the immigrants came from the Rhine Lands which were made up of more than 350 distinct political territories in areas that today belong to Germany, France, and Switzerland.[5] In the colonies, their American neighbors lumped them together and called them "Dutch" (an anglicization of "Deutsch"), "Germans," or "Palatines." In Europe, however, the immigrants considered themselves "Württembergers," or "Palatines," or "Swiss" rather than Germans. Each group spoke a local dialect of German and maintained local customs and traditions.

Nevertheless, immigrants from the Rhine Lands did share several common characteristics. Most of them came from rural villages and were farmers or artisans. They were overwhelmingly Protestant—the majority belonged to either the Lutheran or Reformed churches. Many of the settlers came from political territories where the heads of state were trying to strengthen and consolidate their resources and power. Also, perhaps most influential, they shared the experience of repeated warfare that dominated the region in much of the late seventeenth and early eighteenth centuries.[6]

The large majority of the German-speaking immigrants traveling to the British colonies between 1680–1780 arrived through the port of Philadelphia. The flow of settlers into William Penn's colony can be divided into three periods. During the earliest period, from 1683 until the mid-1720s, roughly 20,000 German-speaking immigrants moved to Pennsylvania. Most of these early settlers belonged to small religious groups (Pietists, Quakers, Mennonites, Dunkers, and Baptists) that were exiled or discriminated against in the Rhine Lands. (Map 5.1) They were lured to the colony by Penn's promises of religious toleration. Some of them, like the Germantown Quakers who came in 1683 and the Mennonites who arrived in 1710, traveled as groups that negotiated with Penn or his agents for tracts of land so that they could settle together.

This picture supposedly shows William Penn greeting an immigrant on the docks of Philadelphia. Frontispiece from *Der Hoch-Deutsch Americanische Calender 1757* (Germantown, 1756). *Courtesy of Library Company of Philadelphia.*

Others, like some of Wistar's shipmates who crossed the Atlantic in 1717, came as individuals or families who had relatives and friends already in the colony.[7]

A series of agricultural disasters in 1709 led to a mass migration to the New World via London from 1709–1710. The British government, anxious to find a solution to the thronging crowds arriving in London, and determined to make better use of its colonial resources, sent more than 3,000 German-speaking settlers to New

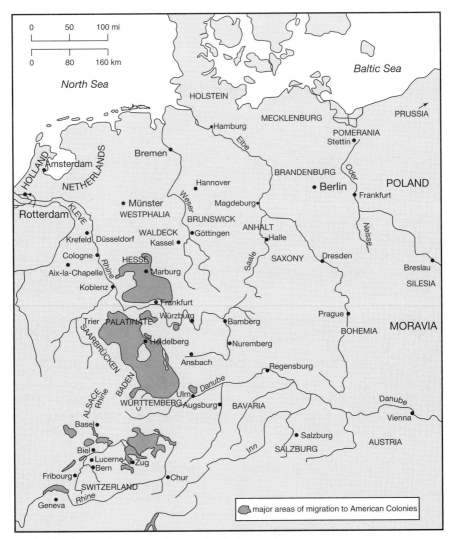

MAP 5.1 Areas of German migration to North America.

York rather than Philadelphia. In New York, the migrants were obliged to participate in a government scheme to produce naval stores, primarily pitch and tar. The British experiment never succeeded in earning grand profits. Nevertheless, the immigrants remained in New York and began to filter into New Jersey and Pennsylvania by the mid 1720s.[8]

About the same time that some of the New York immigrants moved to Pennsylvania, a second period of migration began in Philadelphia. Between 1727–1754, a rapidly increasing number of ships entered the colony's main port, peaking during the period from 1749–1754 when an average of twenty-one ships arrived each year.

While many of the ships carried young, single indentured servants, German-speaking immigrants during this time tended to travel with extended family, neighbors, or friends and they often brought along considerable financial resources. They belonged overwhelmingly to the Lutheran and Reformed churches and usually moved in search of a better standard of living.[9]

Following 1754, the number of German newcomers traveling to Pennsylvania dropped dramatically, signaling the beginning of a third period of immigration. The sharp decline in the late 1750s and early 1760s was, no doubt, the result of the Seven Years War, which made transportation to the colonies difficult. Even after the war ended, though, the number of immigrant ships entering Philadelphia's port never reached the pre-war volume. By the second half of the eighteenth century the Eastern European states of Prussia, Russia, and the Habsburg Empire all competed with Britain in recruiting settlers from Southwest Germany. In many cases, these states offered better incentives for migration than those available in British North America.[10]

Between 1754–1775, when war once again interrupted migration flows, settlers were increasingly young, single men who came alone and with fewer resources than those who had arrived in the 1730s and 1740s. Consequently, larger numbers of immigrants came as indentured servants and worked as day laborers for longer periods of time before buying land. Earlier immigrants had purchased most of the inexpensive land close to Philadelphia, so that new arrivals needed to move further inland to find affordable property. They began to follow other German-speaking colonists south along the Great Wagon Road into the fringe areas of Anglo-American settlement in Maryland, Virginia, and North Carolina. Like those who had come in the earlier period, these newcomers tended to be Lutheran or Reformed (Calvinist) and were motivated to migrate by long-term trends in overpopulation and land scarcity. By the late 1750s, however, a well-developed system for recruiting German-speaking immigrants was also luring potential settlers with the promise of affordable land and abundant labor opportunities.[11]

Although nearly eighty percent of the German-speaking people traveling to British America arrived through the port of Philadelphia, by the eve of American independence nearly all of the colonies included settlers of German descent. (Map 5.2) As we have already seen, immigrants into Pennsylvania and New York spilled over into New Jersey and the Southern Piedmont region. Others, however, traveled directly to Maryland and Virginia through ports on the Chesapeake Bay. By 1760, most of the German-speaking settlers living in South Carolina had arrived through Charleston, and the large majority of those living in Georgia had entered that colony through Savannah.[12] Two groups of southern settlers who differed in significant ways from the majority of German-speaking immigrants were the Moravians of North Carolina and the Georgia Salzburgers. Both groups migrated to the British colonies for religious purposes and both came from regions outside of the Rhine Lands.[13] Even New England had a small minority of German-speaking colonists; there were German settlements in Nova Scotia, Maine, and Massachusetts by 1776.[14]

Thus, as the eighteenth century progressed, German-speaking immigrants settled throughout the British colonies in a wide arc that spanned from Nova Scotia to Georgia. Why had they chosen British America as their destination? What opportunities did they perceive in the colonies? How did the information available to them

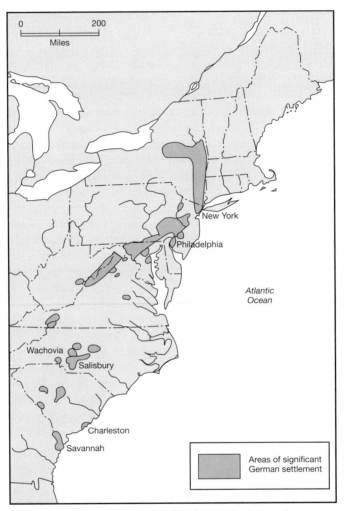

MAP 5.2   Areas of German immigration to North America

change over time? A return to Wistar, the immigrant whose story opened this essay, provides a human dimension to the decision-making process.

EARLY PROMOTIONAL LITERATURE

Wistar's decision to emigrate came early in the eighteenth century, prior to the spread of "Pennsylvania fever," and during the period when a relatively small number of German-speaking settlers migrated to British America. He remarked that part of the reason his departure created so much sadness was that "at that time, it [Pennsylvania] was not so well known as now, so that it was thought one would never more be heard from again, much less seen again."[15] Nevertheless, by 1717, people from the Rhine Lands had been moving to the colonies for over thirty years. The proprietors of individual colonies and their agents were successfully circulating promotional pamphlets and recruiting settlers throughout continental Europe.

Wistar's exposure to this literature and oral information about America shaped both his decision to leave home and his expectations about life in the British colonies. He and other immigrants attributed their choices to divine inspiration but they also acknowledged the influence of books and pamphlets. When asked in 1709 who had told him about the colonies, Philip Adam Hartman from Nassau-Weilburg responded that "God had given him the idea" to emigrate. That same year, another settler stated that he first heard about America from "English agents at Frankfurt and writings brought by them." Johannes Willig "had a book about the Island," as continental Europeans referred to the British colonies. And Johannes Flach had bought a book at Frankfurt for three "Batzen" in which "there was writing about the Island."[16]

For those who either did not own the books or could not read, their friends and neighbors passed on information about America. In 1709, Johannes Linck heard "of books about the Island" through people "from Darmstadt who are going." Another immigrant had "heard of books in Braunfels and at Altenkirchen which Schoolmaster Petri at Reiskirchen brought to the village." A third reportedly heard about the British colonies through people from the Palatinate. Philipps Petri noted that "people everywhere are talking about [the colonies]."[17]

News of British America was spreading across Europe through both the written and spoken word. What were the "books" to which these people referred and how did they portray American opportunities? In 1681, immediately after he received his charter for Pennsylvania, Penn published *Some Account of the Province of Pennsylvania* to recruit settlers. The pamphlet described the colony's landscape and natural resources. He also outlined its constitution, his policies for granting settlers land, the kinds of people best suited for migration, and the preparations required for the long transatlantic journey.[18] Shortly after its initial publication, Benjamin Furly, an English Quaker living in the Netherlands and Penn's agent, translated the pamphlet into Dutch and German for distribution throughout Europe.[19]

Penn's tract was the first in a series of publications printed during the next four decades aimed at potential German-speaking colonists.[20] Among the German-language literature, three works were especially influential. Francis Daniel Pastorius, after traveling to Pennsylvania and founding Germantown in 1683, wrote a series of pamphlets and letters which were published in Europe.[21] Daniel Falkner, who arrived in Pennsylvania with a group of Pietists in 1694, returned to Europe shortly before 1700 as an emissary from the American Pietists "to make known the true state and spiritual condition of the Germans who had emigrated to Pennsylvania," and to solicit aid and recruits.[22] The Pietists were a group of religious reformers who emphasized individual piety, a personal relationship with God, small-group bible studies, and prayer. In some German states they were exiled; in others, they became a part of the state churches. In 1702, Falkner published *Curious Report of Pennsylvania,* which contained the answers to over one hundred questions about the colony.[23] Finally, Josua Kochertal, a Lutheran pastor from the Neckar River Valley, wrote *Detailed and Circumstantial Report about the famous land Carolina which lies in English America* in 1706.[24]

In each case, the author promoted a particular settlement scheme. Pastorius sought to recruit additional colonists on behalf of the Frankfurt Company, a group of Pietist investors who had purchased 15,000 acres of land in Pennsylvania.[25] Falkner collected information and published *Curious Report* in conjunction with Pietist leaders at Halle who were considering sending settlers to the British colonies.[26] Kochertal seems to have acted as an agent for a company of investors hoping to recruit immigrants to Carolina.[27]

INCENTIVES FOR MIGRATION

Each of these tracts provided incentives for Wistar and other German-speaking Europeans to emigrate. First, and not surprisingly, each of the pamphlets promised inexpensive and abundant land.[28] Pastorius claimed that in Pennsylvania, both the wealthy and the poor could obtain property. Those with capital to invest could purchase land at a reasonable rate while those without money could rent it for a penny per acre. Even settlers who could not afford their transportation costs, and instead signed indentures to pay for their trip, could receive fifty acres for an annual rent of a half penny per acre upon the completion of their contracts.[29] Kochertal's descriptions of land in Carolina were even more compelling. That colony's proprietors reportedly guaranteed each head of household fifty acres of land as a gift. If a householder required more land, he could obtain as much as one hundred acres. Householders received their land rent-free for the first three years, and thereafter they only needed to pay a ground rent of an "Englischen Stuber," which, according to Kochertal, was only one-third of the value of a "Kreutzer."[30]

In addition to highlighting the inexpensive cost of land in the British colonies, promoters pointed to its fertility and abundance. Falkner promised that Pennsylvania's land was excellent and that the growing season was comparable to the Palatinate, Magdeburg, or Halberstadt. The colony's rich soil, however, meant that crops grew twice as fast as in Germany. This made a second harvest possible.[31] Kochertal claimed that South Carolina was "one of the most fertile regions which can be found" and was preferable in many places to Germany or England.[32] Furthermore, the vast array of crops and produce that grew in the American colonies seemed to do so with less human energy than in Europe. In Pennsylvania, Falkner observed, peaches and cherries were plentiful and "grew like weeds."[33] Kochertal reported that Carolina's colonists raised grains, rice, and tobacco very profitably, and that wild grapes could be harvested for wine. In addition, other nut and fruit trees simply grew wild, without being planted from seed.[34]

Such reports of natural abundance held particular appeal for people like Wistar. Memories of recent wars were only too vivid. Many of the states along the Rhine River had barely recovered from the devastation of the Thirty Years War (1618–1648) when Louis XIV invaded the Protestant areas with French troops in the 1680s and 1690s. A combination of plundering enemy armies, the provision of foodstuffs for friendly troops, and devastating, harsh winters led to food shortages and crop failures by the first decade of the eighteenth century. At the same time, an expanding population made it difficult for people to find inexpensive land. It is no wonder that the young Wistar, whose father faced difficulty in purchasing land in Waldhilsbach, found the glowing descriptions of the British colonies appealing.[35]

A second incentive prominent in the promotional literature was the non-intrusive government and tax structures of the British colonies. Pastorius, in describing Pennsylvania's government, emphasized that "each year certain persons are elected from the whole people" to the colonial Assembly. These legislators "make the necessary laws and ordinances for that year according to the condition of the time and the people, and thereby prevent encroaching vices."[36] Pastorius also pointed out that elected officials in the colony were chosen by secret ballot, so that "none may know who has voted for, or against, him." He believed this prevented bribery and encouraged honest behavior, since "if anyone has conducted himself improperly this year, a better man may be chosen next time."[37]

Pastorius also stressed the colonists' role in determining taxes. He claimed that "neither the king himself nor his envoys, bailiffs, nor governors may lay any kind of burden or tax upon the subjects, unless those subjects themselves have first voluntarily resolved and consented to give a specified amount." Furthermore, he observed, "no tax may remain in force for longer than a single year."[38] In the Palatinate, subjects paid a whole series of taxes and tithes to the state, local governments, landlords, and the church. In fact, members of Wistar's own village, and many others in the surrounding area, were still required to perform compulsory labor for the Elector, the head of state in the Palatinate.[39] Given their circumstances, Pennsylvania's taxation policies must have seemed a fantasy.

In describing Carolina, Kochertal also stressed low taxes. He claimed that instead of giving local government officials tithes for supporting the clergy, the colonists themselves collected tithes to distribute to their ministers. Almost incredulously, Kochertal added that "the entire annual contribution due to the authorities comes only from the ground rent." The settlers were "otherwise completely freed from all obligations, compulsory labor, serfdom, and all other burdens, whatever they may be named, and the authorities are prepared to give security that it will always remain so in the future."[40] For European villagers like Wistar who were struggling against expanding state bureaucracies and growing tax obligations, Carolina sounded like paradise.[41]

A final incentive colonial promoters used to attract potential settlers was religious toleration. Pastorius promised that in Pennsylvania, "no one sect may raise itself above the others, each shall enjoy freedom of conscience, and no one shall be forced to be present at any public services for the worship of God, and no one shall be disturbed in his belief or religion."[42] Falkner, in providing an overview of religious toleration among all of the British colonies, also claimed that in Pennsylvania, "all sects except the Jews and such as absolutely deny Christianity, are not only countenanced, but they are granted the free exercise of their religion and are undisturbed and protected by the public authorities."[43] He compared this to Maryland, Virginia, and New England, which all allowed the "sects" and Jews to worship in private, but not in public. In his description of Carolina, Kochertal specified that the Lutherans and Reformed as well as the Mennonites would enjoy religious toleration and freedom of conscience.[44]

Religious toleration was a critical incentive in the earliest years of German-speaking migration when Mennonites, Quakers, Dunkers, and Pietists were being harassed and banished from many German states. Pastorius and Falkner were both closely tied to the Pietist conventicles at Frankfurt and Halle, before the movement was fully incorporated into Prussian Lutheranism.[45] The Pietists appealed directly to immigrants interested in religious toleration. Kochertal responded to the tactics that had already proven profitable in Pennsylvania at precisely the time when officials were negotiating another forced exile of Swiss Mennonites.[46] Each of these authors had specific reasons for stressing the broad religious privileges available in the British colonies.

Freedom from an intrusive official church, however, may have attracted a much wider audience among Lutheran, Reformed, and Catholic congregants. Following his invasions of the German states along the Rhine in 1688, Louis XIV forced subjects in the Palatinate and other traditionally Protestant lands to attend Catholic mass. Although the Peace of Ryswick in 1697 brought guarantees of religious toleration for Protestants and Catholics alike, squabbles and conflicts between local clergy intruded constantly into the lives of Palatine villagers. The promise that no one would force them to attend any particular church enticed villagers, even when they did not suffer from overt religious persecution.[47]

WISTAR'S DECISION

The incentives of inexpensive land, low taxes, and religious toleration that Pastorius, Falkner, and Kochertal wrote about undoubtedly influenced Wistar's decision to leave home. Each of the authors was connected to religious communication networks that included areas close to Waldhilsbach, Wistar's home village, and their literature was motivating people to move across the Atlantic. Whether or not he actually read their pamphlets, Wistar would have been familiar with the promises they made.

Pastorius' fellow travelers to Germantown, Pennsylvania were Quakers and Mennonites who were linked to a network of congregations that spanned the area between the Netherlands and Switzerland. Regular communication among the communities evolved as Dutch and Palatine church leaders helped exiled Swiss Mennonites find new homes between 1670–1720. At the same time, English Quaker missionaries traveled up the Rhine convincing Mennonites to join the Society of Friends. Penn's agents funneled promotional literature and information about his colony through these channels, luring settlers across the Atlantic to his province. The Germantown Quakers were the earliest emigrants from towns like Krefeld and Kriegsheim that each had a Mennonite congregation and a new Friends meeting.[48]

By 1710, some of the exiled Swiss Mennonites, who had settled temporarily in the Palatinate, migrated to the Pennsylvania backcountry. Within a few years, they sent Martin Kindig back to Europe to recruit additional emigrants. In 1717, Palatine ministers reported to Dutch religious leaders that 300 Mennonites were traveling to Rotterdam en route to the British colonies.[49] Many of the emigrants came from villages close to Wistar's home. Mennonite families had been living in the area since at least the 1680s, and their numbers had grown with the arrival of Swiss exiles.[50] Wistar's arrival on the same ship with members of this group, and his later business relationships with them, suggests that they were an important source of information prior to his decision to leave home.[51]

Wistar would have known about Pennsylvania from other sources as well. Both Pastorius and Falkner were associated with Pietists at Frankfurt and Halle.[52] In 1706, an itinerant preacher with connections to the same groups of Pietists had created quite a stir when he visited Heidelberg, just a few miles from Wistar's village. He preached to a growing number of people who were convinced their clergy were corrupt, and attended private prayer meetings rather than church services. Palatine church officials, who were in the midst of a difficult transition from a single state religion to three official churches, felt threatened by these "sectarians" who dismissed organized religion.[53] A number of the missionary's followers were imprisoned and sentenced to hard labor before being banished from the Palatinate. Many Pietists from the area eventually moved to Pennsylvania, where they joined the Dunker (Brethren) church.[54] Falkner's *Curious Report* circulated within these Pietist circles and would have been well-known among Wistar's neighbors.

Kocherthal, furthermore, was a Lutheran minister at another village just a few miles from Waldhilsbach. Unhappy with the conditions of the Palatine Lutheran church, he had traveled to London secretly in 1704 to assess the opportunities for emigration. After returning and publishing his pamphlet, he led a group of forty-one people to London in 1708, where they eventually received support from Queen Anne for their transportation to New York. The following year, thousands of emigrants, hoping to find a better life in America, sailed down the Rhine en route to Rotterdam, London, and the British colonies.[55] Many of the 1709 and 1710 emigrants came from towns close to Wistar's home. One group of families left from Leimen and Sandhausen, just a few miles from the hunting lodge at Bruchhausen where Wistar served as a hunter's apprentice. Several of Wistar's shipmates in 1717 had friends or acquaintances who had followed Kochertal's group to New York.[56]

Even closer to home, Anthony Henckel, the Lutheran minister at the church where Wistar's father was a member, determined to leave the Palatinate for Pennsylvania. Henckel had spent years squabbling with Catholic officials over the use of church buildings and property. When he petitioned the consistory (the governing body of the local congregation) for permission to emigrate, he claimed he could not support his family of seven children on the meager income his poor parishes supplied. Oral traditions record that Henckel migrated to New Hanover, Pennsylvania with some of his parishioners the same year that Wistar left.[57]

Wistar did not acknowledge knowing Henckel, nor is there evidence to suggest he established connections with Henckel after he was in the colony. The young man claimed that the only friend who accompanied him to Pennsylvania was Abraham Rhiem. Local and regional officials, nevertheless, remarked upon Henckel's departure. The event also would have been well-publicized among the members of his congregations.[58] It was no accident, therefore, that Wistar decided to leave home at the same time colonial promotional literature was luring so many of his neighbors and acquaintances away from the area.

EXPANDED COMMUNICATION CHANNELS

Promotional literature was one of the primary means for recruiting immigrants during the early period of migration when Wistar made his decision. Religious communication networks were critical for disseminating information about the colonies. However, as early immigrants like Wistar began to write letters home, more first-hand knowledge became available to potential settlers. By mid-century, family and commercial communication supplemented the religious channels through which the early pamphlets flowed. As reliable information increased, so did migration, and, as larger numbers of immigrants arrived, contacts across the Atlantic expanded.

In many cases, letters home from people in America reinforced the same incentives reflected in the promotional literature. One immigrant wrote in 1724 that Pennsylvania was "a precious land with the finest wheat, as well as unusual corn, fine broomcorn, maize, and white beets of such quality as I never saw in Germany."[59] Another one commented on the easily-available land. He promised that "land is not really dear. One takes up 200 acres, promises to pay, by installments, within 10 years, and instead clears off his debt in 5 years."[60] Immigrants frequently expressed surprise at the low taxes and privileges inhabitants enjoyed, and repeatedly referred to British America as a "free land." In 1724, Christopher Sauer stressed that, in Pennsylvania, "neither in the country nor in the city are any imposts known, no duty, no excise, no contribution, in short nothing but a ground-rent of about 20 Kreuzer on 100 acres." He added with amazement that the closest thing in the colony to compulsory labor was that "twice a year the neighbors congregate to repair the roads."[61] An immigrant to New York claimed in 1749 that many paid more for an evening of drinking in a tavern than they paid each year for their annual taxes.[62]

What distinguished immigrant letters from promotional tracts, however, was that they came from trustworthy sources. Family members or friends who had actually been in America confirmed the excellent opportunities in the literature. In 1725, Sauer wrote glowing letters to his acquaintances back home about Pennsylvania's cheap land. "Now we are here in a well-blessed land. There are neither guilds nor burdens from the authorities. My host . . . has fifty acres of fields and forest, for which he must pay the governor one and a half *Reichstaler* yearly. . . . Mr. Güldin has about nine hundred acres, with a rent of two *Reichstaler*."[63] Another newcomer wrote to European family members that his host "came to this country in 1719 and did not bring much with him. Now he has property worth at least 1000 *Florin,* three horses, cows and sheep, hens and sows. . . . There are more people like him who came here in 1719 and now have properties worth 2000 to 3000 *Florin,* and livestock in quantity."[64] Both immigrants painted pictures of wealth unimaginable to their friends living in the war-torn Rhine Lands. Their stories were believable because they had seen the abundance with their own eyes.

Furthermore, early immigrants writing home gave specific information about the labor market that was more current than the earlier literature. One immigrant noted in 1724 that "a reaper earns one *Florin* a day in the summer . . . and the work is not nearly so hard as in Germany."[65] Another sent a glowing report in 1737 about job opportunities in Pennsylvania. He claimed there were no poor people in the colony because anyone who wanted to work could easily support himself: "A day laborer can earn as much as 15 [Swiss] *Shillings* a day in the summer time and 1/2 *Gulden* in the winter. Shoemakers and tailors earn the same. Masons and carpenters earn at least 12 *Batzen* or 1 *Gulden* and the smiths receive very good pay."[66] Although letters may have exaggerated possibilities for work, they were credible because they included exact detail and they came from reliable sources.

Letters home also gave clear instructions about how to prepare for the journey. One immigrant wrote telling his in-laws that they should bring along butter, wheat flour, sausages, and bacon to eat on the voyage.[67] In 1735, Hans Martin wrote to his daughters in Switzerland advising them to pack food that would not make them excessively thirsty, as water on these long voyages was always in short supply. He also recommended bringing good tea, and spices such as cinnamon and nutmeg to take away the bad taste of the water. He noted that sugar was duty-free in Holland, so that they should bring as much as they wanted, and that it was essential to bring along vinegar and wine.[68] The following year, another immigrant recommended to his cousin that anyone who wanted to make the journey should bring along a ham for every two persons and a barrel of vinegar.[69]

Not only did immigrants in the colonies provide lists of provisions for the journey, they gave advice on ways to save and make money. Wistar wrote to a friend considering moving to Pennsylvania with tips on how to earn a profit on the voyage. He recommended that he bring along "good wine, dried fruit and flour and butter and bread and also meat" to sell on the ship. He suggested that the highest profits would be made at sea rather than in port.[70] Johannes Diederich Fahnenstock suggested in 1728 that settlers invest in merchandise to sell, rather than carrying cash. He advised transporting a variety of cloth, new handkerchiefs, new ribbons, lace, pins, and needles. He reported that the best sellers, however, were guns: "A gun that costs there five *Rix Thalers,* will cost here fifteen dollars." He was adamant that "every person ought to bring at least two guns with him—my father-in-law two—Wilhelm two—and Peter two." He warned that immigrants should limit the new merchandise they imported, and pack it in the bottoms of their chests, to avoid paying high customs in England.[71]

Fahnenstock's warning reflects a gradual shift in information channels that took place as German-speaking migration increased. Immigrant letters encouraged new commercial activity that could be illicit because of the settlers' status as non-British subjects and British mercantilist policies. According to the Navigation Acts, settlers could import personal household goods duty-free, but new European merchandise intended for resale was subject to customs. The collection of duties in England was inconsistent, however, and letters home indicate a good deal of smuggling among German-speaking immigrants. In 1724, Sauer claimed that "(t)he Palatines have brought very many goods with them so that many a man has made up to 600 *Florins* by this trip for everything was free because it was not examined in England."[72] The following year, he recommended that "[w]hen one sails here from Holland, one can bring along, of course, much merchandise, as all goods here cost twice as much as over there. . . . If examined by customs in England, it will be confiscated, because the merchants of England do not tolerate it." He slyly added: "They are not supposed to check in the bedsteads, however."[73] By 1737, Wistar was advising his friend that many immigrants were bringing "scythes and straw knives and iron pans" to sell, but he also warned that he should pay the duties on them or risk having his goods confiscated. If he brought pieces of iron stoves, Wistar suggested that "one must put them first in the fire so that they look like old stoves. Otherwise, one must pay high duties on them."[74]

While the extent of smuggling among immigrants is impossible to discern, letters home clearly influenced settlers to bring extra goods to resell in the colonies. The case of one confiscated ship in 1736, one year before Wistar sent advice to his friend on how to avoid paying duties, illustrates the possibilities. When customs officials in Philadelphia seized the *Princess Augusta,* the forfeited contents included 596 scythes, 165 backs for chimneys, 120 pieces of cast iron, 103 large straw knives, 14 drawing knives, a large number of iron and copper kitchen utensils, 23 dozen clasp knives, a variety of other hardware, 2 dozen printed linen caps, 6 pairs of worsted stockings, 4 pieces of striped cotton handkerchief, 19 pieces of bed ticking, additional linens and dry goods, 2 dozen ivory combs, 3 dozen "spectacles" (eye glasses), 32 pocket looking glasses, and 8 flutes. Customs officials claimed that the goods were all new and the immigrants carrying them had failed to pay duties on them in England. After a lengthy hearing before the admiralty court, the judge determined that the goods had been justly confiscated and he ordered them sold.[75]

Illicit trade was only one link between transatlantic trade and German-speaking migration. In addition, early immigrants like Wistar began to import European merchandise regularly; he purchased specific household wares, tools, and German-language books that were expensive or hard to find in the British colonies. In 1732, he ordered guns, knives, ivory combs, silk handkerchiefs, mirrors, eye glasses, copper tea kettles, and lace, among other things, from his business correspondent in the Palatinate.[76] His guns were custom-made for the American market and matched the description of those Fahnenstock had requested several years earlier. Immigrants coming to the colonies often carried his merchandise along with their personal belongings. When customs officials began to systematically search immigrant ships, Wistar sought out ship captains whom he knew would pay the appropriate duties in London to carry his wares. Thus German-speaking immigration created new markets and trade connections.[77]

Wistar's dependence on ship captains to look after his goods reflects another link between trade and migration: the development of a regularized transportation system to carry the increasing number of immigrants leaving for the colonies. Merchant families in Rotterdam and London began to transport German-speaking settlers across the Atlantic as a part of their diverse commercial ventures in the 1730s and 1740s. Ships generally carried immigrants from Rotterdam to London and then to Philadelphia. After unloading their passengers, the ships, loaded with foodstuff, continued on to the Southern colonies and the West Indies, and returned to Europe with rice, sugar, and rum. As the flow of people leaving for the colonies grew, Philadelphia merchants played a larger role in the transportation system, and ships increasingly sailed back and forth across the Atlantic directly between Philadelphia and London. Larger numbers of immigrants also led to increased regulation of the transportation trade in the Netherlands, and a more specialized and highly-competitive system. By the peak years of immigration in the late 1740s and early 1750s, competition and attempts to squeeze ever-larger numbers of immigrants in less and less space aboard ships led to abuses.[78]

One group of participants in this developing specialized trade who were critical in providing information about the colonies were "newlanders"—the term Europeans used for immigrants to the colonies who returned to the continent to transact business or recruit additional settlers. Wistar's business correspondent first mentioned newlanders in his letters in 1735, when the Pennsylvania German with whom he had hoped to ship Wistar's goods did not arrive in Neckargemünd.[79] Two years later, when he sent his friend instructions on what to bring along to the colonies, Wistar lamented that it was difficult to know what to recommend because so many newlanders were returning to Europe and bringing back merchandise. That year he knew of at least twenty-five who set out across the Atlantic. He advised his friend to watch what the newlanders were buying if he wanted to know the best goods to bring along.[80]

Newlanders provided critical conduits for information crossing the Atlantic. For potential immigrants, they could answer specific questions about life in the colonies or about the practical aspects of the transatlantic voyage. As immigrants themselves, they could speak from first-hand experience. Newlanders frequently carried letters from family members who had migrated earlier or returned to fetch those who had been left behind. Whatever their mission, they had knowledge—of markets, transportation systems, people, or colonial conditions—that was critical for transatlantic communication between German-speaking settlers and their homeland. That specialized knowledge allowed some newlanders to become professional agents in the emerging transportation system. As abuses in the system developed, European governments and competitors warned against the vices of these recruiting agents. Perhaps the best known description of the transatlantic voyage for German-speaking immigrants is that of Gottlieb Mittelberger. Written in 1756, Mittelberger provides a discouraging report on the difficulties of journeying to the colonies. He is especially vehement in his warnings against newlanders, whom he calls "thieves of men."[81]

The abuses of the transportation system—by merchants, ship captains, and newlanders alike—and the growing crowds of destitute immigrants arriving on ships cramped with people ravaged by disease began to change the information immigrants wrote in their letters to Europe. As early as 1732, Wistar was sending letters to Europe advising caution in making decisions to migrate. He reported the horrors of one ship which had arrived the previous year. He claimed the voyage had taken twenty-four weeks, and during that time, more than 100 of the 150 people on board had died from hunger and disease. Those who survived reportedly had to pay the unpaid fare for those who had died. Wistar also cautioned potential settlers about the decreasing availability and high cost of land. He warned that those who could not pay for their ship fare "must be sold for 3, 4, 6, to 8 and more years, and serve as slaves; when their time is out they receive nothing but a poor suit of clothing." Any who still wanted to make the journey after hearing his grim tale should "carefully calculate the cost." If they thought they had sufficient financial means, they should then "counsel the matter with God and learn whether it is his agreeable will," and determine whether or not they are willing to face the many difficulties of the journey and relocating. Wistar warned that "no one [should] depend on his friends that may be here, for these have all they can do to get through themselves. Many reckon without their host in this matter."[82] Another group of concerned Pennsylvania German immigrants sent a warning letter that was published in Frankfurt in 1739. They too described the increasingly-difficult conditions of transatlantic voyages and cautioned potential immigrants from being lured by stories of easy prosperity.[83]

⋐ ⋐ ⋐

By mid-century, when the flow of German-speaking immigrants peaked, warnings about devious newlanders, the deplorable conditions on the transatlantic voyage, and the decreasing opportunities for finding inexpensive land in the British colonies spread through the communication channels that had emerged alongside migration.[84] Then the Seven Years War interrupted the steady travel of ships back and forth across the Atlantic. When immigration resumed in the 1760s, potential settlers faced a completely different world of information from 1717 when Wistar had determined to move to the British colonies. Those who decided to migrate in the second half of the century had access to a wide array of choices in destination, and German-speaking settlers lived in nearly every colony. Furthermore, potential immigrants likely heard both positive and negative reports of the journey to the colonies and the opportunities they faced after their arrival.

If all of this information made their decisions more difficult, from Wistar's perspective at least, newcomers had a good chance of hearing from or seeing their family and friends in Europe again. His own decision to leave home when so little was known about Pennsylvania was a part of the process that shaped both migration and communication between British North America and the Rhine Lands. As an early immigrant, he had been heavily influenced by promotional literature and the information from it that circulated orally through the religious networks of the Rhine Lands. After he migrated to Pennsylvania, he became part of the growing communication networks spanning the Atlantic. As Wistar and other immigrants wrote to their families and friends, they provided first-hand accounts that encouraged or discouraged others from moving to British America. His trade transactions carried out by newlanders evolved with the immigrant transportation system and helped to establish regular correspondence between the colonies and Europe. By the time German-speaking migration began to dwindle in the 1760s and 1770s, potential settlers had access to a wide variety of information that came from many different sources and flowed through both secular and commercial channels.

➡ FOCUS QUESTIONS

1. What common background did settlers from the Rhine Lands have?
2. What attractive features did the British colonies possess for German-speaking immigrants?
3. Describe the role of "newlanders" in immigration.

3

THE AFRICAN DIMENSION

Between 1000 BCE, when man started crossing the oceans, and the High Middle Ages, human migration was a one-way process, David Eltis argues. People spread across the globe, but lost touch with their places of origin. Beginning around 1000 CE, this process was reversed as communities were founded that remained attached to their founder states across the sea. The distinguishing mark of transatlantic migration after 1500 was the fact that migrants traveled across the ocean in order to work for others upon arrival. And most of these migrants were not free. Slaves and "servants" with a labor debt who could be bought and sold predominated before the nineteenth century. The composition and direction of these migratory flows was not simply arranged by European entrepreneurs, but also influenced by the migrants themselves.

Within certain margins, slaves were often also able to shape their own lives after arriving in the Americas. In his contribution, Paul Lovejoy focuses on two key factors in the process of community formation among Africans in the New World: ethnicity and religion. Many Africans used ethnic identification as a strategy to resist their ascribed identity as racially inferior slaves. They did not simply fall back upon African practices, but established new identities by forging pan-ethnic groups. On the other hand, Muslims of different ethnic backgrounds identified on the basis of religion. Both factors have to be considered together to get a full understanding of their impact. Thus, ethnicity only contributed to the formation of communities with the help of religious world-views.

Identity and Migration: The Atlantic in Comparative Perspective*

David Eltis

When scholars mention culture and migration in the same sentence, it is usually because they wish to assess the impact of the movement of humans on the structure of societies and the way people live. Diaspora studies of all kinds typically follow this line of investigation. Inquiries into why people move in the first place, by contrast, usually settle fairly quickly into a search for material incentives, or, for some migrations, religious freedom. In fact, the initial impulse to migrate, and the size and composition of the migration, is determined as much by the way people conceive of the social group to which they belong and by its values as it does with the normal human instinct to improve one's well-being. Reversing the usual direction of cause and effect between culture and migration seems particularly important for the early modern Atlantic world, where ocean-going technology brought so many different people from four continents into rather sudden contact with each other. In this essay, group self-perceptions and social values are taken as the starting point of the migration instead of one of the consequences of migration. Nevertheless, to obtain a full appreciation of non-economic factors in the pre-1800 movement of Atlantic migrants, it is first necessary to show how Atlantic migration differed from all previous long-distance movements of people.

From the emigration of homo sapiens from Africa perhaps 100,000 years ago, to the Viking visits to North America, and Chinese and Arab contact with the Indonesian archipelago, migration meant, in essence, the settlement of the globe. In the absence of continuing exchange between old and new communities, migration resulted in continual goodbyes. Ocean-borne migration began about 1000 BCE, and for a further two millennia after this, migrants very seldom returned to their areas of origin. Migrations gave rise to new cultures and societies that remained largely unaware of their place in the increasingly diverse kaleidoscope of humanity. People created identities for themselves without the aid of the "other," a phenomenon almost impossible to imagine in the modern world. The creation of land-based empires in Eurasia and elsewhere periodically slowed or reversed the process of cultural fragmentation. The steady expansion southwards of imperial control in China, culminating in the Chin and Han dynasties, led to consolidation and integration, but these were sub-, not inter-continental phenomena.

*Earlier versions of some paragraphs of this essay have appeared in David Eltis, ed., *Free and Coerced Migrations: A Global Perspective* (Standford: Stanford University Press, 2002): Introduction, and chapter 1; and David Eltis, *The Rise of African Slavery in the Americas* (Cambridge: Cambridge University Press, 2000); chapter 9.

A little over a thousand years ago, the broad pattern of dispersion began to change as people in the far west, the far east, and then the south of the Old World launched extensive transoceanic, or at least trans-maritime, satellite communities whose existence involved the maintenance of retraceable sea-borne connections. Viking trade with the Dorset people of Labrador beginning in the late ninth century, Chinese expansion to the Indonesian archipelago and beyond, and monsoon-based navigation in the Indian Ocean were all predicated on return voyages thousands of miles in length.[1] While the colonization of the globe continued, indeed at an expanding rate, this was a cultural turning point comparable to the revolution that converted hunter-gatherers to settled agriculturalists. Because the problems of sailing were minor compared to overland journeys of equivalent length, reciprocal sea-borne contact began the reintegration of human societies, a process that continues today in the form of cheap air travel and the communication revolution. At some time in the middle of the last millennium, it is likely that the number of languages and cultures in the world that disappeared each year came to exceed those that were created. Thus, conceptions of self at both individual and social levels became tied to ever-changing perceptions of others.

Old World expansion, especially in its western maritime manifestation, has usually been seen as a continuation of global occupation and colonization. However, from the broad perspective adopted here, the diaspora of the people of Western Europe, Western Africa, the Russian Empire, and Southern Asia was not merely an outward movement, it was a critical stage in the conflation and consolidation of the world's people and cultures. After one thousand CE, migration began, once more, to pull together the people of Old and New Worlds, Asia and Europe, and Southern Asia and its archipelago. This was an era that saw the greatest, most concentrated, and longest mass migrations in the human experience up to that time, much of it seaborne and swift by comparison with what had gone before. More important, it necessarily constituted the first time in migration history that some continual contact with the point of departure became possible, either because of additional new arrivals from the area which the original migrants had left, or through written communication. Return became a possibility for many migrants for the first time. Even forced migration eventually resulted in the possibility of return, as in the nineteenth-century cases of the thousands of Yoruba in Brazil who bought their freedom and went back to the area where they had been enslaved, and the descendants of slaves who founded Liberia and Sierra Leone. Return migration of Europeans and Asians— for example, Italians from Brazil and Indians from Mauritius in the Indian Ocean and the Americas—was massive by pre-modern standards. Some eighty-five percent of migrants to the Mascarene Islands off Madagascar elected to go back to India, and in the African case, numerically small though it was, there is growing literature on how Old World identities such as the Yoruba were not just reshaped, but created by the returning migrants.[2] None of these phenomena would have been possible in an earlier era.

While the global mixing of the world's people continues to accelerate in the twenty-first century, it is likely that this process is still in its infancy. Just as eighteenth-century German and Irish migration to North America pointed the way to the mass transoceanic migrations of the nineteenth century, the ethnic composition of free and coerced migration in the four centuries prior to 1900 is a template for migration in the twentieth and twenty-first centuries.[3] No one who has taken a subway ride in New York, London, or Toronto can be in any doubt that modernity today is increasingly associated with the multi-ethnic metropolis, despite government efforts to control migration from the developing world. In the last two decades four-fifths of all U.S. immigrants have originated from non-European parts of the world, and the equivalent ratios for most European countries are only slightly smaller. There are no less than 307 languages spoken in London today by the 25 percent of the city's children who use a language other than English at home. In Amsterdam the figure is 180, and the New York figure is unlikely to be smaller than London's.[4] A multi-ethnic supply of labor appears far more important to the continuation of the modern global economy than to its seventeenth- and eighteenth-century rise.[5]

Intriguingly, while the process of expansion was initially led in the European case by nascent nation states with some degree of ethnic homogeneity, it is also clear that the movement of people that resulted built the base of most multi-ethnic societies in the modern world. Although individuals have moved around so much that there has never been a time when strictly homogenous people formed nations, the mixing of people is greater today than ever before in global history. The future of bloodlines, and in the long-run, religion, as a basis of nationhood does not look secure at this point. Today, as in the last five centuries, mass migration and mixing is triggered mainly by Europe, and what were originally European settlements, yet most people caught in the phenomenon were (and are) not European. The end of this process—a long way off given zero natural rates of population increase and an expanding need for labor in the developed world—is perhaps a fuller integration of the world's people and cultures than has existed since homo sapiens left Africa. Nazi Germany and late twentieth-century Rwanda and Yugoslavia appear as anachronisms on this broad canvas, or, one would hope, the last of this most evil form of ethnocentrism.

Prior to the twentieth century, reintegration of the people of the world advanced most rapidly across the two Atlantic basins. It was dominated by force in the sense that most of those involved did not choose to become migrants. Indeed, transatlantic migration from the sixteenth down to the mid-nineteenth century was strikingly unusual. Return migration and the maintenance of contact between source and host societies made possible a hemispheric "community." Community, in the sense used here, means that everyone living in it had values which, if they were not shared around the Atlantic, were certainly reshaped in some way by others living in the Atlantic basins. As this suggests, events in one geographic area had the potential to stimulate a reaction—by no means just economic—thousands of miles away. In addition, more than half the migrants were involuntary, clearly unwilling to relocate. Trafficking in slaves is as old as slavery itself, but the size of the transatlantic flow and the fact that slaves dominated the populations of most of the receiving areas constituted an unprecedented shift in the history of large-scale migration. Of those migrants who were not forced, a very large number traveled under obligations to others, which meant that the migrant effectively abandoned some basic freedoms for several years after arrival. Table 6.1 presents the data on this pattern. The slaves, of course, are all African. "Servants" includes both indentured and contract migrants, the first entirely European, the second entirely Asian. Both groups obtained a free

TABLE 6.1 **Migration to the Americas: Estimates of Volume and Shares, 1492–1880 (shares in columns 1, 3, 5, and 7 sum to 1; volumes are in thousands)**

	Slaves		Servants		Convicts/ Prisoners		Free persons	
	Total	Share	Total	Share	Total	Share	Total	Share
pre-1580	68	30%	0	0%	3	1%	155	69%
1580–1640	607	67%	52	6%	8	1%	233	33%
1640–1700	829	65%	233	18%	23	2%	191	15%
1700–1760	2846	82%	134	4%	61	2%	450	13%
1760–1820	4325	85%	89	2%	34	1%	650	13%
1820–1880	2296	14%	651	4%	19	0%	13051	81%

Source: David Eltis, "Free and Coerced Migrations from the Old World to New," in David Eltis, ed., *Free and Coerced Migrations: A Global Perspective* (Stanford, 2002).

transoceanic passage in exchange for control over three to seven years of their labor. Because they entered into a contract more or less voluntarily, they were like free migrants; because they could be bought and sold and did not have much control over this process, or the work they were required to perform during the indenture, they were like slaves. Convicts include those sent to French Guiana and Angola (Portuguese *degredados*), as well as the better-known flow of British convicts to North America.

Table 6.1 shows free migration predominated for the first century and again after 1830. For two centuries in between—say 1630 to 1830—coerced migration and migration undertaken under a labor debt to others was by far the most dominant regime under which population movements occurred. Overall, migrants traveling without a labor debt and not enslaved to others were very much in a minority. This raises intriguing questions of how transatlantic migration was for so long associated in the minds of both specialist scholars and the general public with freedom. More substantively, it points to the fact that we cannot begin to explain the nature of Atlantic migration without first taking into account the motives of both migrants and those who organized the migrations, and Africans and Europeans belong to both these categories. Coerced and free migration streams interacted with each other, as did the value systems that made them possible. What makes early modern Atlantic migration particularly different from what had gone before was that, even though such a large proportion of it was coerced—specifically, comprising slaves—the people who supplied the slaves and the slaves themselves had a major determining influence on the existence of the migration, on the numbers of migrants, and who it was that became migrants. Much of the body of this essay is concerned with establishing these propositions.

The fact that transatlantic migration can be grouped according to the labor regimes under which migrants traveled is enough to separate it from other groups of people. It would not occur to historians or demographers to try this kind of grouping

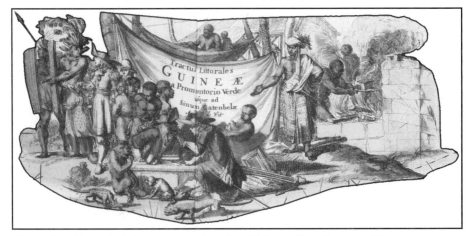

Cartouche with on the left a representation of an African selling slaves to a European merchant. Frederick de Wit, *Atlas* (Amsterdam, ca. 1675). *Courtesy of the Osher Map Library, University of Southern Maine.*

for long-distance population movements before 1500 and after 1900, except possibly for the early Mediterranean slave trade. Indeed, it would not be necessary, in that migrants before and after this period traveled, for the most part, within a common legal framework. The fact that the vast majority of migrants in the period 1500–1850 worked for others at the end of their journey, unlike earlier migrants, helps account for the uniqueness of this period, and also points to the centrality of the demand and supply of labor which formed the basis of the migration. At one level, the direction and composition of the repeopling of the Americas is a function of the relative price of labor, with the relative distribution of free and enslaved people (or the proportion of migrants coming from Europe and Africa) settled by wages and prices of slaves. Although transatlantic migration was the movement of labor from one area to another, economic analysis alone will not tell us why some became slaves and some indentured servants. Moreover, even within labor regimes huge numbers of individuals were excluded from entry into a country and region on non-economic grounds such as race or nationality.

As the opening paragraph has suggested, cultural values and ideologies are of considerable importance in seeking out the fundamental explanations of long-distance population movements. By their nature, these are so entrenched that migrants, and at times those historians who interpret the records they leave, tend to take them for granted. Examples of such shared assumptions underpinning social existence are conceptions of morality, principles of social organization, including attitudes to gender, and issues of identity. It follows that to understand migration, and more particularly the interaction between the flows of free and coerced labor which formed the basis of the repeopling of the Americas, we need to take into account the different values of societies around the Atlantic. More particularly, we need to examine the way groups of people involved in creating a transatlantic community saw themselves in relation to others, and how these perceptions changed over time. No single group was able to impose its values on the early modern Atlantic world, so not only was the composition and direction of migration far more than just an economic story, it was a story shaped by Africans as well as by Europeans.

The basic economic imperatives are well known. At one level, most transatlantic migration before 1830 was impelled not only by the migrants' desires to better themselves, but also by the desire of the European consumer for cheap sugar, the desire of the African elites for imported textiles and metals, and the demographic decline of American indigenous populations which, from the European perspective, meant a shortage of labor. Ocean-going technology brought the European frontier to tropical and semi-tropical areas that for three centuries became the focal point of European expansion (as opposed to European migration). Several products that were either unknown to Europeans (like tobacco), or occupied a luxury niche in pre-expansion European tastes (like gold, but especially sugar), now fell within the capacity of Europeans to produce cheaply. While Europeans came to control the production of such exotic goods, it became apparent in the first two centuries after Columbus that they did not wish to supply the labor that would make such output possible.

In the fifteenth and sixteenth centuries, Europeans came into face-to-face contact with three groups of people who were culturally and physically more different from themselves than any other remote people they had interacted with in the previous millennium. Of two of them, Asians and Africans, they were already aware; the third, American aboriginals, were completely unknown to them. For the Asians, initial contact with the Europeans meant little. Transoceanic mercantile and imperial connections by Asians pre-dated European expansion, and the ability of Europeans to establish land-based empires in Asia, albeit using indirect rule, did not emerge until the second half of the eighteenth century. For Africans, neither the initial Chinese contacts in the east of the continent, nor the much more extended and intensive European interaction in the west, led to loss of territorial control prior to the late nineteenth century, with the exception of western Angola. Indeed, African capacity to resist ocean-borne invaders was probably one of the two key factors which determined that the sugar complex moved across the Atlantic to the Americas after emerging from the Mediterranean, and seemingly island-hopped down the West African coast during the late fifteenth and early sixteenth centuries.[6] The other factor was the willingness of some Africans to sell other Africans as slaves to Europeans. In effect, African strength—the capacity to retain territorial integrity—helped foster the slave trade as Europeans established their plantations in the Americas instead of Africa.

Territorial integrity also meant that African slaves passed into European hands as a result of trade, not conquest. Imagine for the moment an unequal relationship (or no business relationship at all) in the matter of moving slaves to the Americas. Historical examples of this in different contexts include the raids of Romans on the fringes of their empire and Aztecs on the peoples of what is now northern Mexico, that often resulted in a tributary relationship where slaves were handed over in return for an agreement not to attack. In this scenario, Europeans would have organized punitive military raids every so often in order to ensure a flow of "free" labor. In fact, the slaves would not have been free, but the cost of periodic military expeditions would have been much less than the cost of paying elite Africans what amounted to full market value for their human commodities. The number of Africans flowing to the New World would have been many hundreds of thousands greater under these conditions than under one in which market conditions of exchange held.

The largest impact of Africa on the early modern Atlantic world was thus not on culture or labor narrowly defined, but rather on the central geopolitical structure of that world. Atlantic empires based initially in Europe would have had a quite different shape without an African capacity to resist European aggression on mainland Africa. One consequence of the diversion of that aggression to the Americas, as is well known, was European dispossession of the third group of transoceanic people, native Americans. The epidemiological impact of the European invasion destroyed not only native American power structures, it also destroyed a potential labor supply, and of course, increased the demand for alternative labor.

Table 6.1 indicates that most of the early migration to the Americas can be very loosely categorized as free, at least in the sense that it was neither coerced nor bound. We know about the numbers and the geographical distribution of early Iberian migration, but surprisingly little about the terms under which ordinary Castilians and Portuguese came to the Americas prior to the nineteenth century. Spain conquered and then administered an existing empire, the main export of which was precious metals—first looted, and then mined. It is therefore unsurprising that a high incidence of early migrants were soldiers, professionals, and artisans.[7] Spain, and to a lesser degree Portugal, moved into the richest and most populous areas of the New World, and Spanish America exported few commodities compared to later European regimes. It is unlikely that the few native textiles, hides, and plantation products that crossed the Atlantic in the sixteenth century from Spanish America could have justified their transportation costs in the absence of the very high value-to-weight ratios of the bullion which they accompanied.

In Brazil, most of the slaves on the early sugar plantations were Amerindian, and the greater share of African slaves shown in the figures for the 1500–1580 period arrived at the very end of the period, when the gathering demographic disaster triggered the switch from Indian to African labor. Thus, neither Spain nor Portugal initially felt the need for highly elastic supplies of unskilled labor from the Old World. With *corvée* or *mita* labor supplying most of the needs of the Spanish-American mining sector, overall levels of migration were small before 1600, and both the coerced and bound components of that migration were lower than at any point before the mid-nineteenth century.

Perhaps the most important developments for migration in the Atlantic world (certainly for Africans), and more broadly in the saga of European expansion, came in the seventeenth century, rather than with Columbus' contact or the Spanish conquests of the sixteenth century. Three factors reshaped the migrant flow after 1640: first, the Amerindian population reached its lowest point before 1700.[8] Second, at the same time, more intensive production techniques came to be introduced on plantations, specifically gang-labor on Caribbean sugar islands, particularly those occupied by the English. Given the prevalence of small cane farmers and decentralized sugar-growing (as opposed to milling) in early Brazil, the gang-labor system likely did not appear until sugar had been in the Americas for over a century.[9] Before 1800, American plantations were almost synonymous with sugar, since sugar plantations produced about three times more (by value) than non-sugar plantations in the 1770 Caribbean.[10] The work was unpleasant, it was carried out in low-lying unhealthy environments, and, above all, it involved loss of control over the pace at which one worked. All these characteristics ensured that wages would have to be very high to attract voluntary labor. The Portuguese and Spanish who migrated in the early period were not likely of the type to work on sugar plantations. Indeed, no one from any continent would work voluntarily for long periods of time under the kinds of work regimes that evolved in the eastern Caribbean in the mid-seventeenth century. For one and a half centuries, sugar and sugar-products formed by far the most valuable of products exported from the Americas. Neither black nor white, free nor bound could at first sustain a positive rate of natural population growth in the regions most suitable for cultivation. The third development to shape migration was the growing intensity, efficiency, and falling costs of transatlantic contact. The frequency and cost of travel, as well as literacy rates, were such that by the second half of the seventeenth century, for the first time in human history, both people and cheaply produced printed materials speedily crisscrossed vast distances. It is in this sense that there appeared a hemispheric "community."[11]

The above developments facilitated several possible responses to what was, from the European perspective, a labor problem. If Europeans had simply extended the labor regimes which were prevalent in their own part of the Old World to the

New—relied, in other words, on predominantly non-coerced labor—then labor costs would have risen to the point where sugar would not have become a common consumer item as quickly as it did, and the plantation sector of the New World would have grown much slower. A second possible resolution was the employment of forced labor wherever it could be obtained most cheaply—a solution consistent with what many scholars see as the dominant ethos of the merchants at the helm of early modern European expansion. A third possibility, quite different from the second, was to tap what Europeans (and some Africans) came to see as a reserve of coerced labor thousands of miles away from where that labor was to be used, and from where consumers of plantation output and organizers of the plantation complex lived.

There were modest attempts to implement the first and second solutions. More generally, as we shall see, several European countries sent convicts and prisoners against their will to the plantation colonies, where most of them helped produce sugar and tobacco. The U.S. North-West Ordinance (1787) prohibited servitude *except* for those guilty of serious crimes. There was no serious debate over adopting the third option, anymore than there would be today about using free labor rather than, say, a slave trade and chattel slavery to improve company profits, even though there is no reason to doubt the efficiency of the latter. The total absence of serious debate points to the existence, then, as now, of values so widely and deeply held in a community that no discussion of them is deemed necessary. Such values, as well as profit-maximizing behavior, determined both the direction and the composition of migration.

The rise of coerced migration may well have been inevitable in the sense that large-scale migration (several million people over a period of a century or less) could not have occurred in the pre-1800 world unless it *was* coerced. Free migration remained small, or at least very gradual, particularly when expressed as a percentage of source populations. In the Atlantic, the Spanish averaged 2,000 migrants a year in the sixteenth century; the Portuguese 3,000 a year in the eighteenth century; and the English 5,000 a year in the sixty years after 1630. In no period before the nineteenth century is it likely that European migration—including indentured servants—exceeded a five year annual average of 10,000. The white populations of the Americas were not only still small by Old World standards in the mid-eighteenth century despite two and a half centuries of migration, they were also overwhelmingly native-born. Apart from the slave Caribbean and Brazil, these were not migrant societies. After 1820, by contrast, free migrants from Europe averaged 50,000 a year to the U.S. alone.

If coerced migration was inevitable, why was the most severe form of it—the slave trade—confined to migration from Africa and Africans? As already suggested, conceptions of self and community—what the modern literature calls "identity"—are central to determining the form migration takes, who will become migrants, and what their ultimate destination will be. A hemispheric and very long-run perspective suggests that fundamental shifts in how people defined the group in which they lived lay behind the migration patterns described in Table 6.1. It is beyond the scope of this essay to explain these shifts, the aim being merely to note that they happened and to draw some implications for one of the fields of human endeavor affected by such shifts. Constructions of others (or more generally, outsiders) defined and determined the treatment of prisoners of war, lawbreakers, religious and racial minorities, and refugees from advancing armies. The flow of convicts from eastern and western Europe, as well as part of the flow of people into the African slave trade, was shaped by community morality, often reflected in formal legislation. Social mores not only ensured that the convict component of migration would be small (and thus, that the demand for other coerced migrants such as slaves would be greater), but that convicts would have more rights than slaves, and that the convict trade would die out altogether over time—usually in response to pressure from recipient societies in the western case.[12] More broadly, exile came to be regarded as cruel.

The most important shift in values that affected migration was not in the definition and treatment of criminal behavior or religious minorities, however, but rather in conceptions of who should be slaves and serfs. One way to think of this is as a boundary in the mind, as opposed to a geographic or political barrier. Not until the twelfth century could Western European conceptions of the larger society—a grouping of people that, as a minimum, could be counted on not to enslave each other—encompass most of Europe. Before this, an internal slave trade still flourished as people from the north were captured by other Europeans and carried for sale in the south, many, ultimately, to the prosperous Islamic areas. This situation was little different from what existed in Africa. In one sense, the story of transatlantic migration (and eventually abolition of the slave trade and slavery) is a conclusion to the expansion of this sense of identity to incorporate ever-larger geographic and cultural areas. In another sense, the massive and unprecedented flow of racially exclusive coerced labor across the Atlantic is perhaps the result of the differential pace in the evolution of a cultural pan-European-ness on the one hand, and a pan-Africanism on the other. An interlude of two or three centuries between the former and the latter provided a window of opportunity in which the slave trade rose and fell dramatically. For four centuries from the mid-fifteenth century to 1867, Europeans were not prepared to enslave each other, but were prepared to buy Africans and keep them and their descendants enslaved. Given that "Africa" scarcely existed as a concept for Africans in any sense before the nineteenth century, there were always some people living in the subcontinent south of the Sahara who were prepared to enslave others from adjacent or distant societies. The corollary of this is that all people in history have regarded it as morally wrong to enslave and trade some groups with whom they have had dealings—perhaps the basis for abolition has always existed. Between the fifteenth and nineteenth centuries, Europe and Africa simply had different conceptions of the people for whom slavery (and the slave trade) was inappropriate.

In the Atlantic, the peculiar multi-regimed pattern of migration before 1870, as well as the racial basis of the different regimes, is related to the very sudden increase in large-scale inter-continental contact after 1492. Oceans that had hermetically sealed people and cultures from each other sprouted sea-lanes almost overnight. Cultural accommodation between people, in this case between Europeans and non-Europeans, always took time. The big difference was that before Columbus, migrations had been gradual and tended to move outwards from the more to the less-densely populated parts of the globe. After Columbus, western Europe, Central America, West Africa, and eventually much of Asia, all with cities and relatively densely populated, were suddenly thrown together. Before Columbus, cultural accommodation or the emergence of a dominant culture, as with epidemiological adjustment, tended to grow with the migration itself. Columbian contact was sudden, and inhibited any gradual adjustment, cultural as well as epidemiological. A merging of perceptions of right and wrong, group identities, and relations between the sexes, to look only at the top of a very long list of social values, could not be expected to occur quickly in a post-Columbian world. In short, cultural adjustment could keep pace with neither transportation technology, nor the epidemiological consequences of that technology. The result was first the rise, and then, as perceptions of the insider-outsider divide slowly changed, the fall of the transatlantic trade in enslaved Africans. It is hard to conceive of the overwhelming predominance of voluntary migration in the twentieth century—or at least the fact that coercion came to be restricted to refusing entry to a country, as opposed to forcing people to move against their will—without shifts in conceptions of right and wrong, and more inclusive ideas of who should be considered full members of society. Neither expectations of higher profit, nor legal precedent can explain the demise of the migratory regimes that supplied indentured servants, slaves, serfs, prisoners, and contract laborers between 1792 (the decree abolishing the Danish slave trade) and 1939 (when the French finally ended the practice of sending convicts to French Guiana).

Thus, the long coercive interlude in forced transatlantic migration stemmed from the large and important question for which every society in history has provided at least an unthinking answer—which groups are to be considered eligible for enslavement and how does this change over time? If, after Africans had turned the plantation complex away from Africa, it was to be located in the Americas, the answer to who would provide the labor for that complex clearly emerged from a European inability to enslave other Europeans and an African ability to see other African societies as eligible for enslavement and sale into the Atlantic economy. In contrast to Russian, Roman, and some Asian societies, early modern western Europeans and Africans would not enslave members of their own societies, but Africans had a somewhat broader conception of who was eligible for enslavement than Europeans. It was this difference in definitions of eligibility for enslavement that explains the dramatic post-1640 rise of the coerced component of transatlantic migration in Table 6.1. Slavery, which had disappeared from northwest Europe long before this point, exploded into a far greater significance and intensity than it had possessed at any point in human history. The dissonance in African and European identities without which there would have been no African slavery whatsoever in the Americas, had at its root very little of an economic nature. Scholarly failure to recognize the reasons for the rise and fall of direct coercion in migration is due to the fact that cultural values are easily hidden by the economic superstructure. Conceptions of morality lie behind the legislative enactments that send convicts into exile. Communally held conceptions of self and others determine not only who will become slaves, but also where they will be sent and how they will be treated. Constructions of gender, as central to the human psyche as standards of right and wrong and identity (at the level of both the individual and society), are also central to patterns of migrations.

As the above discussion suggests, European and African conceptions of self and community did not remain static. On the African side, the major effect of the African-European exchange that developed out of European contact from the Atlantic

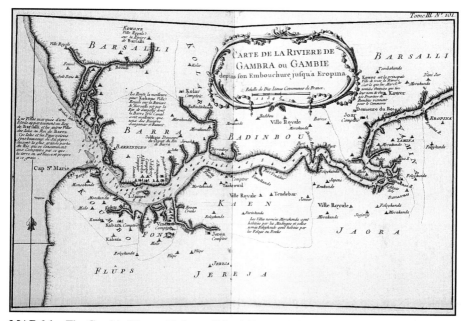

MAP 6.1   The Gambia River with James Island. Jacques Nicolas Bellin, *Le Petit Atlas Maritime. Recueil de cartes et de plans des quatre parties du monde* (Paris, 1764), vol. III-part II. *Courtesy of the Osher Map Library, University of Southern Maine.*

was dramatically different. If Europeans affected African identities it was to encourage an elementary pan-Africanism, rather than to foster tribalism and attach inaccurate ethnic nomenclatures to African groups. The initial and unintentional impact of European sea-borne contact was to force non-elite Africans to think of themselves as part of a wider African group. Initially, this group might be Igbo or Yoruba, and soon, in addition, blacks as opposed to whites. At the most elemental level, by the late eighteenth century the slaves at James Island in the estuary of the Gambia River vowed to drink the blood of the "whitemen." (Map 6.1) In Gorée (Senegal), a little later, one-third of the slaves in a carefully planned conspiracy "would go in the village and be dispersed to massacre the whites." When asked "[w]hether it were true that they had planned to massacre all the whites of the island. . . . [t]he two leaders, far from denying the fact or looking for prevarication, answered with boldness and courage: that nothing was truer."[13] On a slave ship where the slaves were always black, and the crew largely white, skin color tended to define ethnicity.

However, through most of the early modern period, there were limits to such inclusive identities among Africans, which not even the traumatic experience of confinement on a slave ship could breach. Europeans were well aware of this and benefited from the relatively slow development of a broader sense of African-ness or even blackness. Throughout the period covered here, all Europeans used *gromettoes* (castle slaves). Even before Europeans had established their bases on the Gold Coast, they had carried on a successful trade with slaves brought from other parts of

Africa for sale on the Gold Coast. Carrying castle slaves into the area was simply a continuation of this pattern, except that the slaves were now put to work for the small European contingents who took up residence on the coast. The principle was the same as the transatlantic system, however. Slaves were carried far enough away from home to be sold into a strange environment and to people, white or black, whom they could only see as foreigners. Given that all non-slave inhabitants in the new environment were also foreigners, this increased the dependence of the slave on the owner and reduced the possibilities of escape.

The point at which African levels of awareness of European activities began to affect behavior came with the quadrupling of the slave trade during the first three-quarters of the eighteenth century. Although the Atlantic slave trade lasted four centuries, nearly two-thirds of it occurred between the years 1698–1807. In the seventeenth century, there is evidence of European slave captains purchasing slaves from one part of the coast, arming them with clubs, and then using them as "guardians" to help control the bulk of those on board who had been acquired from a different region of Africa. By the end of the second decade of the eighteenth century, the English, at least, were no longer using guardians on the Gold Coast, and the practice slips from the historical record without any discussion. In most African provenance zones, especially the Slave Coast, the Bight of Biafra, and the Angola region on either side of the Congo river, slaves remained under the control of local slave merchants until just prior to embarkation. The latter were, presumably, better able to control the slaves than their European counterparts. Moreover, this was the period when the incidence of slave revolts, especially successful slave revolts on board the ships, increased.[14]

The same outward movement of barriers dividing insider from outsider may be seen within European communities in the Americas. Identifying oneself in relation to the people among whom one lived or, alternatively, did not live, was a universal phenomenon. The plantation Americas, however, especially the Caribbean, quickly came to contain an ethnic mix without parallel in the early modern world. Ethnicity, or nationhood, was a powerful force in the Atlantic even before the arrival of large numbers of Africans in the Americas. Scholars have naturally focused on European-African relations in the Caribbean, or more recently, on similarities and differences between African groups. Whites in the early modern Americas had what Philip Curtin has called the "peculiar European sense of ethnic solidarity."[15] Yet a sense of nation was already highly developed, especially in England, with its common language, centralized administration, and single large city. The colonies that Europeans established in the Americas could never have been "European," as opposed to French, Dutch, English, or Spanish. Overseas settlements were generally more ethnically diverse than were the respective countries that had established them.

The seventeenth-century English mainland colonies came closest to mirroring their Old World antecedents.[16] In what became slave societies, people came together from widely dispersed English locations, though mostly passing through London and Bristol, to form communities. Free migrants to the Chesapeake tended to use family connections.[17] In one of the most widely cited comments on early Barbados, Henry Whistler, who visited the island in 1655 wrote, "[T]his Island is inhabited with all sortes: with English, french, duch, Scotes, Irish, Spaniards thay being Jues. . ."[18]

Despite the influx of non-English, especially Scottish and Irish indentured servants and prisoners, eighty percent of servants before 1650 originated in London. The core English migration to Barbados likely drew on a more limited catchment area than did its Chesapeake counterpart. Jamaica was similar, with more than two-thirds of a sample of 2,077 European immigrants to Jamaica before 1720 coming from London and its immediate environment. A similar pattern is to be found in the French islands. The great majority of seventeenth-century French transatlantic migrants left from La Rochelle, a port on France's Atlantic coast—most of them going to St. Domingue, St. Kitts, and Guadeloupe. Almost half of the *engagés* (French indentured servants) who emigrated came from provinces in the immediate hinterland of La Rochelle.[19]

Between the mid-seventeenth- and late-eighteenth-centuries, European Caribbean populations became more diverse (although in early St. Domingue the opposite occurred, as French migrants replaced freebooters). In the Dutch case, given that few citizens of the Netherlands could be persuaded to migrate, the mixture of people from around the Atlantic basins that lived in the Dutch Antilles and Suriname was always greater than elsewhere.[20] Something of a Huguenot diaspora occurred, particularly to Dutch and English colonies, much of it subsidized in the British Americas.[21] Colonial property owners came from an increasingly wide range of geographic origins. British immigration policies and British military success in acquiring French and Spanish territories after 1756 reinforced this tendency. Part of the increasing diversity came from the slaveholding classes' capacity to absorb into their ranks people who were different from themselves. The most extreme example was in St. Domingue, where, according to a free-colored deputy to the National Assembly, free coloreds owned one-third of all slaves in the colony. After 1789, of course, faced with a tension between slaveowner solidarity and white solidarity, the leading white planters plumped for skin color. The St. Domingue revolution and the ensuing collapse of the plantation regime was due to an unusual fragmentation of the ruling class, as well as the most effective black resistance anywhere in the Americas.[22]

The process can be more finely calibrated in the English colonies than elsewhere. Like all Europeans, the English imposed restrictions on foreigners in their colonies. Paradoxically, Africans were not affected by this process, so that the tendency to base legislation on who a person was, rather than on what that person did, had its largest impact on the Irish rather than on Africans. Because Europeans assumed that only Africans could be slaves, there was no need for legislation that singled them out (as African, as opposed to slaves) for particular treatment. For Africans, the English used a slave code to convert an insider/outsider divide into an apartheid-type legal environment. Restrictions on non-English Europeans tended to be severe when the slave trade was beginning to change the ethnic composition of the new colonies. Later, it declined, both in terms of formal legislation and the application of that legislation, as the influx of Africans reached its peak. The Irish have usually been depicted as remaining at the lowest levels of West Indian society, eventually migrating out of the Caribbean, or at least Barbados and the Leewards.[23] Large numbers remained behind, however. Beginning with the restoration of the right to bear arms in Barbados as early as 1660, the integration process moved farthest in Montserrat. Richard Dunn described the Irish there, comprising over two-thirds of the white population in 1678, as second-class citizens. However, by the time the very detailed 1729 census was taken on Montserrat, they accounted for the largest share of the population of any Caribbean island, and had become the island's major slave-holders and sugar producers. More specifically, they were "on average, bigger planters, and owned more slaves, than did their English counterparts." Further, the Irish were disproportionately represented among eighteenth-century Jamaican office holders.[24] It might be argued that the first great transatlantic Irish diaspora (that of the 1650s) integrated more quickly than some later migrations from Ireland. Integration, indeed, was probably easier in a predominantly slave society (like the Caribbean) than a predominantly free society (like the northern U.S.), though that did not make slave societies any more attractive to immigrants. As in Jamaica, descendants of the 40,000 Irish that moved to Spanish America with Spanish government support in the 1650s filled many official positions in the colonies in the eighteenth and nineteenth centuries, especially in Cuba.[25]

Jewish participation in slave societies followed a similar path. In 1650, the Barbados Assembly passed legislation permitting the immigration of Jews and other religious minorities. Five years later the Barbados Council, in response to a petition, ostensibly put Jews on the same footing as foreigners in England, by resolving that "ye (Jewish) Petitioners behaving themselves civilly, and compartable to ye Government of this Island, and doing nothing tending to ye disturbance of the peace and quiet thereof during their stay, shall enjoy ye privileges of laws and statutes of ye Commonwealth of England & of this Island, relating to foreigners and strangers."[26] Suriname, in English hands between 1651–1667, followed suit and went even further in offering incentives to Jewish migrants.

The contrast with the Portuguese and Spanish colonies is stark. An Italian Capuchin wrote of the extensive forced labor in Portuguese Luanda at this time—he was observing deported Jewish *degredados*, not African slaves.[27] The striking point here is not the contrast between Luanda and Barbados, but rather that when the Barbados resolution passed it was still illegal for Jews even to reside in England. Not until 1656, six years *after* the Council decision, were Jews given the right to take up residence in England for the first time since their expulsion in 1290. This suggests that the Jews sought out, and often found, a measure of civil liberties in the English Americas that was not possible in England itself.[28] They sought the same in the smaller Dutch colonies, and received rather more initially. They remained a small minority everywhere, but were not at the bottom of the socio-economic scale. In Jamaica, the small and urban-based community of Jewish merchants accounted for 6.5 percent of all slaves sold by the Royal African Company between 1674–1708 and it was wealthier, on average, than the English merchant community on the island.[29] In no English possession in the Americas was there complete equality for Jews, nor, indeed, as much equality as existed in the Dutch Caribbean by 1730, but over the course of the slavery era disabilities became fewer.[30]

In summary, the strong pressures on descendants of both Africans and Europeans to search for and stress common bonds with others on the same side of the slave-free divide went further and fastest in the Americas. African nationalities sought out their own kind on seventeenth-century sugar plantations when establishing personal relationships and celebrating the rituals of life, sometimes with the help of slave owners.[31] Even in the very earliest days, there were no counterparts to *gromettoes*, or guardians, in the plantation Americas, whose sole function was to prevent rebellion among those of different ethnicity from themselves. Much less were there recorded instances of slaves of one ethnic group coming to the aid of their owner against another ethnic group, as happened in one seventeenth-century slave ship revolt. For Richard Ligon, who observed the very earliest English plantations, a work force of several nations was potentially troublesome. One estate of 200 hundred slaves was considered well run, "as there are no mutinies amongst them, yet of several nations."[32]

Nevertheless, the rebellions and conspiracies in Barbados later in the seventeenth century show little sign of internecine strife. The Coromantines (from the Gold Coast), most of whom presumably had been brought over as guardians on slave ships, had a prominent role in the Barbados slave conspiracy of 1675, but they were neither acting alone nor were they thwarted by non-Coromantines. The better-known and documented slave conspiracy of 1692 contains no hint of ethnic divisions.[33] In Jamaica, an open land frontier ensured a greater frequency of armed resistance and escape. There is almost a consensus among scholars that slaves from the Gold Coast were over-represented among the rebels, but seventeenth-century documents on Jamaican revolts contain almost no references to the African origins of rebels, and none at all to inter-ethnic strife. As Gold Coast slaves were over-represented among the early Barbados and Jamaican slave populations, Coromantines might have a larger place in the records on rebellions for the simple reason that they had a larger place in islands' slave populations.[34] Maroon communities, seen by some scholars as the ultimate statement of black solidarity against whites, did on occasion organize themselves around concepts of African nationhood. Acceptance of newcomers into such communities, however, had much more to do with geopolitical realities and the survival of the community than with the African origins of newly escaped slaves. In the Jamaican case, division between Spanish- and English-speaking maroons was more important than ethnic divisions between Africans.[35]

Violence at sea was just as important as conflict on land in the Old and New Worlds in shaping migration. European naval warfare, especially between the English and the French, clearly had a major impact on European imperial ventures in the Americas, but as this aspect of the Atlantic story is well known, it will not be pursued further here. Less familiar is the impact of African resistance against all Europeans, not in the geopolitical sense discussed earlier, but in the more direct sense of the slaves themselves resisting confinement and dispatch to the Americas.[36] There are two aspects of this that command attention. The first is the impact of higher transportation costs that followed, from the need to control African slaves who resisted the coerced migration to which they were subjected. Actual revolts may have occurred on ten percent or less of all slave ships, but the fear of the potential devastation from a revolt was constantly present. Owners and captains took basic cost-increasing precautions before they left their home port in terms of numbers of crew, guns, and equipment, but given epidemiological knowledge at the time, they could not protect themselves against the effect of illness without hiring many more men than, except for a minority of voyages, they would strictly require. Captives would often grasp any opportunity to escape or inflict damage on their jailers, however hopeless. It has been estimated that the costs of controlling these unwilling

human cargoes made up approximately eighteen percent of the price of a newly arrived slave in the Americas, and that between 1680–1800, when nearly 6.6 million
slaves left Africa for the New World, the number of people moving across the
Atlantic for Africa would have been nearly nine percent greater in the absence of
shipboard resistance. Put another way, in the eighteenth century alone, resistance resulted in nearly 600,000 fewer slaves crossing the Atlantic, and forced European
consumers to pay higher prices for plantation produce. In effect, Africans who died
resisting the slave traders, as well as those who resisted unsuccessfully but survived
to work on the plantations of the Americas, saved others from forced migration to
the Americas, as well as increasing demand for alternative European labor.

A second aspect of shipboard resistance that had a major shaping influence on
migration was the regional differentials in such resistance that are now apparent. Recent research has revealed a striking geographical pattern with revolts being much
more likely among slaves coming from some African regions than from others.
Three Upper Guinea regions, Senegambia, Sierra Leone, and the Windward Coast,
together with the Gabon region in southern Bight of Biafra, together accounted for
just over ten percent of all slave voyages leaving Africa. However, over forty percent
of the voyages with slave revolts came from these regions. All other African regions
either had about the same share of slave revolts as slave exports, or substantially
fewer revolts than their share of slave exports would lead us to expect. It is hard to
avoid the suggestion that European slave traders avoided trading in those areas of
the coast where they were likely to face the most troublesome (from the European
perspective) human cargoes. Indeed, it is clear that slave trading in such areas became intensive only when the slave trade was at its peak volumes, and when slaves
were harder to obtain all along the other areas of the African littoral. This finding is
all the more striking when the geographic relation of Upper Guinea to both Europe
and the Americas is taken into account. In terms of both distance and time—in other
words, taking into account winds and ocean currents—Upper Guinea is much closer
to both Europe and the key slave markets in the Americas than is the rest of the
African continent. Other things being equal, it should have been an area preferred,
rather than avoided, by European slave ships. Once more Africans, this time the non-
elite, heavily influenced the pattern of transatlantic migration. In this case, it was
both the volume of that migration that was affected—as noted above, anything that
increased costs reduced the number carried across the Atlantic—and more impor-
tantly, the direction. West-Central Africa, the Bight of Biafra, and the Bight of Benin
supplied most of the slaves arriving in the New World, in part because Europeans
avoided Upper Guinea.

Combining these various effects means that the African capacity to resist and
deal with Europeans as equals resulted in well over one million Africans preserved
from the stark alternatives of death on the middle passage or a life on a plantation in
the Americas. African power relative to Europe may have helped ensure a plantation
complex in the Americas rather than Africa itself, but that power also put a cap on the
number of slaves carried across the Atlantic. As we have shown, it was not just the
numbers of slaves carried across the Atlantic that Africans helped shape; it was also
the direction and structure of the trade. The regional distribution of the slave trade

was just as much a product of Africa as of Europe. In addition, while Africans made up the vast majority of all migrants to the New World before 1800, free and coerced, the fewer Africans carried, the greater the demand for alternative forms of labor and alternative sources of migration—specifically European.

From the broad perspective, the coercive phase of transatlantic migration had proved to be a long interlude. By the twentieth century, the re-emergence of voluntary migration (with no legally enforceable ties between migrant and future employer at the end of the migration) was complete. In 1770, very few could be found to question the dominance of the slave trade as the chief means of supplying labor to the Americas (or anywhere else). A century and a half later, there were even fewer to question the idea that free migration was the only morally justifiable way to organize long-distance migration. It is essential, however, to see the evolution of this long interlude and the broader shaping of the Atlantic world in terms of interaction between societies in Europe, the Americas, and Africa, even though imperial power resided in Europe before 1750, and political power in the hands of those of European descent for a long time thereafter. The major historical lesson is that coerced migration has reinforced the racial divide in slave societies. In societies where slaves are of minor importance or do not exist, however, the opposite is likely to happen in the long run, in that migration fosters more broadly conceived conceptions of self and the immediate group in which one lives. Feedback from slavery and the slave trade, as well as resistance from the slaves themselves, helped this process along in societies that were not built around slavery, until what were, ultimately, two conceptions of group identity faced off in the nineteenth century. The more inclusive of the two—the one shared by slaves and free blacks, it should be noted—prevailed. Slavery and the slave trade have produced bitter race relations, but have also created a more multi-cultural and pluralistic Americas than could have existed without them. As the reintegration of human societies in the world, begun one thousand years ago, accelerates in the new millennium, the apparently innate desire of humans to identify themselves with some, and differentiate themselves from others (apparently part of the same process), will no doubt continue. Despite the horrors of the twentieth century, the prospect of malevolent social consequences from this tendency seems set to diminish.

➠ FOCUS QUESTIONS

1. Why did the "sugar complex" not take root in Africa?
2. How did changing values affect migration?
3. In what ways did slave rebellions on board ship affect the slave trade?

Trans-Atlantic Transformations: The Origins and Identity of Africans in the Americas

Paul E. Lovejoy

In both Africa and the Americas, ethnicity and religious affiliation provide distinct categories which were essential in the identification of the enslaved population, as they were for all sections of society.[1] In the context of slavery, ethnicity and religious affiliation are often thought to have overlapped to a considerable extent, although as Maureen Warner-Lewis has argued, ethnic and religious plurality was common.[2] Thus, Yoruba slaves are readily identifiable through religious practices, particularly their association with *orishas* (the deities, who mediated between Olorun, the supreme god, and mortals) and *Ifà* (the god of divination). *Orisha* worship was associated with Christianity and known as *santería* (the religious system venerating the deities, which were identified with certain Catholic saints). Similarly, Ewe/Fon are associated with *vodun* (a religion whose beliefs and rituals centered on the worship of spirits), and while obeah (a belief system involving the casting of spells, as well as healing by means of herbal or animal medicine) is sometimes associated with Akan, and more recently perhaps with Igbo origins, the ethnic/religious overlay is again apparent. In the context of some "creole" societies in the Americas, there is disagreement over the African roots of particular religious practices and beliefs, in which ethnic origins and religious observance are considered to be intrinsically linked. This essay is an attempt to distinguish religious and ethnic factors in the process of identification and community formation under slavery.[3]

Religion and ethnicity offered related but contrasting mechanisms for group identity that must be examined in historical context. Despite confusion in the scholarly literature, I would contend that both religion and ethnicity served to integrate individuals of diverse backgrounds into communities and social networks of interaction that were products of the slave trade. Both ethnicity and religion "creolized" slaves in the sense that these conceptual frameworks provided individuals with various means of establishing social relationships under the oppressive conditions of slavery. The perception that sometimes equates religion and ethnicity is misleading, however. Both religion and ethnicity required individuals to subordinate previous identities in favor of a new, shared level of consciousness as slaves in a racialized context. Where that increased consciousness began to develop is open to question, and it is here that the distinction between religious and ethnic identification offers a key to understanding patterns of slave identification as "resistant responses" to racial slavery.[4]

In contrast to many enslaved Africans who adjusted to slavery in the Americas by establishing new identities as members of pan-ethnic groups such as Igbo/

Calabari/Calabali or Lukumi/Nago/Aku/Yoruba, enslaved Muslims banded together on the basis of religion, not ethnicity.[5] The contrast between these situations suggests that ethnic and religious factors sometimes reinforced community structures, culture, and patterns of resistance, but in the case of Islam, ethnic identification was subordinated to the religious community. The question then becomes: what was the relationship of other ethnic identities to religious affiliation; did ethnicity develop as subordinate categories in larger religious brotherhoods? In understanding the process of "creolization," the contrast between the pan-ethnicity of the Yoruba and the subordination of ethnicity to Islam is striking, especially since many Yoruba were also Muslims, revealing tensions in group consciousness. This contrast highlights the conflicting strategies of those slaves who used religious observance to reinforce and intensify ethnic identification, and those who overlooked ethnic differences when individuals proclaimed themselves Muslims.

In Islamic societies, ethnic categories were associated with slavery, indeed, ethnic identification was associated with free status as well. Being Muslim also implied an ethnic affiliation, and sometimes more than one ethnic identification through parents. The complexity of ethnic identification, it is suggested here, resulted in a similar process of socialization that is comparable to what has sometimes been called the process of creolization in the Americas.[6]

'CHARTER' GENERATIONS AND THE ORIGINS OF SLAVE CULTURE

I take as a starting point the idea that recognizable communities of slaves with a shared culture evolved in Africa, across the Atlantic, and in different parts of the Americas. These communities included Yoruba (Lukumi/Aku/Nago), Kongo, Igbo, and Muslims, often identified as Mandingo. The questions that I am asking attempt to identify the principles that were fundamental in the establishment of these trans-Atlantic communities. Following the lead of Ira Berlin, what were the basic or 'charter' principles that determined community formation and group identity?[7] However, I also follow Douglas Chambers in allowing for stages of creolization, since the continued arrival of people from an emergent homeland had the effect of reinforcing certain charter principles, at least in the case of Igbo slaves.[8] The questions I wish to ask are: where and how were the charters established? The case of Islam suggests that the charter could have been established in Africa itself, while Yoruba identity seems to have emerged in Africa and the diaspora in tandem. These contrasts suggest that people adjust by association with a larger community, but exposure to that community might occur anywhere along the slave route. We cannot presume to know *a priori* the extent to which such adjustment was forced or voluntary as a form of resistance, why and how people chose one strategy of survival over another, and when.

In examining the charter generation of trans-Atlantic port communities, Berlin raises the issue of layers of adjustment and identify formation, which intersected with religion and ethnicity. According to Berlin, "The assimilationist scenario assumes that 'African' and 'creole' were way stations of generational change rather than cultural strategies that were manufactured and remanufactured and that the vectors of change moved in only one direction—often along a single track with Africans inexorably becoming creoles. Its emphasis on the emergence of the creole— a self-sustaining, indigenous population—omits entirely an essential element of the story: the charter generations, whose experience, knowledge, and attitude were more akin to that of confident, sophisticated natives than of vulnerable newcomers."[9]

By "charter generations," Berlin refers to the early generations of contact between western Africa, Europe, and the Americas, which did not experience the deracination of plantation slavery. Berlin contrasts the history of this charter generation of Africans, with its links across the Atlantic world, with the relative isolation and deracination of plantation slavery. I am suggesting, however, that other charter principles crossed the Atlantic, not just those affecting Berlin's "Atlantic creole," and that the process continued in later generations, especially in contexts of relatively concentrated immigration. The formation of communities under slavery could and did rely on common linguistic and cultural backgrounds in the establishment of pan-ethnic groups, and religion was frequently a mechanism of social integration within the slave community. However, the interface was not uniform.

In determining ethnicity, the charter principle seems to have been based on common language. Yoruba, Igbo, and other languages facilitated communication, even as ethnic and geographical distinctions recognized in Africa often continued. Nonetheless, ethnicity allowed internal differentiation among slaves within a system subordinated to racial categories. The difficulty in analyzing ethnogenesis emerges in considering religion, because ethnicity sometimes was tied to a religious category, as in *vodun*, and sometimes religion could serve as a pan-ethnic force of community development; Islam was a religion that inherently did so. Moreover, the Islamic case suggests that some slaves, at least, had complicated ethnic backgrounds. In Islamic West Africa, the role of long-distance trade and relocations through slavery strongly influenced ethnic and religious formation. Even elites were of mixed origins because of the widespread practice of concubinage, which required women to be of slave origin, that is, non-Muslims and almost always ethnically distinct. In response to the racial categorization of slavery in the Americas, it can be seen, religion could transcend issues of ethnicity. Factors of ethnicity and religion created a spiral, or circular, effect on the development of slave society, with both ethnicity and religious affiliation defining and explaining the other.

Religion and ethnicity overlap but are not coterminous, although religion can be one dimension of ethnicity, so that at times religious observances have been given an ethnic assignment. For many people actually involved, it seems, the idea of "religion-in-the-making" predominated, in which tradition was being manipulated or created as a defensive response to the subordination and oppression of slavery. Religion, therefore, sometimes has been inclusive of many influences, some of which generated distinctions that are thought to have had an ethnic basis. The traditional religion associated with African survivals is often syncretic and modern, and should be considered to reflect the modification of tradition in a changing historical context. This modernizing form of tradition stands in contrast with Islam, which was traditional in the sense that the practice of Islam in West Africa was replicated under slavery as much as possible. This conservative reliance on tradition emphasized the pillars of faith, the use of Arabic, literacy, and an identifiable dress code. This contrast in the forms of adaptation as characterized in religious behavior is also reflected in the methods of self-identification through ethnic designations. The emergence of super-ethnic groups like Yoruba/Aku/Luckumi/Nago or Calabari/Igbo accompanied the modernizing process of religious synthesis. Often, ethnically based sub-groups shared religious orientations. Ethnicity operated within a religious world-view that integrated people of diverse backgrounds into recognizable communities. By contrast, Muslims brought with them a sense of community, which was re-established upon identification of Islamic symbols and expressions. Once a new arrival who was Muslim came in contact with another Muslim, the community surfaced. The generation and maintenance of this sense of community originated in Africa, in contrast to the development of pan-ethnic Yoruba and Igbo identities. This difference reflected the situation in West Africa, where sub-ethnic distinctions among Yoruba and Igbo were more important than a common identity, whereas for Muslims, identification with Islam was more important than ethnic distinctions.

Which cultural and religious orientations proved most adaptive to the conditions of slavery varied, and which resulted in the greatest chance for survival is open to question. Islam almost disappeared, despite attempts at self-preservation, while other religions flourished in the post-emancipation era. Despite the concentration of Muslims in Bahia, and pockets of Islam in Jamaica, North America, and Haiti, Islam only emerges after the ending of slavery in even more scattered locations. The presence of Islam has been continuous, but it has been weak. Other religious traditions have proven to be more vibrant and adaptive, as in *candomblé*, *santería*, and *vodun*. Unlike Islam, these religions had a tradition of incorporating other traditions and practices, thereby showing that religion has ways of accommodating people of different ethnic identities. Hence in St. Domingue, *vodun* appears to have included a Kongo component, although the basic religious structure and vocabulary are from the Slave Coast. In Brazil, lay brotherhoods allowed ethnic organization within a religiously derived structure of Christianity, so that *candomblé*, of West-Central African origin, became the means of consolidating Nago ethnicity. In all cases, ethnicity and religion played off each other, but in the case of Islam there was something different; Islam stands apart as a mechanism for integrating people to the community. The cloak of Christianity provided the cover for the transformation of specific African religious practices and beliefs into new forms which are not consistent with a static, generic traditional African religion. The way that Yoruba ethnicity evolved in Brazil, Cuba, Sierra Leone, and the Nigerian hinterland indicates that the interaction between religion and ethnicity was often complex. Who is Yoruba is better answered by what language is spoken, rather than by religious affiliation, which in the nineteenth century could be *orisha*, Islam or Christianity, or indeed combinations thereof.[10]

ETHNICITY AND SLAVERY IN THE AMERICAS

Another area of analysis that is particularly fraught with ahistorical generalizations concerns issues relating to ethnicity.[11] With few exceptions, the study of slavery in the Americas has tended to treat ethnicity as a static feature of the culture of slaves. Twentieth-century ethnic categories in Africa are often read backwards to the days of slavery, thereby removing ethnic identity from its contemporary political and social context, and how that might affect analysis and projections. Michael Mullin, for example, is certainly correct in noting that "tribal" is no longer "good form," but in my opinion "ethnicity" is not "a euphemism for tribal," as he claims.[12] The concept of ethnicity is a particularly valuable tool for unraveling the past because it is a complex phenomenon tied into very specific historical situations. For example, Hall's account of Africans in colonial Louisiana traces the movement of a core group of Bambara from Africa to Louisiana, although the details of this population displacement, especially the chronology of enslavement in West Africa, have yet to be reconstructed adequately.[13] What does it mean that Bambara arrived in Louisiana in the eighteenth century? To answer this question requires a detailed study of how the term Bambara was used in different contexts at the time, not only in Louisiana but also in other parts of the diaspora and in West Africa. Specific ethnic identifications had meaning only in relation to the boundaries that separated different ethnic categories from each other, including the political, religious, and economic dimensions of these differences and how these changed over time. Certainly, historical associations with Africa were also essential features of these definitions of community, and rather than being static, the links with Africa were seldom disconnected from events across the Atlantic.

Ethnicity underwent redefinition in the Americas. On the one hand, European observers developed categories for African populations which involve problems of interpretation: the Chamba of slave accounts refers to the Konkomba and Gurma of the upper Voltaic region, not the Chamba of the Benue River basin in Nigeria; Gbari are an ethnic group referred to as Gwari by Hausa-speakers, but Gambari is a Yoruba term for Hausa; Nago is a sub-section of Yoruba speakers but was sometimes used as a generic term for Yoruba; Tapa refers to Nupe. These labels had meanings that have to be deciphered in context. In the Sokoto Caliphate, conversion to Islam often meant becoming Hausa, since many probably were non-Hausa in origin. The imposition of European labels for African populations further compounds the problem, since these were not necessarily the names used by enslaved Africans themselves. As the study of ethnicity in Africa has demonstrated clearly, ethnic identities can only be understood in context of the times; present ethnic categories cannot be applied backwards in time any more than present religious practices can be.

A brief guide to ethnicity in the context of slavery in the Americas would include a discussion of a dozen or so ethnic groups of ethnic clusters, including the following: Wolof; Mandingo/Bambara; Akan/Koromantin/Coromantine; Gbe/Mina (Allada/Fon/Ewe/Mahi); Yoruba (Nago/Aku/Lukumi); Igbo (Carabali/Calabari); Ibibio (Moco); various Bantu groups, including Kongo and Mbundu (Kongo/Angola); and Muslims from the central Sudan (Hausa/Nupe/Borno). Gbe is actually a modern linguistic term to refer to the cluster of languages that includes Fon, Allada, Ewe, and Mahi; historically the term Mina was sometimes used to designate these people, especially in Brazil, although that term itself has to be deciphered carefully because it was used to mean different things in different contexts.[14] There were numerous other ethnic groups; the Upper Guinea coast was characterized by a great number of groups, and some parts of the interior were lumped together as Chamba (Konkomba/Gurma), and although few in number, the Fulbe (Fulani/Peul) also stand out. This list may seem like a bewildering number of ethnic groups to the non-specialist, but in the African context, it is relatively few. Indeed, a dozen ethnic concentrations compares favorably with the concentration of European populations in the Americas, which included Spanish, Portuguese, English, Dutch, French, Danish, Irish, Scots, and Jews, at least. If absolute numbers of people are considered, moreover, many more Africans than Europeans crossed the Atlantic before the middle of the nineteenth century. The usual assumptions that Africans came from far more diverse backgrounds than Europeans is therefore only part of the story. The nature of enslavement guaranteed that isolated communities and small-scale societies were targeted, so that it can be expected that the backgrounds of people were, indeed, diverse. However, in most cases, enslaved individuals from isolated backgrounds followed trade routes, and, temporarily at least, remained with people whose language, cuisine, and culture were imposed upon them. Moreover, many of the enslaved came from near the coast, from societies and states that were influenced by the demand for slaves across the Atlantic. Hence, people who understand the Akan language (Twi), one of the Gbe languages, Yoruba, Igbo, Ibibio, Kikongo, and Kimbundu were concentrated in sufficient numbers in some places that these languages survived, often for longer than a generation, because of the continued influx of new arrivals who spoke the same languages or dialects of those languages. Again, the number of African languages is about the same as the number of European languages that spread to the Americas, although the African languages tended to be distributed more widely, while European languages, arising from political power, were more concentrated, and thereby became the common languages of expression, despite the development of creole forms of these languages as well. Those enslaved individuals from Africa did not come from theoretically pure ethnic groups, but had experienced complicated and disruptive interaction with their enslavers and the merchants who took them to the coast. Slave owners in Africa considered how best to exploit the value of their human chattel, which might well mean keeping individuals in Africa as slaves, not just selling them to European ships. Ethnicity cannot be considered a static concept, although in some essentialist sense, ethnicity often implied a degree of continuity that was ancient and primordial, in the same sense that English, French, German, and other European ethnicities are often considered.

A study of ethnicity among the enslaved population of the Americas can be achieved in several ways: first, by considering the regional origins of the enslaved population leaving Africa and the destinations of that population; second, by examining plantations records, wills, and other documents in the Americas; and third, by studying the detailed records collected by the British anti-slave trade patrols of the nineteenth century. The regional origins of the enslaved population, which can be calculated from the voyage database developed by David Eltis, David Richardson, and Stephen Behrendt, allows a chronological and regional breakdown of the slave trade to the Americas. In broad outline, their breakdown enables an identification of the principal ethnic groupings, confirming numerically the relative importance of different coastal regions and allowing a correlation with political events in the interior, and hence, the determination of the affected populations.[15]

The various demographic data that have been selected to display the range of ethnicities under slavery demonstrate that there were heavy concentrations of people of similar regional or ethnic background. Hence, the port of York in Virginia received the bulk of its imported population from the Bight of Biafra between 1718–39 (Table 7.1); of those whose regional origins are known, 7,600 people came from the Bight of Biafra, out of a total population whose origins are known of 14,218, representing 53 percent of the population. Since the majority of these people were either Igbo or had learned to speak some Igbo before arriving in Virginia, it is hard to imagine that there was not an important Igbo presence in the early cultural development of the tidewater area.[16] As the Virginia data reflects, regional categories become standard in the study of the slave trade, and are now further codified in the voyage database that is likely to be the statistical source of most demographic data on the slave trade for some time to come. In the Virginia case, the problems with the standardized divisions do not matter very much. However, for certain purposes, the Gold Coast and the Bight of Benin can be combined conceptually because of extensive interaction along the coast, and between the coast and the interior, which also overlapped. Senegambia, Upper Guinea, and Sierra Leone can be combined, too, both because even in combination the far western Sudan and the Guinea coast provided relatively few slaves, except in specific contexts, and because the overlap with the interior and along the coast was considerable. By contrast, Angola is too broad a category, and it makes sense to distinguish between Cabinda and the Loango coast to the north of the Congo River, and Luanda and Benguela and their subsidiary ports to the south of the Congo (Map 7.1). The Bight of Biafra stands out as a region that is relatively distinct, but there were links with the Gold Coast and Sierra Leone that qualify this generalization.

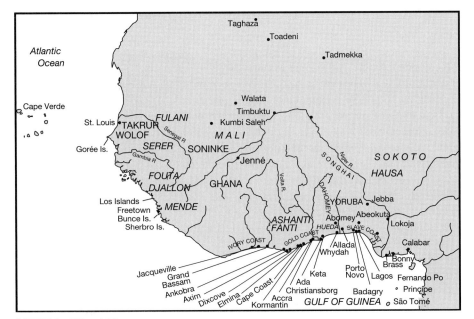

MAP 7.1 West Africa.

TABLE 7.1 Geographic Origins of Africans Entering Port York, Virginia, 1718–1739

Origin	1718–1726 *(%)*	1728–1739 *(%)*
Bight of Biafra	60	44
Angola	5	41
Gold Coast	13	5
Senegambia	4	10
Madagascar	9	-
Windward Coast	7	-
Sierra Leone	1	-
Total, Known Origins	8,400	5,818
Origins Unknown	213	2,968
Percent Unknown	3	34

Source: Allan Kulikoff, "The Origins of Afro-American Society in Tidewater Maryland and Virginia, 1700 to 1790," *William and Mary Quarterly* 35 (1978): 226–259, table on p. 232, citing *Documents Illustrative of the Slave Trade to America*, Elizabeth Donnan ed. (Washington, D.C., 1930–1935) IV: 183–185, 188–204.

Considerable diversity in ethnic origins is recorded in plantation records, as revealed in plantation records for St. Domingue (Tables 7.2–4), census records and inventories for Bahia (Table 7.5),[17] and slave registration data for Trinidad,[18] but again all these cases display considerable ethnic concentration. Moreover, the St. Domingue data reveals considerable variation in the gender composition of the enslaved population as organized by ethnicity (Table 7.4), and the Bahian data demonstrates that ethnic categories carried over into the freed population.[19] The Bahian material also allows a comparison of urban and rural slave populations and ethnic identifications. Each of these cases suggests that information on ethnicity, religion, and gender exists that can be used to reconstruct the impact of the slave trade on the emergence of the new societies in the Americas, and that this analysis can be informed through the exploration of ethnic and religious concentrations and their significance in connecting the history of the diaspora with the history of Africa.

The ethnicity, religion, and culture of the enslaved population kept changing. Before the abolition of the trans-Atlantic trade in enslaved Africans, new slaves were constantly arriving, and thereby infusing slave communities with new information and ideas which had to be assimilated in ways that we do not always understand at present. There is often confusion in the identification of language, culture, religion, place, and political entities, any of which could be, and was, used as a

TABLE 7.2   Ethnic Composition of African-Born Slaves, Sugar Estates, St. Domingue

	North *(1778–1791)*	**West** *(1785–1791)*	**West** *(1796–1797)*
Senegambia			
Senegal	1.4	1.5	1.7
Bambara	4.0	3.0	3.5
Fulbe (Poulard)	0.7	0.8	0.5
Mandinke	3.0	0.5	1.0
Upper Guinea Coast			
Kissi	0.4	0.0	0.1
Susu (Sosso, Tini)	1.2	0.2	1.6
Mesurade/Canga	2.5	0.7	0.2
Cap Lao	0.0	0.9	1.6
Other	6.3	5.4	4.5
Gold Coast			
Côte d'Or	0.9	0.1	0.1
Bandia, Banguia	0.0	1.5	1.1
Koromantin (Caramenty)	0.0	0.7	2.4
Mina	3.4	3.0	0.2
Bight of Benin			
Gbe (Arada, Fon, Foeda Adia)	15.9	16.0	17.3
Yoruba (Nago)	8.9	16.1	18.6
Bariba/Borgu (Barba)	0.8	0.8	1.6
Tem (Cotocoly)	0.3	1.8	3.2
Gurma (Tiamba/Kiamba)	2.5	2.5	2.7
Nupe (Taqua, Tapa)	0.8	1.3	3.0
Hausa (Aoussa/Gambary)	0.7	4.9	4.3
Bight of Biafra			
Igbo (Ara, Arol)	2.5	5.6	7.2
Ibibio (Bibi)	0.0	0.0	0.4
Anang (Moco)	0.0	0.1	0.1
West-Central Africa			
Congo	40.8	31.3	21.0
Mondongue	2.5	0.8	1.5
Mozambique	0.6	0.8	1.0
N slaves	2,143	1,059	2,641

Source: David Geggus, "Sugar and Coffee Cultivation in Saint Domingue and the Shaping of the Slave Labour Force," in *Cultivation and Culture: Work Process and the Shaping of Afro-American Culture in the Americas*, Ira Berlin and Philip Morgan, eds. (Charlottesville, 1993).

TABLE 7.3 Ethnic Composition of African-Born Slaves, Coffee Estates, St. Domingue

	North *(1778–1791)*	West *(1785–1791)*	West *(1796–1797)*	South *(1796–1797)*
Senegambia				
Senegal	0.7	2.0	2.2	2.5
Bambara	2.0	5.9	6.2	5.9
Fulbe (Poulard)	0.4	0.2	0.6	0.9
Mandinke	2.9	0.0	0.3	1.6
Upper Guinea Coast				
Kissi	0.2	0.0	0.0	0.2
Susu (Sosso, Tini)	0.3	0.2	1.0	1.4
Mesurade/Canga	0.9	0.2	0.6	2.2
Cap Lao	0.0	2.8	0.8	0.0
Other	2.5	2.8	3.3	2.6
Gold Coast				
Côte d'Or	0.7	0.0	0.1	0.3
Bandia, Banguia	0.0	0.0	0.8	0.0
Caramenty	0.0	0.7	0.4	0.0
Mina	1.0	0.4	1.2	2.7
Bight of Benin				
Gbe (Arada, Fon, Foeda, Adia)	10.1	5.7	10.3	5.4
Yoruba (Nago)	5.5	9.2	12.2	9.3
Bariba/Borgu (Barba)	0.1	0.0	0.4	0.3
Tem (Cotocoly)	0.0	1.1	2.3	0.6
Gurma (Tiamba/Kiamba)	1.1	1.5	2.1	2.0
Nupe (Taqua, Tapa)	0.5	0.7	1.4	0.6
Hausa (Aoussa/Gambary)	0.4	1.8	2.7	2.4
Bight of Biafra				
Igbo (Ara, Arol)	2.3	10.5	8.8	13.0
Ibibio (Bibi)	0.0	1.8	1.5	2.3
Anang (Moco)	0.0	0.0	0.3	1.3
West-Central Africa				
Congo	63.9	47.3	35.3	36.0
Mondongue	0.1	2.6	2.9	2.0
Mozambique	4.2	2.6	2.4	4.1
N slaves	973	457	1,578	1,576

Source: David Geggus, "Sugar and Coffee Cultivation in Saint Domingue and the Shaping of the Slave Labour Force," in *Cultivation and Culture: Work Process and the Shaping of Afro-American Culture in the Americas*, Ira Berlin and Philip Morgan, eds. (Charlottesville, 1993).

TABLE 7.4   Sex Ratios of Selected African Ethnic Groups in St. Domingue, 1721–1997

Region and Group	Sex Ratio	Sample	Percent
Senegambia	214	1,380	10.3
Bambara	278	718	
Senegal	156	379	
Mandingue	167	192	
Poulard (Fulbe)	163	71	
Sierra Leone	84	206	1.5
Sosso/Tini (Susu)	91	128	
Timbou (Jalonka)	57	58	
Windward Coast	120	253	1.9
Mesurade/Canga	110	124	
Gold Coast	151	633	4.7
Mina	136	441	
Caramenty	208	79	
Bandia (Guang)	143	73	
Slave Coast	99	4,552	34.1
Gbe (Ewe/Fon)	66	1,962	14.7
Arada	69	(1,694)	
Adia	89	(119)	
Foeda	51	(103)	
Fond	48	(46)	
Nago (Yoruba)	87	1,580	
Chamba/Gurma (Thiamba/ Kiamba)	191	297	
Cotocoli (Tem)	116	166	
Bariba/Borgu (Barba)	155	84	
Hausa (Aoussa, Gambary)	1,588	287	2.1
Nupe (Taqua/Tapa)	324	161	1.3
Bight of Biafra	103	1,245	9.3
Igbo	97	1,129	
Bibi (Ibibio)	186	83	
Central Africa	166	4,928	37.0
Congo	168	4,561	
Mondongue	144	283	
South-eastern Africa	219	137	1.0
Mozambique	231	129	
Total	133	13,334	

Source: David Geggus, "Sex Ratio, Age and Ethnicity in the Atlantic, Slave Trade: Data from French Shipping and Plantation Records," *Journal of African History*, 30:1 (1989): 32.

TABLE 7.5 Ethnic Designations of Slaves in Bahia (1775–1815)

Designations	Number	Percent
Bight of Benin		44.3
Gbe (Jeje)	104	
Yoruba (Nagó)	100	
Benin	4	
Savaru	1	
Mina	40	
Côte de Mina	15	
Central Sudan		10.6
Nupe (Tapa)	12	
Bariba/Borgu (Barbá)	1	
Hausa	50	
West-Central Africa		45.1
Angola	167	
Congo	4	
Benguela	93	
Sao Tomé	3	
Mondubi	1	
Gabon	1	
Sub-Total	596	100
Other		
Gentio de la Côte	270	
Africain	13	
de la Côte	2	
Total	881	

Source: Maria Inês Côrtes de Oliveira, Retrouver une identité: Jeux sociaux des Africains de Bahia: (vers 1750–vers 1890), Thèse pour le Doctorat en Histoire, Université de Paris-Sorbonne (Paris IV), 1992, 98, citing Testament et inventaires après décès: Chartes de Liberté; Enquête du Calundu de Cachoera; Liste des Africains résidant dans la Paroisse da Penha.

proxy for ethnicity. An analysis of facial and body markings, and who had these and who did not, can help to identify the backgrounds of people. In the nineteenth century, the movements of former slaves, both before British abolition and especially afterwards, continued trans-Atlantic contacts, thereby complicating issues of ethnicity and ethnic identity. Being Nago in Bahia in the early nineteenth century was not the same as being Yoruba in West Africa, but uncovering the differences and what these labels meant at the time is a major task whose undertaking must inform any analysis of the slave condition.

METHODOLOGICAL PROBLEMS

The interaction and interconnections of religion and ethnicity as identifying mechanisms raise problems of methodology in the reconstruction of the history of the African diaspora.[20] The discussion of slave religion and ethnic identity has tended to be static, not careful in using empirical documentation to substantiate speculation derived from anthropology. The difficulty is trying to avoid telescoping history, which thereby disguises the integrative forces of religion in transcending ethnic divisions.

The technique that many scholars have adopted in overcoming the supposed paucity of sources is the application of anthropological observations from the twentieth century to the past.[21] "When correlated with later anthropological accounts," according to Raboteau, "some of the distortion and confusion can be neutralized (though it would be naïve to assume that some modern accounts of African religions do not also suffer from bias)."[22] Can anthropological insights be used without verification through the usual methods of historical scholarship? Without the verification of contemporary documents, the findings of anthropology are nothing more than speculation. Unfortunately, specialists of slavery in the Americas have generally failed to document their analysis of religion and culture on the basis of the lived experiences of the enslaved Africans themselves.[23] In discussing Igbo customs and practices, for example, Sterling Stuckey uses twentieth-century data to demonstrate the continuity and longevity of African customs and practices, but he does not establish how and when culture was transferred.[24] The result is bad anthropology and even worse history. A critical examination must use the same rigorous historical methodology that characterizes other areas of history.

In Raboteau's words, the issue is "the question of the historicity of 'traditional' African cultures."

> Can it be assumed that African cultures and religions have not changed since the close of the Atlantic slave trade a century ago? To simply use current ethnological accounts of African religions without taking into account the possibility of change is methodologically questionable. Due to pressures from without—intensified Muslim and Christian missions, European imperialism, Western technology and education—the growth of African nationalism during the late nineteenth and twentieth centuries, African traditional religions have changed and continued to do so. . . . Besides external pressures to change, there are also indigenous processes of change within traditional African societies themselves.[25]

Despite Raboteau's caution, the examination of religion is usually treated in static terms; it is not shown what people believed and how they expressed these beliefs in different times and places, not even in Raboteau's work. Nor has there been sufficient attempt to demonstrate how religion was related to ideology and political structures in Africa and how this changed in the Americas. Instead, the concept of traditional African religion has been presented as an unchanging force that was all-embracing over vast parts of the African continent; observations from a variety of sources are merged to fabricate a common tradition that may or may not have had legitimacy. For want of historical research, the religious histories of Africans from the Bight of Benin, the Bight of Biafra, Kongo, and the interior of Angola are accordingly reduced to the meaningless concept of traditional (Map 7.2). Hence, the concept "traditional" has little functional or analytical use.[26]

The same standards of historical reconstruction should apply to the study of the African religious tradition as are applied to the examination of the impact of Christian missions and evangelicalism and the spread of Islam. Unlike the study of traditional African religion, the conversion of slaves to Christianity in the Americas has been the subject of extensive research. Consequently, scholarly analysis has not been prone to ahistorical generalizations, except with respect to the African background. Until recently, moreover, the African contribution to the spread of Christianity in the Americas was overlooked. As John Thornton has demonstrated, some Africans from Kongo and Angola were already Christians before reaching the Americas, and hence enslaved Christians were also a factor in spreading the faith among slaves in the Americas.[27] Thornton's discovery indicates that the interaction between African religious traditions and Christianity was more complex than previously thought. Moreover, the context for analyzing the conversion to Christianity includes Africa as well as Europe and the Americas. Clearly, the complexities of African religious history are blurred because there has been little research done on this important topic. The possible exception is the study of Islam among slaves, where the historical context of enslavement has sometimes been identified with concurrent political developments in West Africa.

The approach that is developed here attempts to situate ethnicity in historical context, demonstrating the ways in which culture changed, especially in diaspora. Nonetheless, the relationship of diaspora to homeland influenced the conceptions of ethnicity. People had to live in the present, and when that was under conditions of slavery, there was not much place for nostalgia. Ethnic labeling and stereotyping are only one component of the slave experience, but unraveling what these meant in historical context can help to unravel how the enforced migration of slavery shaped the cultures of the Americas, and indeed of Atlantic Africa. Ethnicity and religion are to be deciphered for specific situations because their deconstruction is the methodological means of reconstructing how the African diaspora came into existence, thereby making more sense out of the creole forms that the various components of the diaspora have developed.[28]

CREOLIZATION IN CONTEXT

Creolization can be perceived as a process of integrating overlapping ethnicities—European and African, as Earl Lewis does—but it is not clear how African history fits into the picture.[29] The term creole is thought to derive from the Portuguese

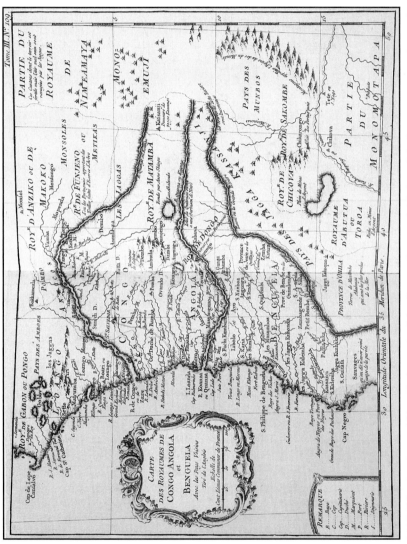

MAP 7.2 Southwest Africa. To the north of the Congo River are Cabinda and the Loango coast, to the south the Angolan capital Luanda and Benguela. Jacques Nicolas Bellin, *Le Petit Atlas Maritime. Recueil de cartes et de plans des quatre parties du monde* (Paris, 1764), vol. III-part II. *Courtesy of the Osher Map Library, University of Southern Maine.*

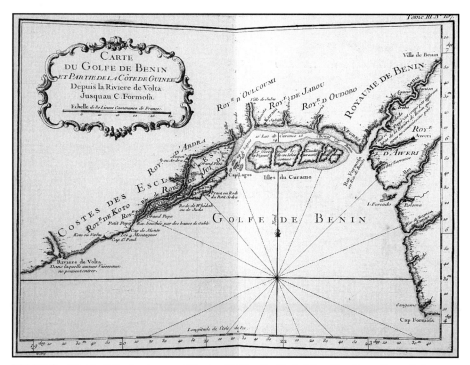

MAP 7.3   Bight of Benin. Jacques Nicolas Bellin, *Le Petit Atlas Maritime. Recueil de cartes et de plans des quatre parties du monde* (Paris, 1764), vol. III-part II. *Courtesy of the Osher Map Library, University of Southern Maine.*

crioulo, which according to Berlin, originally referred to someone of African descent born in the Americas, although recently this etymology has been challenged by Warner-Lewis, who suggests a Bantu origin for the term.[30] By extension, the term has been applied to people of European descent as well, and sometimes specifically to the racially mixed offspring of Africans and Europeans. In 1968, Kamau Brathwaite articulated his idea of creolization as "the process . . . which is a way of seeing the society, not in terms of white and black, master and slave, in separate nuclear units, but as contributory parts of a whole." For Brathwaite, creolization was the cultural process that occurred under slavery in tropical plantation colonies: "[W]ithin the dehumanizing institution of slavery . . . were two cultures of people, having to adapt themselves to a new environment and to each other. The friction created by this confrontation was cruel, but it was also creative. The white plantations and social institutions . . . reflect one aspect of this. The slaves' adaptation of their African cultures to a new world reflects another."[31]

Brathwaite envisioned creolization as the emergence of "authentically local institutions" and a "little tradition" among slaves, that reflected a division within Jamaica between two *separate* traditions, one African and inferior, and the other European and superior. Cultural polarity was the basis of the "creole", which was defined more by its divisions than its similarities, and hence was not a "plural" society that evolved "increasingly common values." Brathwaite's creole falls along an "histori-cally affected social-cultural continuum . . . [with] interrelated and sometimes over-lapping orientations."[32] The idea can be traced back at least as far as Philip Curtin's *Two Jamaicas.*[33]

As Mintz and Price developed the concept, creolization was meant to empha-size the cultural creativity of the enslaved in the Americas, and it involved a process of adjustment under slavery that was remarkably fast. According to Mintz and Price:

> The beginnings of what would later develop into "African-American cultures" must date from the very earliest interactions of the enslaved men and women on the African continent itself. They were shackled to-gether in coffles, packed into dank "factory" dungeons, squeezed to-gether between the decks of stinking ships, separated often from their kinsmen, tribesmen, or even speakers of the same language, left bewil-dered about their present and their future, stripped of all prerogatives of status and rank . . . and homogenized by a dehumanizing system that viewed them as faceless and largely interchangeable.[34]

However, their hypothesis that "distinctive, 'mature' African-American [i.e., Creole] cultures and societies probably developed more rapidly than has often been as-sumed," indeed "within the earliest years of slavery," is not proven, as they admit.[35] Indeed, the assertion compounds the difficulties with their basic assumption that African culture could not be conveyed to the Americas because of the heterogeneity of the enslaved population and for want of appropriate institutions. The extent to which culture dissipated in the course of the trans-Atlantic crossing has to be demon-strated for specific historical situations, with documentation, not assumed *a priori*, nonetheless. Despite the reservations of Mintz and Price themselves, subsequent stu-dents of slavery have frequently assumed lack of evidence was confirmation of rapid creolization.[36]

Creole, or Krio, was also used in West Africa to describe the population of mixed ancestry in Sierra Leone, and subsequently along parts of the West African coast.[37] The origins of this usage derive from the use of the term for essentially linguistic purposes, deriving from Portuguese pidgin, as noted above; the pidgins spoken along the coast were trade languages often specifically identified with people of mixed European and African origins, including former slaves from the Americas. As in the Americas, the term suggests that people had diverse origins, and hence a new identity emerged that more or less effectively amalgamated these differences. Unlike the way the term is often used in the study of slavery, Krio emerged as an ethnic designation.

Hence the various uses of creole present a problem in analysis: originally re-ferring to American-born people of African descent, whether or not racially mixed, by extension, the term became associated with culture, and creole was applied to mixed populations, whether of African descent or not, as long as they were born in the Americas. The problem with the term is establishing the parameters of its use; in some constructions, birth was essential in establishing the boundary, but Berlin has demonstrated that birth was not always essential. According to Berlin, Atlantic cre-oles designates:

> Those who by experience or choice, as well as by birth, became part of a new culture that emerged along the Atlantic littoral—in Africa, Europe, or the Americas—beginning in the 16th century. It departs from the notion of "creole" that makes birth [in the Americas] definitive. Circumstances and volition blurred differences between "African" and "creole" as defined only nativity. "African" and "creole" were as much a matter of choice as of birth. The term "Atlantic creole" is designed to capture the cultural transformation that sometimes preceded generational change and sometimes was unaffected by it.[38]

Berlin is describing the hybrid culture of the Atlantic rim, centered on port towns, and adopting one or another pidgin forms of a European language.

STAGES OF CREOLIZATION

The emphasis of Mintz and Price on the rapid creolization of newly arrived slaves from Africa poses special problems. Stephan Palmié, as a result, asks for greater attention to historical context in criticizing the idea that synthesis was rapid and occurred early.[39] Palmié argues that:

> Despite its theoretical sophistication and methodological soundness, the "rapid early synthesis" model suggested by Mintz and Price fell short of stimulating a thorough historicization of African-American anthropology. Instead, and quite contrary to these authors' intentions, it sometimes seems to have encouraged hypostatising the concept of creolization to a degree where it allows glossing over history in a manner reminiscent of an earlier inflationary use of the concept of "acculturation". This tendency . . . not only trivializes the question of how exactly "creole" synthesis was achieved, but also obscures the formidable problems presented by cases where covariational* "adhesions" might plausibly be attributed to Atlantic transfer–not necessarily of concrete forms, but of organizational models.[40]

Since creole could refer specifically to the mulatto population, as well as all others born outside of the native lands of their parents or grandparents, whether in the Americas or elsewhere, it is worthwhile distinguishing among Creole populations, carefully isolating the use of the concept as a linguistic designation for dialects (pidgins) from its use in a cultural context. These various usages suggest that population mixture implicitly denies ethnic purity. From this perspective, the process of creolization could be realized as quickly as Mintz and Price have argued, or much more gradually, even in stages.

---

*A covariational relationship exists when two phenomena occur together, but no information is yielded about which is the cause and which the effect.

An analysis of the gradual process of incorporation, in contrast to the rapid adjustment postulated by Mintz and Price, was developed by Fernando Ortiz as early as 1916. Ortiz described this process as transculturation: "*transculturation* . . . expresses the different phases of the process of transition from one culture to another . . . [which] does not consist merely in acquiring another culture [i.e., *acculturation*] . . ., but the process also necessarily involves the loss or uprooting of a previous culture, which could be defined as *deculturation*."[41]

Such a view suggests phases of creolization, in contrast to the model of Mintz and Price postulating an initial, sudden introduction to creole culture by the mass of newly imported, deracinated African slaves. Ortiz's problem is that he did not know enough African history; he saw the reformulation of African norms in the context of Cuba, as Palmié has recently summarized, but he, and indeed his successors, failed to allow for the possibility of ongoing interaction across the Atlantic, even during the days of slavery.[42] The flow of culture for these analysts is one way only, from Africa to the Americas, and then in the context of ethno-destruction. The dichotomy that is perceived is between African retention, whether specific survivals or generalized cultural responses, and the European imposition of an early form of colonialism. This was a colonialism of what? What were the origins of the enslaved? How were people enslaved? What were their perceptions? Was the severance from natal Africa as dramatic and severe for all, as claimed? The recognition of the importance of African culture, even if not analyzed in historical context, does indeed call into question one of the basic assumptions of the Mintz/Price model. It suggests, as Berlin calls the first generation of enslaved Africans in each American colony, a charter generation, I would assume. Douglas Chambers has attempted to describe the different, but continuous, processes in terms of primary and secondary creolization, the initial stage emphasizing the high proportion of African-born slaves and the latter stage indicating a predominance of American-born slaves in the population.[43]

At first consideration, the description of creolization as a gradual process of cultural transference, subject to adjustment through resistance response, seems to explain the emergence of a hybrid culture dominated by an American-born population; new arrivals had to assimilate to a common American or creole culture and society (cultures and societies?). I contend that these qualifications of the creolization model still skip over African history. Palmié asks "how exactly historical human agency makes the respective (formal and functional) variables 'stick' in specific instances." By "agency," Palmié is referring to the ability of enslaved people to determine their own fate. Unless the extent to which people could shape their surroundings with reference to the African past has to be addressed, according to Palmié, the creole theory "evades the issue of systemic articulations that may . . . reveal single observational units to be part and parcel of larger, encompassing historical processes operating on a transatlantic scale." The historical context is crucial, but Palmié does not allow for enough interaction across the Atlantic, even in the case of *ekpe*. The history of *ekpe*, or *abakuá*,* in Cuba and in the interior of the Bight of Biafra were certainly connected, but why is it assumed that influences only flowed one way, most especially in

---

*A cult that derives from the Efo and Efik peoples of the Cross River Delta in present-day Nigeria.

identifying institutions that Mintz and Price claim could not have crossed the Atlantic? The location of acknowledged exceptions in the nineteenth century does not alter the critique. Perhaps there were similar, long-standing cultural and historical traditions that lasted as long, but dating from an earlier period, that now no longer exist in a recognizable form. The question then becomes what is the rate of creolization; was it a question of sudden creolization, being born in the Americas and achieved within a generation, or did the variety of conditions that occurred under slavery result in more complex patterns? Perhaps the connections with Africa were stronger than Mintz, Price, and others of the creole school have assumed.

In identifying individual enslaved Africans and following their route into slavery, the creolization model is challenged to explain individual life histories. These histories reveal that individuals were enslaved most often for political cause, and occasionally for more narrowly defined judicial or religious reasons, rooted in specific places at exact times. How and why they reached the Americas has to be analyzed in historical context, using rigorous historical methodology. Also, individuals reflected communities, whether particular towns and settlements were destroyed during the act of enslavement or not. The idea of stages of creolization is tempting; it is a move in the right direction, but does not go far enough because it does not recognize that agency was always present, and that adjustments to enslavement began at the point of enslavement. The presence of agency flowed across the Atlantic in both directions.

CONCLUSION

In exploring ethnicity and religion as charter principles in the formation of the African diaspora, I am suggesting that Africans moved across the Atlantic in identifiable patterns which were understood in ethnic and religious terms. However, the recognition of ethnicity and religion as essential in the self-identification of enslaved Africans is not sufficient; each must be understood in terms of process and change. Locating where the process of community redefinition occurred is the question. Those models of creolization and transculturation that emphasize the extent of adaptability in the Americas cannot explain the role of Islam in the diaspora. Certainly, a similar process of creolization shaped communities, including both slave and free, in West Africa. Enslaved Muslims in the Americas had already undergone this transition. In West Africa, ethnic plurality characterized Muslim society. Through enslavement, conversion, and migration, people of diverse ethnic backgrounds came to identify with Muslim culture. Pan-ethnic groups similar to those familiar in the Americas emerged in this situation. Hausa, Mande, and Borno indicated such super-ethnic groups.

The Muslim experience suggests that religion and ethnicity both played a role in the cultural adaptations under slavery and the emergence of what might be called the "cultures of servility," which in their social forms required the subordination of the enslaved population. In that subordination was also contained the basis of resistance. This process was underway along the trade routes and in the ports of western Africa. Both ethnicity and religious affiliation enabled individuals to establish new relationships under slavery, and at the same time allowed them to establish themselves within the structure of slave society. Moreover, I would contend that the development of a trans-ethnic religious framework subordinated issues of ethnicity within the slave community. In the case of Islam, this subordination of ethnicity to the larger community had already occurred in Africa and was transposed to the Americas. Other religious movements, such as vodun, candomblé, IFÁ, and santería, evolved in a trans-Atlantic milieu, as promoted by the regular and continuous interaction across the Atlantic in their development. Unlike Islam, however, ethnic categories became associated with chapters of these religions, and hence ethnic categories emerged within the context of the religious framework.

➡ FOCUS QUESTIONS

1. Describe the ways in which ethnicity and religion creolized Africans in the New World.
2. What are charter principles and which does Lovejoy identify?
3. How does Lovejoy criticize existing models of creolization?

4

IMAGINATION

The discovery of America presented European historians with an extraordinary problem. How was this new hemisphere, never mentioned in the Bible, to be perceived? What evidence was trustworthy? It required centuries for historians of the metropolitan core (England, France, and the Netherlands), whose "knowledge" of America began with sixteenth-century fables of indigenous Americans with tails and three eyes, and who stridently rejected the legitimacy of American sources both indigenous and Spanish, to gradually come to terms with this issue.

Benjamin Schmidt's "The Purpose of Pirates" offers us a portrait of America which was deliberately distorted by the Dutch for their own political purposes. Taking the horrific accusations of the Dominican Friar Bartolomé de Las Casas' *Brief History of the Destruction of the Indies* at face value, the Dutch, who were themselves struggling for liberation against the Spanish, we see how history can be employed as a political instrument. The Dutch gave massive publicity to Las Casas' accusations of Spanish brutality, as they did to the reports of the pirate Alexander Exquemelin, whose views appeared in his famous book *The Buccaneers of America.* Schmidt concludes that the employment of Las Casas and Exquemelin demonstrates "the remarkable plasticity and convenient malleability of America during the age of discovery."

Jorge Cañizares' essay "Whose Center and Whose Periphery" reflects on the process by which Europeans gradually came to accept the authenticity of both indigenous and Spanish colonial sources. Initially indigenous American sources were automatically rejected, for they were presented, not in writing, but rather in pictographic symbols. Europeans from the metropolitan core also rejected the work of Spanish historians as being "stuffed with impossible facts [and] absurd exaggerations." Over two centuries, however, as Europeans visited America, and as Spain's own historical prowess grew, particularly with the founding of the Archivo de Indias, which brought together a treasure trove of routine colonial reports, Europeans from the metropolitan core came to value and appreciate the work of indigenous Americans and Spanish colonial historians.

Whose Centers and Peripheries? Eighteenth-Century Intellectual History in Atlantic Perspective

Jorge Cañizares-Esguerra

Around 1580, as the Spanish Dominican Diego Durán researched his history of the Aztecs,[1] he found himself confronted with two contradictory accounts of the death of Moctezuma. The traditional account from Spanish sources contended that the Aztecs themselves had stoned Moctezuma to death. Indigenous sources, however, told a dramatically different story; namely, that the emperor and several other Aztec nobles had been stabbed to death by the Spanish conquistadors. Although this account was an obvious challenge to Spanish official historiography, Durán himself saw no choice but to accept it, for the story was recounted in native documents recorded in indigenous scripts and texts. Despite the generalized doubt about the reliability of Amerindian informants, Durán, like most Spaniards, believed that indigenous documents in non-alphabetical scripts kept trustworthy historical records.[2]

European intellectuals in the eighteenth century, however, held strikingly different views on the accuracy of indigenous historical sources. For example, in 1787 an anonymous British reviewer argued that a history of the Aztecs recently published in Italy by the Mexican Jesuit Francisco Clavijero (1731–1787) made no sense; it was a book "stuffed with impossible facts [and] absurd exaggerations." The reviewer derided histories like Clavijero's because they drew most of their facts from Mexican indigenous records, which, the reviewer argued, were primitive paintings, not writings, and therefore utterly unreliable. "All the history, therefore, anterior to the conquest by Cortés . . . [should be] receive[d] with very great distrust."[3]

To be sure, lack of belief in non-alphabetical scripts was part of the skeptical mood that characterized the Enlightenment. In the following pages I describe how the history of the New World was written on both sides of the Atlantic in the eighteenth century. The skepticism that dominated the "age of reason" took on different meanings in different places. In Western Europe it generated new forms of reading, assessing, and validating testimonies and new forms of writing history that drew upon non-literary, material evidence. In Spain it prompted scholars to create new, more reliable narratives based on primary documentation, which in turn led to the formation of one of the largest specialized repositories of primary sources in the world, the Archive of the Indies. Finally, in Spanish America, skepticism was turned against its most ardent European promoters. Spanish American scholars questioned the ability of European observers to ever comprehend the past and nature of the New World.

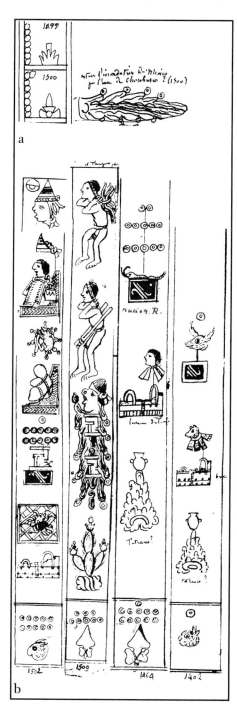

Entries recording events that took place in the Central Valley of Mexico around 1500 C.E.: (a) *Histoire mexicaine depuis 1221 jusqu'en 1594;* (b) Codex en Cruz. These copies belonged to León y Gama. *Courtesy of the Bibliothèque Nationale, Paris.*

The great intellectual, cultural movements of the modern world like the Renaissance, the Enlightenment, and Romanticism are often presented as European inventions, passively and derivatively consumed everywhere else. The story that follows demonstrates the problematic nature of such an approach. In the age of Enlightenment, when it came to new ideas on how to write the history of the New World, there was as much intellectual creativity in the colonial peripheries as in the metropolitan core.

In Western Europe, skeptics not only questioned the reliability of Amerindian sources, they also doubted the credibility of earlier Europeans observers. In the 1781 edition of his widely read *Histoire philosophique des deux Indes,* for example, the Abbé Guillaume-Thomas Raynal (1713–1796) argued that all Spanish accounts of the New World were "confusing, contradictory and full of the most absurd fables to which human credulity could ever be exposed."[4] For Raynal the conquistadors were plunderers, not dispassionate observers. In an earlier edition, Raynal had suggested that the only way to save any surviving historical records from the destruction and oblivion to which they had been subjected was to allow philosophers like Locke, Buffon, or Montesquieu to visit the New World.[5] Clearly, by the third quarter of the eighteenth century the sources that Europeans had traditionally used to interpret the past of the Americas—translations of documents recorded in indigenous scripts and travel accounts by conquistadors, missionaries, sailors, and colonial bureaucrats—were considered unreliable. Many intellectual and cultural developments help explain this curious burst of skepticism.

One problem presenting itself to historians of pre-Columbian America was the reliability of the Bible as a historical source. The Scriptures had long been assumed to be the sole surviving, accurate historical record of the human race. Since the second half of the seventeenth century, however, skeptics had begun to question its authority and credibility. As humanist antiquarians unearthed ancient sources, including ancient Egyptian chronologies, and as the Jesuits made Chinese classical texts available in translation, it became clear that the chronologies of Hebrews and heathens could not be easily reconciled. Eighteenth-century conservative luminaries, such as the Neapolitan scholar Giambattista Vico (1668–1744) and the Anglican Bishop of Gloucester William Warburton (1698–1779), pursued a defensive strategy to safeguard the Bible's authority. Chinese ideograms and Egyptian hieroglyphs, long considered the repositories of ancient historical knowledge, lost their luster and prestige. Vico and Warburton argued that non-alphabetical scripts represented a more primitive stage in the evolution of mental faculties. Thus, in the debates over the reliability of Biblical chronologies, Chinese and Egyptian sources were discarded and Amerindian pictograms came to exemplify the first stage in the evolution of writing. The primitive Amerindian paintings were seen as products of a child-like mentality, the initial phase in the evolution of the mental faculties. No wonder, then, that in 1787 Warburton was so willing to dismiss documents recorded in Mesoamerican scripts.

If academic debates over biblical chronology account for the loss of credibility of Amerindian sources in the eighteenth century, the intellectual elitism that characterized the Enlightenment helps explain why earlier reports of the New World were also considered untrustworthy. When Raynal called on philosophers to visit and report on the New World in order to replace the unreliable testimony of earlier Spanish witnesses, he was simply following a convention of his time. In his groundbreaking 1755 study of the origins of social inequality, Rousseau characterized the so-called European "age of discovery" as one of lost opportunities. According to Rousseau, missionaries, traders, soldiers, and sailors had not truly studied the foreign societies they visited and conquered, for they had failed to go beyond appearances. A new category of travelers was needed, Rousseau insisted, one whose "eyes [are] made to see the true features that distinguish nations."[6] Rousseau, therefore, invited the leading intellectual luminaries of his age to set sail and become philosophical travelers.

When Rousseau and Raynal called into question the reliability of typical European accounts of foreign societies, they were simply echoing the learned consensus of their age that the observations of untrained individuals were not trustworthy: witnesses left to their own devices failed to make accurate observations. This was one of the tenets of the "age of reason," which divided the world into two unequal parts: on one hand, the fear-stricken, deluded majority; and on the other, the reasonable few, whose minds had been trained to understand the world accurately.

Cornelius de Pauw (1739–1799) typifies the authors north of the Pyrenees, who, in the second half of the eighteenth century, sought to write histories of the New World while dismissing earlier Amerindian and European testimonies. De Pauw was a prolific author from the Southern Netherlands, whose *Recherches philosophiques sur les américains* (Philosophical Inquiries on the Americans, 1768–1769) proved extremely influential. The book was structured as a series of essays evaluating previous reports on the New World. Utterly skeptical of the power of the untrained mind to observe accurately, De Pauw set out to demonstrate that contradictions plagued existing literature on the history of the Americas. Take, for example, his analysis of the Inca Garcilaso de la Vega's *History of the Incas* (1609). Owing to Garcilaso's dual heritage as the son of a Spanish conquistador and an Inca princess, which gave him access to the most learned and accurate contemporary testimonies from both European and indigenous sources, Garcilaso had enjoyed a reputation as the foremost authority on the history of the Incas since the early seventeenth century. In De Pauw's hands, however, Garcilaso's history appeared riddled with contradictions.

Garcilaso had maintained that the Inca kept their records in quipus (knotted strings), not alphabetical writing. He had also argued that the great legislator, founder of the Inca dynasty, Manco Capac, had turned the savages of Cuzco into civilized agriculturists, and that the eleven rulers who followed Manco Capac had all been sage and prudent, spreading civilization and a humanely religious solar cult throughout an Inca Empire that expanded through gentle conquest. Garcilaso, finally, had argued that the Inca had established palaces, cities, universities, and astronomical observatories, as well as pious and prudent laws. De Pauw read Garcilaso carefully and attacked many of his premises. According to De Pauw, it was inherently contradictory to maintain that the Inca enjoyed wise laws while they lacked writing, for laws existed only when written and codified. According to De Pauw, unwritten rules were not laws because they changed according to the whim of the times and the imagination of tyrants. There were other serious logical flaws in Garcilaso's narrative. The claim that one man, Manco Capac, had single-handedly transformed highland savages into civilized creatures in one generation was outrageous. For evidence, De Pauw cited the Jesuit missions of Paraguay, the most recent example of a successful transformation of savages into settled civilized agriculturists. The achievement of civilization in Paraguay had required no less than fifty years and the imposition of harsh policies to prevent the Amerindians from escaping. Societies, De Pauw argued, are not transformed by leaps, but like nature, evolve in sequential stages—evenly, harmoniously, and slowly.

Drawing upon this principle of slow social progress, De Pauw maintained that Garcilaso's chronology of the Inca did not make sense. Garcilaso had argued that forty years after the death of Manco Capac, astronomical observatories had been built in Cuzco to determine solstices and equinoxes. To evolve from a state of savagery to sophisticated astronomical knowledge required more than forty years. Finally, based on the notion of the harmoniously integrated evolution of social institutions, De Pauw insisted that the Inca could not have had an advanced agricultural society without having at the same time iron, money, and writing - which they all lacked. Garcilaso had presented Inca rulers as patriarchal yet prudent, preoccupied with the welfare of the majority, but how could rulers have been prudent and gentle, De Pauw wondered, when the Inca had never developed institutions to check and balance the power of their monarchs? A fair, gentle patriarch was a contradiction in terms. So, too, was the idea that the Inca fought "just wars" even as they engaged in conquest. Even if one conceded to Garcilaso that Manco Capac had in fact been fair, prudent, and gentle, what were the chances, De Pauw sardonically asked, that twelve such statesmen should appear in succession? De Pauw applied the same unrelenting critical techniques to tear apart previous versions of the history of the Americas.[7]

If the views of learned authors such as Garcilaso, who had ably synthesized the testimonies of both Amerindians and Europeans, proved untrustworthy, how then should scholars write the history of the New World? Western European authors were not merely content with dismissing as sources translations of records written in indigenous scripts. Nor were these scholars satisfied with demonstrating logical inconsistencies in the accounts of travelers, missionaries, sailors, and colonial bureaucrats. Some philosophers, like the Frenchman Charles-Marie de La Condamine (1701–1774) chose to go to the New World and study first-hand the land and its peoples, thus doing away with bothersome intermediary textual authorities. As the eighteenth century unfolded, witnesses trained in the new European sciences arrived in the Americas in ever greater numbers.

In addition to on-site research, however, another option existed for scholars who did not trust the older accounts. Some European authors set out to reconstruct the past of the New World conjecturally, using non-literary, material evidence. Rousseau, for example, tried to do away with all evidence from literary sources. Paying lip service to the reliability of the Bible as an accurate account of the past, Rousseau turned to nature for insights, drawing endlessly on evidence from animal behavior to fill in the gaps in his evolutionary narrative of society and the causes of inequality. In addition, authors like De Pauw, who found suspect all previous accounts of the past of the New World, turned to nature for evidence upon which to build alternative histories of the Americas.

De Pauw offered a new conjectural history of the lands and peoples of America based entirely on facts from geology, geography, animal distribution, and some old-fashioned medical theories. De Pauw found evidence pointing to an early geological catastrophe in America: fossil bones of gigantic animals; earthquakes and active volcanoes still rocking the earth; sea-shells strewn over all the low valleys; ores of heavy metals protruding on the surface of the land. According to De Pauw, there were also substantial indications that the New World was a humid, putrid environment: the lesser number, smaller size, and monstrous appearance of quadrupeds; the degeneration of foreign animals; the successful development of "watery" plants from the Old World such as rice, melons, citrus, and sugar cane; the proliferation of insects and reptiles; the abundance of poisonous plants such as curare, whose virtues only the savage knew; the American origin of syphilis (humanity's scourge). De Pauw concluded that a flood had suddenly transformed a continent of big animals and ancient civilizations into a land enveloped by miasmas. America's coldness and humidity, in turn, had emasculated its fauna and peoples. Drawing on an ancient medical tradition that assumed that males were "drier" than females, De Pauw argued that the Amerindians were effete. The Amerindians were millenarian inhabitants of the continent who, as a consequence of the flood that destroyed the New World, had become humid and insensitive, incapable of feeling passion and sexual urges, which, in turn, explained why, upon arrival, Europeans had found an allegedly sparsely populated continent.[8]

The eighteenth century witnessed many other conjectural histories of the New World. One of the leading historians of the age, the presbyter William Robertson (1721–1793), rector of the University of Edinburgh, published his *History of America* in 1777. Rather than drawing upon geology and geography, Robertson made use of the new science of political economy as he sought to cast Amerindians as the missing link in the history of the evolution of human societies. By the eighteenth century, Spain had become a weak imperial power, reviled and ridiculed in Europe. Criticism of Spain, to be sure, was not new. In the Middle Ages, Europeans had represented Spain as a threatening frontier where Jews and Muslims roamed undisturbed. In the sixteenth century, as it consolidated a formidable overseas empire at the outset of the Reformation, Spain came to be both admired and despised. The figure of the intolerant, greedy, cruel Spaniard, dedicated to killing Amerindians and Dutchmen, came to life in the hands of Protestant printers. In the seventeenth century, Spaniards were commonly represented not only as cruel bigots but also as ignoramuses, and Spain was depicted as a country firmly controlled by superstitious friars.[9] While resisting these cartoonish representations, Spanish authorities and intellectuals were concerned about Spain's decline. Efforts to reform the economy and open the empire to new ideas were first attempted as early as the 1620s under the aegis of the Count-Duke of Olivares (1587–1645), but gained momentum after the War of the Spanish Succession (1701–1714) when a new dynasty, the Bourbons, replaced the Habsburgs on the throne.

Reforms also extended to historiography. In debates which lasted from the 1740s until well into the 1790s, intellectuals argued that previous accounts about the history of the Americas were utterly unreliable. Some authors, like the Count of Campomanes (1723–1803), substituted the conjectural histories offered by Northern

European authors like Robertson for all previous available narratives. Others, however, came up with alternatives deeply rooted in Spain's own intellectual traditions.

Juan Bautista Muñoz (1745–1799) typifies the authors who, in the eighteenth
century, turned to the scholarship of Spanish humanism for inspiration. Muñoz
inherited a corpus of critical Valencian scholarship, including the writings of such
luminaries as Juan Luis Vives (1492–1540) and Gregorio Mayans y Siscar (1699–
1781), Muñoz's own mentor.[10] Drawing upon this tradition, Muñoz rejected all previous accounts of the history of the New World. Muñoz did not think that existing
narratives of America were unreliable merely because they were translations of
records in indigenous scripts. Nor did he limit himself to the argument that previous
accounts were doubtful because ignorant travelers, missionaries, sailors, and bureaucrats had written them. The older narratives, Muñoz maintained, were untrustworthy
because they lacked a solid foundation. Since archival sources had not been written
with the intention of moving audiences to support specific political agendas—as
most printed documents usually are—Muñoz advocated the writing of new histories
that were largely based on unpublished, primary documentation. Much earlier than
German historian Leopold von Ranke (1795–1886), Muñoz considered painstaking
archival research a pre-condition for writing history.

No adequate archive existed, so Muñoz set out to organize one. Over a period
of twenty years, he carefully put together one of the greatest collections of documents and manuscripts on the Spanish colonization of the New World.[11] Muñoz also
persuaded the minister of the Council of Indies, José de Gálvez, to create the
Archivo de Indias (Archive of the Indies) in the early 1780s.[12]

Muñoz envisioned himself as a Descartes of American historiography, doing
away with previous textual authorities through methodical doubt, and as a Bacon of
historical method, reconstructing knowledge upon solid foundations based on the
painstaking collection of facts. He thought that within the archives of Spain would be
found the answer to each and every one of the charges leveled by foreigners against
the nation. Muñoz was a patriot who thought that the truth about the deeds of Spain in
the New World could only emerge after the exhaustive accumulation of new documentary evidence. According to Muñoz, the sheer amassing of sources would demonstrate that the negative European portrayal of Spain was simply innuendo, deliberate
manipulation of the truth, and biased interpretation of the available information.

Although in his first forays into the archives Muñoz despaired of finding any
logic behind the thousands of stored documents, he slowly began to find order. In the
many documents and manuscripts lying unpublished on the shelves of archives and
private libraries, he found evidence that Spain had transformed the history of navigation and commerce. The documents also seemed to reveal what the rest of Europe
had most denied: the profound contributions that Spain had made to the store of universal knowledge. The many unpublished travel reports of the sixteenth and seventeenth centuries, the countless geographical surveys (particularly those sponsored in
the later sixteenth century under Philip II), and the various manuscripts on natural
history, demonstrated Spain's significant contributions to natural history and geography. The many letters, reports, and trials of colonial bureaucrats and the prolonged
and well-documented discussions addressing the issue of laws for the colonies, on
the other hand, proved the prudence and philosophical depth of Spanish colonial

legislation, "a precious monument of human wisdom." The numerous unpublished ethnological studies of indigenous peoples, Muñoz argued, indicated that colonial laws had been hammered on the anvil of sound anthropological knowledge. The many documents related to the Church demonstrated that the conquest had never been merely motivated by greed. According to Muñoz, these documents also revealed that the civilization created by Spain in the Indies was a harmonious whole in material and spiritual balance. This search for evidence of the wisdom of Spanish legislation and of natural history observations was the organizing principle behind the invaluable collection of primary documents that Muñoz gathered in some hundred and fifty stout volumes over the course of twenty years.[13]

As in Europe, there was much support in Spanish America for the writing of new historical narratives. Yet these new histories of America were significantly different from those that appeared on the other side of the Atlantic. Spanish Americans, to be sure, tried to offer alternative accounts in which the inhabitants of the New World did not appear as degenerate and effete, as conjectural historians like De Pauw had presented them. In the process, Spanish American writers also articulated a powerful and creative critique of Eurocentric forms of knowledge. Spanish American authors, for example, exposed the shortcomings and limitations of the new European philosophical travelers, who had been arriving in ever increasing numbers to the New World. Spanish American intellectuals maintained that foreign travelers were unreliable sources because they tended to be ignorant of native languages, gullible, and easily manipulated by savvy local informants: so much for the boasted skepticism of the observers from Western Europe.

The work of Antonio León y Gama (1735–1802) exemplifies the distinctly patriotic scholarship that appeared in eighteenth-century Spanish America. León y Gama first articulated his views on the limited ability of outside observers to understand the past and the nature of the New World in a debate over the curative power of lizards. A flurry of speculation and clinical experimentation greeted the public of Mexico in 1782 when the leading physician of the Audiencia (high court and council) of Guatemala, José Flores, published a treatise claiming to have discovered that the raw meat of lizards cured cancer.[14] The discovery triggered a medical controversy in the capital of Mexico. Some physicians proved through clinical trials that the lizards were in fact poisonous, not curative. León y Gama, however, denounced these clinical trials as having either administered the wrong lizards to patients, or mishandled the ones that were curative. Drawing on the works of Francisco Hernández, the sixteenth-century savant sent by Philip II to compile a natural history of the New World, León y Gama maintained that several distinct species of lizards, some of them indeed poisonous, existed in central Mexico. The physicians who conducted the trials that proved the lizards poisonous might have failed to identify the correct species or, worse, might have mishandled the right ones, turning them poisonous. Great care and great knowledge was needed to identify the correct species. Once the right lizard was caught, León y Gama argued, it had to be fed only with the appropriate local insects; all females, particularly those pregnant, had to be discarded; finally, the lizard had to be treated gently, for if irritated it could become poisonous. The amount of knowledge that these techniques demanded from physicians was extraordinary. Doctors needed to know the natural history of the area in order to identify, feed, and treat the curative lizards properly. The message behind León y Gama's treatise was that only those who knew the local fauna and flora in all its exquisite detail and intricacy were qualified to use the lizards. Those ignorant of the bewildering details of Amerindian lore would never be able to master their curative powers.[15]

In the 1790s, in a different debate, this time over how to read Mesoamerican scripts, León y Gama maintained that outsiders had failed to understand the meaning of Amerindian sources for the same reasons that they had failed to grasp the importance of the curative power of lizards, namely, superficial acquaintance with the great complexities of Amerindian knowledge. By demonstrating the difficulty of reading Aztec documents, León y Gama set out to show the degree of linguistic and scientific knowledge required to handle this material appropriately, knowledge that only insiders could ever hope to master. León y Gama used Nahuatl documents recorded in indigenous scripts to make his case.

Nahuatl historical sources, León y Gama argued, ranged from widely accessible historical documents to arcane records that stored secret knowledge. He offered a few examples. *Codex histoire mexicaine depuis 1221 jusqu'en 1594,* on the one hand, indicated that the flood of Tenochtitlan occurred in the year "eight flint" (1500 CE).

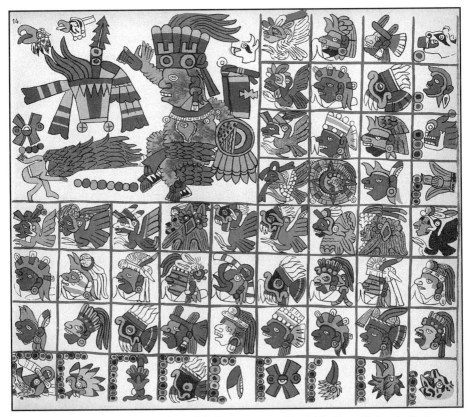

Detail of the ritual calendar Tonalamatl Aubin. *Courtesy of the Bibliothèque Nationale, Paris.*

Although it located this event in equally rough fashion in the same year, the *Codex en Cruz*, on the other hand, dated other events using a finer grid. It recorded, for example, the dates of birth of the monarch of Texcoco, Nezahualcoyotl (1402 CE), his son Nezahualpilzintli (1464 CE), and the ruler Quauhcaltzin (1502 CE).

Sources such as *Codex histoire mexicaine,* León y Gama maintained, had been written for the masses, because they required only a superficial acquaintance with writing techniques and astronomical knowledge. Sources such as the *Codex en Cruz,* on the other hand, were addressed to more knowledgeable and sophisticated audiences, for they demanded familiarity with the hieroglyphs of deities and towns, as well as an exquisite command of multiple calendrical counts. A third type of source, such as the ritual calendar *Tonalamtl Aubin,* could only be read by highly trained religious specialists. With hundreds of symbols and obscure references to celestial phenomena and deities, sources such as *Tonalamtl Aubin* demanded from their intended audience complete command of both theological subtleties and astronomy.[16]

Complicating the picture of different documents for different audiences, there stood the additional problem of the nature of the logograms* and ideograms† used by Amerindians to record their annals. According to León y Gama, logograms and ideograms often alluded to local objects accessible only to a privileged few. An extensive knowledge of local natural history, León y Gama argued, was needed to understand the logograms of town names. The names of towns in such documents as the *Codex Cozcatzin* and the *Codex histoire mexicaine* could not be read without having first gained vast knowledge of the natural history of central Mexico. The names of Cimatlan, Tulan, Papatztaca, and Huexotzinca in these codices are denoted by logograms with the images of local shrubs, trees, and flowers. According to León y Gama, some logograms were simply too idiosyncratic and undecipherable, as in the case of references in the *Codez Cozcatzin* to the town of "Teyahualco," whose rebus image León y Gama challenged anyone to explain. Even more upsetting for those who sought a shortcut to the interpretation of Amerindian documents, was the fact that some towns with similar Nahuatl names were identified with the same logograms in different documents. This, León y Gama argued, was the case of "Atempa" in the *Codex Cozcatzin* and "Atenco" in *Matrícula de Tributos.*

If to read the name of towns in Aztec sources required at times knowledge beyond the reach of common mortals, the reading of the name of rulers was even more difficult. According to León y Gama, the signs used to refer to rulers did not merely allude to the sound of their names, but also to some aspects of their moral character. The fact that the logogram of the ruler Quauhcaltzin in *Codex en Cruz* was a caged eagle. León y Gama argued, was of little use for those who knew that the logograms of the last Mexica monarch Quauhtemotsin, the Acolhua lord Quauhtletcohuatzin, and the lord of Coyuacan Quauhpocatzin were also represented as eagles in other sources. The eagles representing these rulers, however, showed subtle differences; their beaks appeared either shut, open, or giving off smoke, and their eyes were gazing up or down. According to León y Gama, such subtle distinctions were allusions

---

*A logogram is a symbol or letter representing an entire word (e.g., $ for dollar).
†An ideogram is a symbol or character representing an idea or thing.

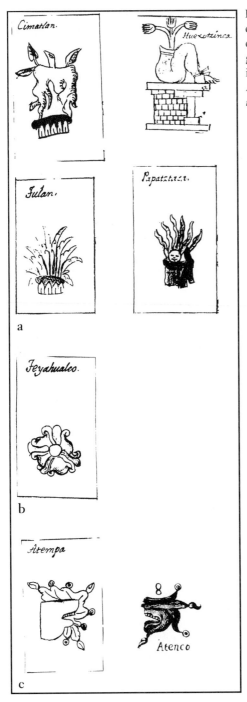

Pictograms for Mesoamerican towns in indigenous sources used by León y Gama to demonstrate the difficulty of establishing general rules for the reading of Mesoamerican scripts. Codex Cozcatzin and Codex Azcatitlan. *Courtesy of the Bibliothèque Nationale, Paris.*

to some aspect of the moral character of these rulers that had been understood only by a handful of retainers. The logic behind these correlations, therefore, was now beyond the understanding of any mortal, including any late-colonial native elites.[17]

León y Gama's reading of Mesoamerican codices was subtle and sophisticated. Notwithstanding his faith in the curative power of lizards, León y Gama's insistence that there were different types of indigenous sources and that each required a vast amount of contextual information of linguistics and local natural history to be read, was unique for his age. León y Gama brought to bear learned humanist and antiquarian sensibilities to the reading and interpretation of sources in non-alphabetical scripts. His approach contrasts dramatically with the heavy-handed techniques of contemporary Western European conjectural historians. Radically different historiographical techniques seemed to have developed in each of the three areas of the Atlantic world discussed in this chapter, each paradoxically "modern" in its own way. Although Spanish America and Spain itself are traditionally considered peripheries to an eighteenth-century North Atlantic core, the scholarship produced by authors like Juan Bautista Muñoz and Antonio León y Gama are proof that the skepticism of the Enlightenment took on different meanings in different settings. Most studies of the Enlightenment, however, have failed to realize that the ideas produced by a handful of great French, British, and German writers were not simply "transmitted" to the rest of the world, where they allegedly were either vigorously consumed or forcefully rejected. We have seen in the preceding pages that the same intellectual tools were used in different ways in Europe north of the Pyrenees, Spain, and Spanish America. If in the skeptical "age of reason," non-Iberian authors created new and sophisticated forms of reading and invented the genre of conjectural history, Spanish writers anticipated the great insights of nineteenth-century German scholarship as they went about creating archives and histories based solely on primary sources. Scholars in Mexico took yet another route; they articulated a formidable critique of the limitations of knowledge that European skeptics were bound to face in the Americas. Oddly enough, it was colonial scholars like León y Gama who put together the most sophisticated historical monographs on the Americas created in the Enlightenment. When it came to affairs of the mind, there were no colonial peripheries and metropolitan cores in the "age of reason."[18]

➡ FOCUS QUESTIONS

1. When French, Dutch, and English historians wrote about the Americas in the seventeenth and eighteenth centuries, they tended to dismiss Spanish and indigenous American sources. Why?

2. What leads Cañizares to conclude that, in the writing and understanding of the history of the Americas, "there was as much intellectual creativity in the colonial peripheries as in the metropolitan core"?

The Purpose of Pirates, or Assimilating New Worlds in the Renaissance

Benjamin Schmidt

FIRE IN AMERICA

For so many of its unfortunate inhabitants, America, during a painfully long stretch of the sixteenth and seventeenth centuries, had become an excruciating place to be. America was unpleasant—indeed, blisteringly and searingly so, since fire would seem to have been the torment of choice for those intruders who made it their business to tyrannize the New World. "The way they normally dealt with the native leaders and nobles," writes one indignant observer, "was to tie them to a kind of griddle, consisting of sticks resting on pitchforks driven into the ground, and then grill them over a slow fire, with the result that they howled in agony and despair as they died a lingering death." In another instance, as related by another observer—who, like the first, emphasized his status as an eyewitness to those grisly events that he so carefully narrated—the reader learns that local leaders "were tied to wooden spits placed between two fires and then roasted alive, as one roasts a pig." All of this was done solely, adds the author (with a fine sense of Herodotean wit), to induce the inhabitants to reveal the whereabouts of more pigpens for plunder. Fire, in fact, broke out all over the New World during these years, and usually for purposes that can aptly be called diabolic. "Others were crucified by these tyrants," writes our second source, "and, with kindled matches, were burned between the joints of their fingers and toes. Others had their feet put to the fire, and thus were left to be roasted alive." In a strikingly similar passage, the first-cited author describes the manner in which natives of the West Indies would sometimes be tied up, in a sitting position, with fires lit under their outstretched feet. This torture was applied to one unfortunate soul "until all of the marrow ran out through the soles of his feet and he died." Only in America, as they say.[1]

Or rather, only in the America of the Dutch imagination, since both of these accounts derive from the fiery presses of the Netherlands, where the New World featured prominently and forcefully throughout the Dutch Golden Age (ca. 1570–1670). This essay enlists texts such as these to explore a central chapter in early modern cultural geography: how observers of the sixteenth and seventeenth centuries imagined a part of the world that they had never seen—and, in most cases, hardly intended to visit. The newly identified continents of America had two distinct functions for early modern Europeans. In the wake of the epochal voyages of the

Renaissance, Europeans came into contact, on the one hand, with an immense and hitherto unexplored hemisphere in the West—the Americas, North and South—which became the focus of intense colonization efforts by the imperial powers of the day. On the other hand, Europeans contended with an immense and influential body of literature *describing* America—travel accounts, illustrated histories, tropical geographies, epic poetry, decorative maps, and so forth—which conveyed, in an immediate and often striking form, the meaning and message of the so-called New World. While not among the primary colonizers of the Americas, the Dutch did play a critical role in the production of Americana (books, maps, and other, especially published, matter on America), and this afforded them a leading role in the articulation of what the New World's discovery, conquest, and settlement would come to stand for. They did so, above all, through texts, not unlike the two sources quoted above.

There are three simple points that can be made about these remarkable—and remarkably similar—passages, about the original texts from which they derive, and about their relevance to the early modern conception of the New World. First and most basically, it should be emphasized that both of these sources are *Dutch,* with the muted qualifier that the first-cited, and perhaps the second as well, were not actually composed by born-and-bred Netherlanders. They count as Dutch texts, however, in the crucial sense that both were edited, printed, and promoted in the Netherlands, in conjunction with the massive production of other Dutch Americana. They share with each other and with numerous likewise-produced texts, a pronouncedly Netherlandish vision of the New World: an image of cruel destruction and savage violence—"tyranny," as it was so often termed—perpetrated upon innocent natives of America. That is to say, both texts echo a distinctly Dutch discourse of America. The first derives from Bartolomé de Las Casas' *Brevíssima relación de la destruyción de las Indias* (Short account of the destruction of the Indies), which, though quietly printed in Seville in 1552, gained great prominence only after its publication in Antwerp in 1578. It was this Dutch-language edition, quickly followed by another, this time French-language edition, in 1579 that set off an avalanche of Lascasian texts published over the next half century, primarily in the Low Countries. In time, the *Brevíssima relación* became the single most printed work on America to circulate in early modern Europe—and a bestseller, more generally, among early modern readers. The second text, published precisely one century after the first, appeared originally in Dutch. Alexander Olivier Exquemelin's racy tale of Atlantic piracy, *De Americaensche zee-rovers* (The buccaneers of America), rolled off the presses of Amsterdam in 1678. It enjoyed astonishing popularity thereafter, translated into all of the major European languages—English, French, German, and Spanish—and printed in dozens of editions over the coming century. Though the author's biography remains imprecise—some historians place his birth in Huguenot northern France, while others have made the case for Holland—the language and form of the book are indisputably Dutch.[2]

That both works enjoyed such outstanding popularity, particularly (if not exclusively) in the Netherlands, is but one of many similarities, though the second point to be made has to do with their differences—in this case, of genre, subject, and date. To begin with the last and most straightforward of these: the two accounts debuted in 1578 and 1678, respectively, neatly symmetrical years that also happen to bookend the Dutch Republic's Golden Age. They deal, however, with subjects not normally juxtaposed: the Spanish conquest of America (or *conquista*) in the case of Las Casas, and Anglo-French piracy in the case of Exquemelin. In many ways these subjects are, generically speaking, utterly dissimilar. The one deals with military conquest and colonial expansion, and it fits most naturally under the rubric of imperial history (albeit with overtones of tragedy). The other relates tales of picaresque adventure and, though more awkwardly categorized, comes closest in genre to the travel (or naval) narrative. (The *Buccaneers of America* was among the pioneering forms of pirate literature, the father of a very impressive lineage of works of fiction and nonfiction, among them Daniel Defoe's enormously successful *History of the pyrates* of 1724.) The accounts, however, share a good deal as well: both detail the exotic geography of the Atlantic World, both enumerate the inestimable riches of the Atlantic World, and both underscore the unimaginable cruelty of the Atlantic World. Also, the respective vignettes of violence so resemble one another that, although relating wholly distinct stories of America, the two narratives end up sounding singularly alike. Thus, the shared fetish for fire.

This leads to a final point that relates to the purpose of these texts and their role, more broadly, within the political history of the Netherlands. The years of the two first-editions mark the dramatic rise and equally precipitous fall of the Dutch Republic from the stage of European history—the earlier date coinciding with the Dutch uprising against Habsburg Spain, the latter registering a calamitous war waged against England and France, and the consequent onset of the Republic's economic, political, and cultural decline at the twilight of the Golden Age. The two texts likewise indicate the beginning and end of a vigorous process of cultural geography, by which the new, and newly embattled, United Provinces (as the Dutch Republic was officially known) formulated and promoted an appropriately Dutch vision of the world. Literature was the medium for this exercise of geographic construction, or "fashioning": a sustained pattern of representation, by which certain circles in the Republic actively and strategically shaped the globe, forging a particular vision of America and of their own nation's relation to affairs abroad. Describing other parts of the world—geography, broadly understood—served the Dutch as a means of self-definition. Attention, above all, to the New World, that most malleable of continents, fit Dutch designs perfectly, since America's discovery (by Europe, at least) had taken place during a period that overlapped with the Dutch revolt against Spain and emergence of the Republic, and thus lent itself conveniently to this process. American conquistadors and buccaneers looked largely alike because the Dutch chose to see them so.

The imaginative maneuver of the Dutch vis-à-vis America offers a prime example of how geography could work in early modern Europe, and how representations of the expanding globe came to reflect debates closer to home. Concern with place veered subtly toward politics and polemic, and description turned easily into self-definition—notably in Dutch works on the New World produced in the late sixteenth and seventeenth centuries. This was done primarily in print—textual, visual, cartographic—and this essay will examine specific samples of American literature as a way of illustrating broader patterns of cultural production. The focus will be America's place within the Dutch Republic, yet the arguments extend, more generally, to the operation of geographic fashioning in Renaissance Europe. To be sure, the exercise of describing other lands—and doing so creatively, even in ways that push a specific agenda—is hardly new to the Netherlands or to the Renaissance. What makes the early modern Dutch case so exceptional, however, is the way it matches the politically novel situation of Republic, which came into political being during this period, with the geographic novelty of America, which came under European purview over approximately the same era. Extraordinary times called for extraordinary measures, as it were; and events in the early modern Netherlands encouraged a remarkable expansion, by the upstart Republic, of both its political and geographic horizons.

DUTCH REVOLTS

America arrived in the Netherlands at a most opportune moment: coincident with the Dutch Revolt, which commenced in the final third of the sixteenth century. News of the New World had circulated in Northern Europe, of course, from the moment of Columbus' first reports in 1493. What had changed in the Netherlands was the quantity of news and, more critically, the quality of reports, which were now more strenuously shaped by Dutch authors and editors with a specific audience in mind. If accounts of America's "discovery," of the Spanish conquest, and of the New World natives were commonly printed in Antwerp from the beginning of the sixteenth century, the tenor of these descriptions and the images they projected of rapacious Spanish "tyranny" took off in the 1560s and 1570s, by which time Antwerp itself was sacked by Spanish troops (in 1576). The revolt of the Dutch against their Habsburg overlords instigated a shift in the representation of the Habsburg adventure overseas; the image of Spanish troops, whether in America or Antwerp, had darkened. Indeed, the explosive account of Las Casas arrived at a distinctly acute moment in the history of the Revolt, its publication culminating a ferocious war of words against the Spanish regime in the Netherlands.

Some basic background: The Dutch struggle against Spain broke out in 1566, when a collection of lesser nobles confronted the Habsburg regent, Margaret of Parma, about the conduct of the Spanish Inquisition in the Low Countries. From this relatively minor, in many ways parochial, and essentially political dispute—one of the regent's councilors dismissed the motley band of nobles as "beggars" for their presumptuous approach of the regent on such a matter—developed a far deeper crisis over the conduct of government and the reformation of religion in the Low Countries. Concern over the conduct of the Inquisition, in this way, sparked a broader conflict over the power of centralizing authorities and the form of religious practice and tolerance in the Netherlands. The flare-up soon enough became a firestorm when, later that year, religious iconoclasm broke out, fueled by a minority of the Calvinist faithful with grievances against the Catholic regime. The chaos that ensued—condemned, in fact, by Dutch nobleman and Spanish governor alike—induced the king, Philip II, to send his veteran commander, the duke of Alba, to stamp out the flames of heresy and revolt. The high-handed policies of Alba made a bad situation worse. His notorious tribunal, nicknamed the Blood Council, injudiciously targeted the merchant and noble classes, while his hefty Tenth Penny (a levy paid on transactions of goods) recklessly taxed the lower orders at a moment of widespread economic depression (there had been a series of droughts in the preceding years). Religious and governmental grievances thus transformed into widespread social and economic protest and, by the end of the decade, full-fledged political revolt.[3]

Revolts do not necessarily spell revolutions, let alone wholesale changes of regime, and the Dutch uprising began relatively modestly. Alba's unwise and largely unpopular government notwithstanding, scholars now understand that the majority of the population of the Low Countries remained, well into the 1570s, faithful to the traditional authorities. This is a crucial historiographic point and one that sometimes gets lost, especially on American audiences bred on the heroic accounts of John Lothrop Motley and his nineteenth-century New England compatriots, who tended to place the rise of the Dutch Republic within the context of the rise of that other mercantile, democratic, and Calvinist republic to the west—the United States (which happened to have had excellent relations with the Netherlands in the 1770s and 1780s).[4] These American historians, for their part, took their cue from the Dutch rebels themselves, who cannily exploited the printing presses to present what was essentially a civil war—half of the nation, at least, favored the old regime—as a pious and patriotic resistance to a tyrannical overlord.

Propaganda, that is to say, played a critical part in this pioneering, and in many ways modern, political movement. Above all, the rebels sought to diminish and blacken the reputation of the Spanish government, and they did a masterful job of conjuring an oppressive, colonial government from the Habsburg regime in Brussels and the royal court in Madrid. To establish the fact of Spanish misrule and tyranny, the patriotic party further lit upon the idea of citing America—sixteenth-century colonial America—which became for them the prime model of enemy perfidy. Why America? First, because reports of American brutalities, lately committed by the conquistadors, had been trickling back to Europe; second, because the very distance and plasticity of the New World allowed for still-greater literary leverage and imaginative embellishment; and third, because the hard-pressed rebels, desperate by this time to gain some sort of support, chose to project their enemy's enemy—the oppressed natives of America—as their friend. The specter of Spanish cruelties in the Andes and Mexico was raised, accordingly, to rally Dutch troops in Antwerp and Malines. A sympathetic image of the innocent Indian was propagated, in this manner, as part of a broader campaign against the universal monarchy of Habsburg Spain.

Bartolomé de Las Casas' *relación* fit this strategy perfectly. While the Dutch nobles could complain that "the Spanish seek nothing but to abuse our Fatherland as they have done in the New Indies," they could do so, in the 1560s at least, with relatively little detail.[5] The much-cited "example of the Indies" remained just that in the early years of Dutch propaganda: a sensational, if still somewhat vague, reference to the notorious conduct of Spain in Central and South America. In Las Casas' account, however, the rebels discovered an exhaustive and surprisingly lurid catalogue of tyrannies—recorded by a Castilian cleric, no less[6]—that was certain to enliven their prose—and it did. From the late 1570s, pamphleteers and printmakers began to vilify the enemy in the blackest of terms, citing the goriest of details, fingering the most ignominious of perpetrators, and enumerating the most staggering fatality figures from Spain's misdeeds abroad. Topoi of Spanish tyranny in America—textual and graphic themes that recurred with almost rhythmic regularity—emerged, proliferated, and ultimately became codified in Dutch rhetoric of these years. This is perhaps most notable in the widely circulated and politically prominent *Apologie* (1581) of the rebels' leader, William the Silent, and in the *Plakkaat van Verlatinge* that was drawn up by the States General (their official "declaration of independence"). Both were signal documents of the Revolt, and both made conspicuous use of American imagery by way of strengthening their brief against the Habsburg authorities. Graphic images played a part, too, in the fiercely anti-Habsburg campaign carried out in prints, maps, and other visual media.

It would be difficult to overemphasize the profound impact and sensational effect of Las Casas in the Netherlands. It was not just the staggering volume of printed editions of the *Brevíssima relación*—nearly one Dutch-language edition churned out every other year for the next half century (twenty-three from 1578–1638), and still more if one counts the multiple French and Latin editions that would have appealed to the multilingual population of the Low Countries. Nor was it the remarkable diversity of form of these texts—some literal translations from the Spanish, others poetic renditions composed in lively doggerel, and still others in the almost emblematic form of abbreviated text paired with woodblock image. (There was even a Las Casas-derived map of America, with the Spaniard's eye-witness descriptions matched with a Caribbean geography.) Rather, it was the way Lascasian rhetoric and imagery became so finely interwoven into the fabric of Dutch discourse, political and historical no less than polemical and geographical. The prose of Las Casas inspired the polemicists of the Netherlands, who lifted language and motif from the *Brevíssima relación* in order to color their accounts of the revolt. Descriptions of events in the New World and events in the Netherlands thus merged into a single, seamless narrative decrying the global tyrannies of Spain. The patriotic version of the Revolt, like the Lascasian version of the *Conquista,* told a startling tale of Habsburg colonial violence perpetrated against innocent and oppressed natives—of the Netherlands and the Americas alike.

Thousands of words could be cited to underscore the mutual borrowing and energetic intertextuality traded between Dutch histories of the Revolt and Dutch descriptions of America. In this case, however, the proverbially worthy picture (or two) makes the point perhaps more effectively, and certainly more graphically. The first illustrated Dutch-language edition of Las Casas appeared in Amsterdam in 1609 (a crucial year, not coincidentally, in Dutch-Spanish truce negotiations, when anti-Habsburg polemicists in the Netherlands were beating the drums of war especially loudly). This slim and inexpensively produced volume had a remarkably simple format, designed to bring the message of Las Casas to the broadest possible audience. Each page included an engraved scene (the number of these varies among specific editions) coupled with a brief and vaguely rhyming caption, which were meant to narrate, in both word and pungent image, the history of Spain's engagement in America. The illustrations themselves contain, to the modern eye at least, shocking material. The one meant to depict the "Roasting of the Nobles"—the engraving that correlates, more or less, to the passage cited at the opening of this essay—is fairly typical for the volume. A writhing body is shown strapped to a wooden grill over which stands an armored Spanish *halberdier* supervising two assistants, one of whom feeds, and the other of whom stokes, the flames rising beneath the victim. In the background, one can witness a second, equally appalling vignette of violence, as another helmeted and mustachioed—that is, plainly Spanish—figure brutally hatchets the hands off Indian men and women, who are shown walking away with crudely amputated and still bleeding limbs. Another engraving contains, among other cruelties, the image of a soldier dashing an Indian baby into a boulder (meant to illustrate the pathological sadism of the Habsburg troops); and yet another depicts a native child, sliced into halves, being fed by a Spaniard to his dog, a scene meant to dramatize the treatment by the Catholic invaders of unbaptized Indian children.

Collectively, these images are almost unbearable to look at. They are also almost certainly the product of creative reconstruction, since the Dutch artist who drafted them had probably not been to America and had no direct contact with the long-deceased author of the text, Bartolomé de Las Casas. They bear little resemblance, moreover, to the mostly Caribbean and Mexican settings which they purport to reproduce. The backdrops are done indiscriminately, and the generic looking "Spaniards" of the foreground torment somewhat bland-looking figures that are meant to stand for American Indians (the latter are generally featureless and minimally clothed by European standards). Yet the engravings are carefully and purposefully designed all the same. Rather than a faithful rendition of the New World, they offer the Dutch engraver's and publisher's imaginative projection of America and the settings of these events—and, for that matter, the Dutch engraver's imaginative reconstruction of the tyrannies themselves, which derive only loosely from the *Brevíssima relación*. This is not to say that the images are somehow incorrect. They are "true," though mostly to the distinctly Dutch sense of what took place in America—which was imagined to somehow mirror events taking place back in the Republic.

This explains the striking resemblance that the American scenes bear to altogether different sets of images representing Habsburg military action in the Netherlands. Compare, in this regard, the Lascasian "Pit of Horrors" of the 1609 volume to an engraving produced for Johannes Gijsius's popular *Oorsprong en voortgang der Neder-landtscher beroerten ende ellendicheden* (Origin and expansion of the Dutch troubles and miseries), an early history of the Revolt that appeared in 1616.[7] The pile of naked, skewered bodies in the Dutch history book is meant to represent the 1576 "Spanish Fury," a signal event from early in the war when Habsburg troops went on a rampage in the city of Antwerp. As in the Las Casas engraving, which illustrates the Spanish treatment of the natives of Guatemala, the Antwerp scene features innocent women and children strewn in a heap, the flailing victims of both engravings throwing their arms to the heavens in their feeble defense against Spanish swords. The grisly abomination against women and children displayed in both the Las Casas-derived "Tyrannies against Mother and Babe" (in this case, set in Yucatán) and the Dutch historical print, "Murder in Oudewater" (again, from the history of Gijsius) once more share motifs: the horrific mutilation of children (and their identically denuded mothers), the casual mayhem in the background, and even the architecture of the scenes, both of which are set in open buildings that fill the left half of the respective prints.

These prints and others like them convey a matching tale of tyrannies committed by a single Spanish enemy. The victims are the dually suffering inhabitants of the Low Countries and America, and the message is of a unity of historical experience— and, by implication, of purpose and future strategic interest. Dutch publishers were

"Pit of Horrors" from Bartolomé de Las Casas, *Den Spiegel der Spaensche tyrannye gheschiet in West Indien* (Amsterdam, 1620). *Courtesy of Universiteitsbibliotheek Amsterdam.*

joining the narratives of America and the Netherlands as a way of adopting, through the mechanism of geography, an ally in the war against Spain. If the point had not been made clearly enough, there appeared in 1620 a single publication that combined both histories under the broad banner *Den Spiegel der Spaensche tyrannye,* or The Mirror of Spanish Tyrannies. The first half of the volume "reflected" (as the title metaphorically suggested) the tyrannies of the West Indies, while the second featured those of the Low Countries. In truth, though, the two were by now utterly self-reflective, visually no less than rhetorically. Both narratives conveyed a single message of Habsburg perfidy. Both conveyed sympathy for the abused natives, and both offered the Dutch reader the hope that, with their American cousins-in-suffering, they would soon slay the dragon of Habsburg universal monarchy.

THE PURPOSE OF PIRATES

The *Spiegel der Spaensche tyranny* was the latest, and in many ways most emphatic, representation of Spanish cruelty to roll off the presses, and it marked something of a turning point, both in the history of Dutch representations of America and in the

"Antwerpen" from J. Gijsius, *Spaensche tirannye in Nederlandt* (1620). *Courtesy of Universiteitsbibliotheek Amsterdam.*

history of the Dutch Republic. The dazzling *Mirror of Spanish Tyrannies* published in Amsterdam saturated the market around 1620, an astonishing eight editions appearing in the space of three years—a veritable literary explosion in the context of early modern publishing. These were the very years during which the war with Spain had resumed after the Twelve Year Truce (1609–1621), and one imagines that the publication of Las Casas—with vivid illustrations in 1609, at the start of the Truce, and in multiple "patriotic" editions in 1621, at the close of the Truce—was meant by the Dutch war party to drum up Hispanophobic fervor. That the warmongers expended such extraordinary efforts in this regard suggests, however, that support for an already half-century old military struggle had declined. This, in fact, was the case, and, after the initial flood of publications and propaganda, the traditional flow of anti-Spanish rhetoric began to subside.

Dutch representations of America also shifted in these years (the middle decades of the seventeenth century), though for reasons that had less to do with domestic politics than with international affairs. With the resumption of military activities in 1621, the Republic also commenced colonial activities in the West—colonization happened to be one of the most contentious issues of truce negotiations—with the foundation of the Dutch West India Company (WIC). A brief three

"Moort tot Oudewater" from J. Gijsius, *Spaensche tirannye in Nederlandt* (1620). *Courtesy of Universiteitsbibliotheek Amsterdam.*

years later, Amsterdam merchants successfully established a settlement at the tip of Manhattan christened New Netherland, and, by 1630, Dutch forces gained a toehold in Brazil that would expand into the colony known as New Holland. The image of the New World also underwent rapid and radical change in these years. As the war against Spain transformed from a desperate, national struggle for survival to a protracted, and in many ways peripheral, foreign policy issue, the need to carry out a front-line propaganda campaign diminished. The theme of Spanish tyranny receded from the public's purview, and so too did the propagandistic images of these tyrannies. Moreover, the idea of a Dutch alliance with their enemy's enemy—the notion that the Dutch might join as brothers-in-arms with the natives of America, since they both opposed Spanish colonial rule—was now put to the test, as the Dutch began to arrive on the shores of the New World and to establish bona fide contacts with the American Indians. Needless to say, this was a test that they largely failed. Not unlike the Spanish, French, or English, the Dutch fought their own wars against the Indians; and they also engaged in their share of abuses of native rights and lands. In fact, the failures garnered sufficient attention by the middle of the century that critics of Dutch colonial policy seized upon the motifs of tyranny and innocence in America, only to invert these images to sabotage the initiatives of a lately beleaguered WIC. It

Engraving "Mother and Child" from Bartolomé de Las Casas, *Den Spiegel der Spaensche tyrannye gheschiet in West Indien* (Amsterdam, 1620). *Courtesy of Universiteitsbibliotheek Amsterdam.*

was now the Dutch West India Company, in the eyes of its critics, that tyrannized in America by restricting free trade, persecuting colonial challengers, and, most damning, by savaging their neighboring Indians.

The fascinating transmutation of Dutch colonial rhetoric in this period is a subject that lies beyond the scope of this essay. All the same, it is worth drawing attention to the stubborn staying power of the twin topoi of tyranny and innocence, which remained prominently associated in Dutch minds with America. Indeed, both motifs resurface in the second half of the century, though this time in connection with an altogether different literary form, namely the new genre of pirate literature. Again, a brief bit of historical background: The Peace of Westphalia ended the Eighty Years War in 1648 and ushered in a period of relative stability for the Republic vis-à-vis Spain. In the meantime, though, Dutch relations with England soured, and three bitter Anglo-Dutch conflicts occupied the Republic's attention from 1652–1678. The final of these conflicts (1672–1678) involved the French as well, as the Sun King, Louis XIV, joined forces with his Stuart counterpart, Charles II, to quash the upstart Republic. The Netherlands, once again, faced a patriotic struggle— at sea against the English, on land against the French, and in the printing presses against both. Transformations taking place in the New World also altered the political and polemical landscape. By the early 1650s, the Dutch colony in Brazil had

Frontispiece from *Den Spiegel der Spaensche tyranny geschiet in West-Indien* (Amsterdam, 1620). *Courtesy of Universiteitsbibliotheek Amsterdam.*

fallen to the Portuguese, who, in the topsy-turvy world of Baroque diplomacy, had themselves broken off from Spain (in 1640), though, in matters strategic, they harbored little sympathy for their enemy's former enemy, the Dutch. New Netherland, too, had switched hands. Following years of British encroachments from both New

England in the north and Virginia in the south, it succumbed in 1664 to the fleets of the duke of York and was baptized anew, New York.[8]

Under these revised circumstances, what became of the image of the New World? The 1678 publication of Alexander Exquemelin's *De Americaensche zee-rovers* (The buccaneers of America) announced the dramatic reappearance of America in the Netherlands—and, for that matter, the literary debut of the so-called buccaneer.[9] There had existed, of course, prior descriptions of pirates and their close cousins, privateers, in various early modern media. The pirate had an important role to play on the late Elizabethan and early Jacobean stage (this in the wake of Drake and Ralegh's exploits); and a similar literary character made frequent appearances in English and Spanish "romances"—fictional narratives considered to be precursors of the modern novel.[10] A mid-seventeenth-century prose account of *The Beginning, Middle, and End of Piracy* (*'t Begin, midden en eynde der see-roveryen;* 1659) that enjoyed enormous popularity in the Netherlands offered a thrilling tour of the high seas and the rogues who inhabited them. The publisher's bold pronouncement notwithstanding, however, piracy did not quite end at this point. The middle decades of the seventeenth century may have denoted, if anything, the climax of Caribbean piracy, and Exquemelin's splashy account—recording the activities of mostly English and French privateers and introducing the catchy neologism "buccaneer"—almost certainly marked the crest of the genre in the Netherlands and beyond. "Perhaps no book in any language was ever the parent of so many imitations and the source of so many fictions," wrote the esteemed, nineteenth-century bibliographer, Joseph Sabin.[11] Robinson Crusoe, as it turned out, was but a few years away.

Exquemelin's account looked *back,* however, and in a very self-conscious way, to an earlier narrative style and to an existing literary type, namely the Spanish *conquistador,* as articulated by the Dutch-produced Las Casas. The 1678 reader of Americana, like that of 1578, found him- or herself in a New World of appalling violence. The *Americaensche zee-rovers,* that is, narrates a chilling tale of harsh and cruel adventure, the volume's unruly protagonists slashing, harassing, and burning their way to blood-curdling infamy. The English and French pirates whom Exquemelin describes, much like the *conquistadors* chronicled earlier by Las Casas, make their living through violence. The American landscape, as depicted by Exquemelin, is characterized by the same "inhuman cruelties," the same "ingenious torments," and the same "unprecedented tyrannies" that Las Casas, too, could only inadequately describe. His landscape is similarly strewn with mutilated body parts—noses and ears, tongues and testicles—left behind by similarly "bloodthirsty devils" who persecute their victims, in both cases, just for sport. In the later account, as in the earlier, marauding thugs alight from their vessels to burn, flay, rape, slash, gouge, garrote, and most basically hunt down the natives like—and, according to both accounts, with—dogs. It is a wonderful irony that the "natives," in the case of Exquemelin, are most often the Spanish creole descendants of Las Casas' *conquistadors,* the sixteenth-century hunters having become the seventeenth-century hunted.

Early modern Europe, it should be recognized, was itself a fairly bloody terrain. In an age of eighty- and thirty-year wars, of reckless religious iconoclasm and political revolt, of habitual urban riots and plunderings of the countryside, one might be tempted to say that thuggishness and violence were the norm, and that the uncanny

Frontispiece from Alexander Olivier Exquemelin, *De Americaensche zee-roovers* (Amsterdam, 1678). *Courtesy of Universiteitsbibliotheek Amsterdam.*

correspondence of cruelties in these two accounts is merely coincidental. Yet the Dutch publishers of Exquemelin would seem determined to dismiss such doubt by presenting the buccaneer narrative in terms so remarkably Lascasian—so remarkably akin to the form and style in which Las Casas had earlier been presented in the

Netherlands—that the juxtaposition of the texts would have been obvious. Language and motifs, characters and events, episodes and outcomes all seem deliberately interchangeable.

While many literary passages and rhetorical devices could be cited to make this point, a picture, once again, will save a thousand words. The engraved frontispieces of Exquemelin's and Las Casas' texts, commissioned expressly by Dutch printers for these volumes, were designed to distill for the reader their volumes' themes. In this case, the two prints also bear a remarkable similarity in theme and format, both depicting what the respective titles designate, identically, as the "inhuman cruelties" (*onmenselijke wreedheiden*) committed in America. The Las Casas print originates from a much-copied edition published in Amsterdam in 1620 by Jan Evertsz Cloppenburg who, as head of the printing press, played a critical role in the volume's ultimate look. The duke of Alba posing on the right and Don Juan of Austria (who was Philip II's half-brother, sent to command the Spanish troops in the Netherlands in the late 1570s) occupying the left, stand amidst evidence of their combined barbarities, the first surrounded by scenes of the Revolt, the second by images of the *Conquista*. In the *Zee-roovers* print (produced for the printer and bookseller Jan ten Hoorn), the niche-portraits represent an English and a French buccaneer—so the title itself implies—encompassed by vignettes of American tyrannies. Each of the pirates tramples a victim. The figure on the right threatens a feather-clad Indian ("innocenter"), who supplicates with a fist full of pearls; while the left-hand figure taunts a Spaniard, who begs for his life. Judging from the surrounding depictions of destruction and mayhem, neither probably received mercy; for the New World resembles, in a most visible way, a landscape of tyranny. Both prints show the reckless violence of the New World; both show the pervasiveness of torture and torment abroad; and both show the eruption of fire throughout the land. Both images describe a landscape of unremitting and therefore morally significant cruelty, which has come to identify, in both frontispieces and in corresponding texts, the meaning of America.

Or so it appeared from the Netherlands. At the twilight of their Golden Age, as at its dawn, the Dutch imagined the New World as a locus of tyranny, since it suited their purposes to do so. In the late sixteenth and early seventeenth centuries, the America articulated by the new Republic provided an effective means to vilify Spain. Las Casas represented but one of the numerous, polemical texts used by the rebels to project a geography of opposition in the distant New World, where the natives' suffering served as a dire warning to the Netherlands. A full century later, America still retained its reputation for violence and cruelty, though this time it featured the latest nemeses of the Republic, England and France, as perpetrators of tyrannies abroad. The purpose of pirates in 1678 resembled the purpose of *conquistadors* in 1578: to discredit the opponents of the Republic, in the one case the regime of Philip II, and in the other the invading troops of Louis XIV and Charles II. More generally, the purpose of cultural geography in the nascent Dutch Republic was to seek support abroad for evolving agendas at home. Dutch representations of the New World mirrored political concerns in the Old, and, owing perhaps to the unique circumstance of the Republic, mirrored them in exceptionally vivid ways. The process of geographic fashioning in the early modern Netherlands, and particularly the appropriation of the

New World, attests to the exceptional agility and outstanding ingenuity of the Republic's promoters. It also demonstrates, finally, the remarkable plasticity and convenient malleability of America during the age of discovery.

➥ FOCUS QUESTIONS

1. Why did Netherlanders find it so politically useful to expose the sins of the Spanish occupation of the Americas?
2. Discuss this paradox: How was it that Las Casas, whose aim was to ameliorate Spain's treatment of indigenous Americans, became instead the father of the Black Legend of Spain in America, whose net effect was to give moral support to the interventions of other European colonialists, and hence even more exploitation and abuse of the American Indian?
3. Schmidt's essay is about "assimilating new worlds in the Renaissance." How did Europeans who had never been to America imagine it? What lesson does that teach us about how we imagine the unknown, the unfamiliar, in our own era?

NOTES

Introduction: The Rise and Transformation of the Atlantic World by Wim Klooster

1. J.H. Parry, *The Age of Reconnaissance: Discovery, Exploration and Settlement, 1450 to 1650* (Berkeley: University of California Press, 1981), 5.
2. Felipe Fernández-Armesto, *Before Columbus: Exploration and Colonization from the Mediterranean to the Atlantic, 1229–1492* (Philadelphia: University of Pennsylvania Press, 1987), 152.
3. Jacques Bernard, "Trade and Finance in the Middle Ages, 900–1500," in *The Fontana Economic History of Europe: The Middle Ages*, ed. (n.p.: Collins/Fontana Carlo M. Cipolla Books, 1972), 274–338: 285. Luís Adão da Fonseca, "The Discovery of Atlantic Space," in *Portugal, The Pathfinder: Journeys from the Medieval toward the Modern World 1300–ca.1600*, George D. Winius, ed. (Madison: The Hispanic Seminary of Medieval Studies, 1995), 5–18: 9–10.
4. Carlo Cipolla, *Guns, Sails, and Empires: Technological Innovation and the Early Phases of European Expansion 1400–1700* (1965; New York: Barnes & Noble Books, 1996), 76–78. Richard W. Unger, "Portuguese Shipbuilding and the Early Voyages to the Guinea Coast," in *The European Opportunity.* An Expanding World: The European Impact on World History 1450–1800, Felipe Fernández-Armesto, ed. Volume 2 (Aldershot: Variorum, 1995), 43–63: 46–47, 53.
5. Pablo E. Pérez-Mallaína, *Spain's Men of the Sea: Daily Life on the Indies Fleets in the Sixteenth Century*, trans. Carla Rahn Phillips (Baltimore and London: The Johns Hopkins University Press, 1998), 129–135.
6. Dr. Samuel Johnson, quoted in Marcus Rediker, *Between the Devil and the Deep Blue Sea: Merchant Seamen, Pirates, and the Anglo-American Maritime World, 1700–1750* (Cambridge: Cambridge University Press, 1987), 258.
7. Ivana Elbl, "The Overseas Expansion, Nobility, and Social Mobility in the Age of Vasco da Gama," *Portuguese Studies Review* 6:2 (Fall/Winter 1997–98), 53–80: 54–56. David Birmingham, *Trade and Empire in the Atlantic, 1400–1600* (London: Routledge, 2000), 28–29.
8. George D. Winius, "The Work of João II," in *Portugal, The Pathfinder: Journeys from the Medieval toward the Modern World 1300–ca.1600*, George D. Winius ed. (Madison: The Hispanic Seminary of Medieval Studies, 1995), 89–120, ibidem, 91–92.
9. Fonseca, "Discovery of Atlantic Space," 14.
10. Parry, *Age of Reconnaissance*, 90–93. Patricia Seed, "Jewish Scientists and the Origin of Modern Navigation," in *The Jews and the Expansion of Europe to the West*, Paolo Bernardini and Norman Fiering eds. (New York and Oxford: Berghahn, 2001), 73–85, 79–80.
11. C.F. Beckingham, "The Quest for Prester John," in *The European Opportunity.* An Expanding World: The European Impact on World History 1450–1800, Felipe Fernández-Armesto, ed. Volume 2 (Aldershot: Variorum, 1995), 175–194: 183–184. Moran Cruz, Jo Ann Hoeppner. "Popular Attitudes Towards Islam in Medieval Europe," in *Western Views of Islam in Medieval and Early Modern Europe: Perception of Other*, David R. Blanks and Michael Frassetto, eds. (New York: St. Martin's Press, 1999), 35–81:

63–64. L.N. Gumilev, *Searches for an Imaginary Kingdom: The Legend of the Kingdom of Prester John,* translated by R.E.F. Smith (Cambridge: Cambridge University Press, 1987. Original ed. 1970).

12. Bernard, "Trade and Finance," 276. Seymour Phillips, "The outer world of the European Middle Ages," in *Implicit Understandings: Observing, Reporting, and Reflecting on the Encounters between Europeans and Other Peoples in the Early Modern Era,* Stuart Schwartz, ed. (Cambridge: Cambridge University Press, 1994), 23–63, ibidem, 39.

13. J.D. Fage, *A History of Africa* (London: Hutchinson University Library for Africa, 1978): 77.

14. Ivor Wilks, *Forests of Gold: Essays on the Akan and the Kingdom of Asante* (Athens: Ohio University Press, 1993), 1–39. Susan Keech McIntosh, "A reconsideration of Wangara/Palolus, Island of Gold," *Journal of African History* 22 (1981), 145–158.

15. Wilks, *Forests of Gold,* 22–28.

16. Ralph A. Austen, "Marginalization, stagnation, and growth: the trans-Saharan caravan trade in the era of European expansion, 1500–1900," in *The Rise of Merchant Empires. Long-distance Trade in the Early Modern World, 1350–1750,* James D. Tracy, ed. (Cambridge: Cambridge University Press, 1990), 311–350, 320. Eltis, *Rise of African Slavery,* 150–151.

17. P.E. Russell, "Castilian documentary sources for the history of the Portuguese expansion in Guinea in the last years of the reign of Dom Afonso V," in *Portugal, Spain and the African Atlantic, 1343–1490: Chivalry and Crusade from John of Gaunt to Henry the Navigator* (Aldershot: Variorum, 1995), XII: 1, 17.

18. Cf.: Frederick J. Pohl, *Prince Henry Sinclair: His Expedition to the New World in 1398* (New York: Clarkson N. Potter, 1974).

19. Alfred W. Crosby, Jr., *The Columbian Exchange: Biological and Cultural Consequences of 1492* (Westport: Greenwood Press, 1972), 66–68, 176–188.

20. Jared Diamond, *Guns, Germs, and Steel. The Fates of Human Societies* (New York and London: W.W. Norton, 1997), 160, 162.

21. Noble David Cook and W. George Lovell, "Unraveling the Web of Disease," in *"Secret Judgments of God": Old World Disease in Colonial Spanish America,* Noble David Cook and W. George Lovell, eds. (Norman: University of Oklahoma Press, 1992), 213–242: 216–222. Alfred W. Crosby, "Virgin Soil Epidemics as a Factor in the Aboriginal Depopulation in America," *William and Mary Quarterly*, 3rd series, 33:2 (April 1976), 289–299.

22. Robert McCaa, "Spanish and Nahuatl Views on Smallpox and Demographic Catastrophe in Mexico," *Journal of Interdisciplinary History* XXV:3 (Winter 1995), 397–431, 409, 419–420.

23. Neal Salisbury, *Manitou and Providence: Indians, Europeans, and the Making of New England, 1500–1643* (New York and Oxford: Oxford University Press, 1982), 101–105. Arthur E. Spiess and Bruce D. Spiess, "New England Pandemic of 1616–1622: Cause and Archaeological Implication," *Man in the Northeast* 34 (Fall 1987), 71–83: 71.

24. One historian claims that Europe's population may have shrunk by two-thirds between 1320 and 1420: David Herlihy, *The Black Death and the Transformation of the West,* Samuel K. Cohn, Jr., ed. (Cambridge: Harvard University Press, 1998).

25. The Portuguese, for instance, shipped Beothuk Indians from Newfoundland to Lisbon in 1501, and shortly thereafter French explorers sent back other North American natives who were presented to crowds in Rouen. P.E. Russell, "Some Socio-Linguistic Problems Concerning the Fifteenth-Century Portuguese Discoveries in the African Atlantic," in *Portugal, Spain and the African Atlantic,* XIV: 12. Harald E.L. Prins, *The Mi'kmaq: Resistance, Accommodation, and Cultural Survival* (Forth Worth, Texas: Harcourt Brace College Publishers, 1996), 50–51. Cf. Geoffrey Symcox, ed., *Italian Reports on America 1493–1522: Letters, Dispatches, and Papal Bulls,* translated by Peter D. Diehl (Turnhout: Brepols, 2001), 56.

26. Quoted in: Prins, *Mi 'kmaq,* 44.
27. *Politics,* 1254a, 1253b, in: William Benton, ed., *The Works of Aristotle,* Volume II (Chicago: Encyclopaedia Britannica, 1952), 447. Cf. David Brion Davis, *The Problem of Slavery in Western Culture* (New York and Oxford: Oxford University Press, 1966), 69.
28. Arnold J. Bauer, "The Colonial Economy," In *The Countryside in Colonial Latin America* Louisa Schell Hoberman, and Susan Migden Socolow, eds. (Albuquerque: University of New Mexico Press, 1996), 19–48: 27.
29. Hilary McD. Beckles, "The Colours of Property: Brown, White and Black Chattels and their Responses on the Caribbean Frontier," *Slavery & Abolition* 15 (1994), 36–51: 41–43. William B. Taylor, *Drinking, Homicide, and Rebellion in Colonial Mexican Villages* (Stanford: Stanford University Press, 1979), 15–16, 21–22.
30. Cheryl English Martin, "Indigenous Peoples," in Hoberman and Socolow, *Countryside in Colonial Latin America,* 187–212: 191–194.
31. Robert S. Grumet, *Historic Contact: Indian People and Colonists in Today's Northeastern United States in the Sixteenth through Eighteenth Centuries* (Norman and London: University of Oklahoma Press, 1995), 76. Salisbury, *Manitou and Providence,* 56–57.
32. Salisbury, *Manitou and Providence,* 12.
33. Ida Altman, and Reginald D. Butler, "The Contact of Cultures: Perspectives on the Quincentenary," *American Historical Review* 99:2 (April 1994), 478–503: 495.
34. Jaime Jaramillo Uribe, "Mestizaje y diferenciación social en el Nuevo Reino de Granada en la segunda mitad del siglo XVIII," *Anuario Colombiano de Historia Social y de la Cultura* II (1965), 21–50: 30.
35. Juan Marchena Fernández, *Oficiales y soldados en el Ejército de América* (Sevilla: Escuela de Estudios Hispano-Americanos, 1983), 127.
36. Kirti Chaudhuri, "A recepção europeia da expansão," in *História da Expansão Portuguesa,* Francisco Bethencourt and Kirti Chaudhuri, eds., Volume I: A Formação do Império (1415–1570) (s.l.: Temas e Debates e Autores, 1998), 512–533: 514, 518–520.
37. Renate Pieper, *Die Vermittlung einer neuen Welt: Amerika im Nachrichtennetz des habsburgischen Imperiums, 1493–1598* (Mainz: Philipp von Zabern, 2000), 39–49.
38. Pieper, *Vermittlung einer neuen Welt,* 47, 142–143, 155.
39. Diogo Ramada Curto, "A literatura e o império: entre o espírito cavaleiroso, as trocas da Corte e o humanismo cívico," in Bethencourt and Chaudhuri, *História da Expansão Portuguesa,* I: 434–454: 438–439.
40. Quoted in Elizabeth Eisenstein, *The Printing Revolution in Early Modern Europe* (Cambridge: Cambridge University Press, 1983), 87.
41. Maria Fernanda Alegria, João Carlos Garcia, and Francesc Relaño, "Cartografia e viagens," in: Bethencourt and Chaudhuri, *História da Expansão Portuguesa,* I: 26–61: 42–43.
42. Chaudhuri, "Recepção europeia," 514. Peter Burke. *Antwerp, A Metropolis in Comparative Perspective* (Antwerpen: Martial & Snoeck, 1993), 42–44, 47–48, 53. Cf. Werner Waterschoot, "Antwerp: books, publishing and cultural production before 1585"; and Paul Hoftijzer, "Metropolis of print: the Amsterdam book trade in the seventeenth century," in *Urban Achievement in Early Modern Europe: Golden Ages in Antwerp, Amsterdam and London,* Patrick O'Brien, ed. (Cambridge: Cambridge University Press, 2001), 233–248, 249–263.
43. Lyle N. McAlister, *Spain and Portugal in the New World 1492–1700* (Oxford: Oxford University Press; Minneapolis: University of Minnesota Press, 1984), 455–456.
44. Peter Burke, "America and the Rewriting of World History," in *America in European Consciousness, 1493–1750,* Karen Ordahl Kupperman, ed. (Chapel Hill: University of North Carolina Press, 1993), 33–51: 42.
45. Fernández-Armesto, *Before Columbus,* 234–236.
46. In the Middle Ages, the religious distinction had itself replaced a contrast between 'Romanitas' ('Roman-ness') and various kinds of barbarism: W.R. Jones, "The Image of the

Barbarian in Medieval Europe," *Comparative Studies in Society and History* 13 (1971), 376–407: 405. In a similar vein, it has been suggested that the Europeans' sustained interaction with African slaves in the Americas made them stress what they had in common with each other. David Eltis, *The Rise of African Slavery in the Americas* (Cambridge: Cambridge University Press, 2000), 242.

47. John Hale, *The Civilization of Europe in the Renaissance* (New York: Athenaeum, Toronto: Maxwell MacMillan Canada, New York: Maxwell MacMillan International, 1994), 359–362.

48. Elliott Horowitz, "The New World and the Changing Face of Europe." *Sixteenth Century Journal*, XXVIII: 4 (1997), 1181–1201: 1181, 1188.

49. Anthony Pagden, *European Encounters with the New World: from Renaissance to Romanticism* (New Haven and London: Yale University Press, 1993), 132.

50. Hale, *Civilization of Europe*, 371.

51. Sabine MacCormack, "Limits of Understanding: Perceptions of Greco-Roman and Amerindian Paganism in Early Modern Europe," in Kupperman, *America in European Consciousness*, 79–130: 87.

52. Burke, "Rewriting of World History," 44. Auke van der Woud, *De Bataafse hut. Verschuivingen in het beeld van de geschiedenis (1750–1850)* (Amsterdam: Meulenhoff, 1990), 109. Jennifer D. Selwyn, "'Procur[ing] in the Common People These Better Behaviors": The Jesuits' Civilizing Mission in Early Modern Naples 1550–1620," *Radical History Review* 67 (1997), 4–34: 24.

53. James Lockhart, "Sightings: Initial Nahua Reactions to Spanish Culture," in *Implicit Understandings: Observing, Reporting, and Reflecting on the Encounters Between Europeans and Other Peoples in the Early Modern Era,* Stuart B. Schwartz, ed. (Cambridge: Cambridge University Press, 1994), 218–248: 218–219.

54. Pagden, *European Encounters,* 10.

55. Mary Helms, "Essay on objects: Interpretations of distance made tangible," in Schwartz, *Implicit Understandings,* 355–377: 371, 373.

56. John Block Friedman, *The Monstrous Races in Medieval Art and Thought* (Syracuse: Syracuse University Press, 2000), 9–21.

57. Frank Lestringant, *Mapping the Renaissance World: The Geographical Imagination in the Age of Discovery,* translated by David Fausett, with a foreword by Stephen Greenblatt (Berkeley and Los Angeles: University of California Press, 1994), 78.

58. P.E.H. Hair, "The Use of African Languages in Afro-European Contacts in Guinea: 1440–1560," in P.E.H. Hair, *Africa Encountered: European Contacts and Evidence 1450–1700* (Ashgate: Variorum, 1997), VI: 17.

59. Walter Ralegh, *The Discoverie of the Large, Rich and Bewtiful Empyre of Guiana, with a relation of the great and Golden Citie of Manoa (which the Spanyards call El Dorado)* (London, 1596), 10. Thomas Suárez, *Shedding the Veil: Mapping the European Discovery of America and the World* (Singapore: World Scientific, 1992), 43–44. Miguel Acosta Saignes, *Vida de los esclavos negros en Venezuela* (Havana: Casa de las Américas, 1967), 127.

60. Neil L. Whitehead, "Introduction," in *The Discoverie of the Large, Rich, and Bewftiful Empyre of Guiana,* Walter Ralegh, transcribed, annotated and introduced by Neil L. Whitehead (Norman: University of Oklahoma Press, 1997), 75.

61. D.A. Brading, *The First America: The Spanish Monarchy, Creole Patriots, and the Liberal State, 1492–1867* (Cambridge: Cambridge University Press, 1991), 14. James Romm, "Biblical History and the Americas: The Legend of Solomon's Ophir, 1492–1591," in *The Jews and the Expansion of Europe to the West,* Bernardini and Fiering, 27–46: 30–31. Salo Wittmayer Baron, *A Social and Religious History of the Jews,* 2nd revised and enlarged ed., XV (New York and London: Columbia University Press, Philadelphia: The Jewish Publication Society of America, 1973), 339–340. In the nineteenth and twentieth centuries, archeologists occasionally claimed to have found the mysterious land of Ophir in various parts of Africa, including the border area of present-day Zimbabwe and Mozambique: Werner Keller, *The Bible as History: A*

Confirmation of the Book of Books (New York: William Morrow and Company, 1956), 199.

62. Brading, *First America,* 196–198. García was certainly not the first author who tried to establish the Jewish origins of natives. He was not even the first Dominican, since father Diego Durán preceded him in the sixteenth century. See *The History of the Indies of New Spain,* Diego Durán, translated, annotated, and with an introduction by Doris Heyden (Norman, Okl., and London: University of Oklahoma Press, 1994), 3–10.

63. Yosef Hayim Yerushalmi, *A Jewish Classic in the Portuguese Language* (Lisbon: Fundação Calouste Gulbenkian, 1989), 26.

64. Elisabeth Levi de Montezinos, "The Narrative of Aharon Levi, alias Antonio de Montezinos," *The American Sephardi. Journal of the Sephardic Studies Program of Yeshiva University* VII-VIII (1975), 62–83. David S. Katz, *The Jews in the History of England 1485–1850* (Oxford: Clarendon Press, 1994), 113.

65. Alfred Padula, "Innocence and Empire: Dutch Imperialism in the Age of Pieter van der Keere," in *Reading the New World: Interdisciplinary Perspectives on Pieter van der Keere's Map Nova Totius Terrarum Orbis Geographica ac Hydrographica Tabula* (Amsterdam, 1608/36), Matthew H. Edney and Irwin D. Novak, eds., (Portland, Maine: Osher Map Library Associates, 2001), 9–16: 13.

66. K.G. Davies, *The North Atlantic World in the Seventeenth Century* (Minneapolis: University of Minnesota Press, 1974), 56.

67. Ida Altman and James Horn, "Introduction," in *"To make America": European migration in the early modern period,* Ida Altman and James Horn, eds. (Berkeley and Los Angeles: University of California Press, 1991), 1–29: 14.

68. František Svejkovsky, "Three centuries of America in Czech Literature, 1508–1818," in *East Central European Perceptions of Early America,* Béla K. Király and George Barany, eds. (Lisse: The Peter de Ridder Press, 1977), 33–55: 46.

69. David B. Quinn and A.N. Ryan, *England's Sea Empire, 1550–1642* (London: Allen & Unwin, 1983), 168.

70. David Cressy, *Coming Over. Migration and Communication between England and New England in the Seventeenth Century* (Cambridge: Cambridge University Press, 1987), 192–193.

71. Frank Lestringant, "Geneva and America in the Renaissance: The Dream of the Huguenot Refuge 1555–1600," *Sixteenth Century Journal* XXVI:2 (1995), 285–295. Bertrand Van Ruymbeke, "Le refuge atlantique: la diaspora huguenote et l'Atlantique anglo-américain," in *D'un Rivage à l'Autre. Villes et Protestantisme dans l'Aire Atlantique,* Guy Martinière, Didier Poton, and François Souty, eds. *(XVIe-XVIIe siècles)* (Paris: Imprimerie Nationale, 1999), 195–204: 196.

72. Isaac Jogues, "New Netherland in 1644," in *The Documentary History of the State of New York,* 4 vols. E.B. O'Callaghan, ed. (Albany: Van Benthuysen, 1851), 15.

73. Willem Frijhoff, *Wegen van Evert Willemsz. Een Hollands weeskind op zoek naar zichzelf, 1607–1674* (Nijmegen: SUN, 1995), 581.

74. Cole Harris, "European Beginnings in the Northwest Atlantic: A Comparative View," in *Seventeenth-Century New England. A Conference Held by The Colonial Society of Massachusetts, June 18 and 19, 1982,* David D. Hall and David Grayson Allen, eds. (Boston: The Colonial Society of Massachusetts, 1984), 119–152: 121, 124. James Horn, *Adapting to a New World: English Society in the Seventeenth-Century Chesapeake* (Chapel Hill and London: University of North Carolina Press, 1994), 147.

75. A.J.R. Russell-Wood, "Fluxos de emigração," in: Bethencourt and Chaudhuri, *História da Expansão Portuguesa,* I: 224–237: 235–236. Ida Altman, "A New World in the Old: Local Society and Spanish Emigration to the Indies," in Altman and Horn, *To make America,* 30–58: 37.

76. Alexander V. Berkis, *The Reign of Duke James in Courland 1638–1682* (Lincoln, Nebraska: Vaidava, 1960), 77.

77. Pérez-Mallaína, *Spain's Men of the Sea,* 215.

78. Altman, "New World in the Old," 38. Auke Pieter Jacobs, "Legal and Illegal Emigration from Seville, 1550–1650," in Altman and Horn, *To Make America,* 59–84: 67.

79. A recent article gives these figures for migration to the Thirteen Colonies: 1607–1699: 96,600 indentured servants, 66,300 free migrants, and 2,300 convicts, prisoners and political exiles; 1700–1775: 103,500; 151,600; and 52,200, respectively. Aaron S. Fogleman, "From Slaves, Convicts, and Servants to Free Passengers: The Transformation of Immigration in the Era of the American Revolution," *Journal of American History* 85:1 (June 1998), 43–76: 44 (Table 1). Indentured servitude did not exist in the Portuguese empire and was virtually absent from Dutch America because of the small home populations and the need to defend the numerous colonies these countries had across the globe. Soldiers were preferred to settlers. Cf. Timothy J. Coates, *Convicts and Orphans: Forced and State-Sponsored Colonizers in the Portuguese Empire* (Stanford: Stanford University Press, 2001), 186–187.

80. David W. Galenson, *White Servitude in Colonial America: An Economic Analysis* (Cambridge: Cambridge University Press, 1981), 13–14. John J. McCusker and Russell R. Menard, *The Economy of British America 1607–1789. With Supplementary Bibliography* (Chapel Hill and London: University of North Carolina Press, 1991), 240, 242. Altman and Horn, "Introduction," 8. Cf. Debien, G., *La société coloniale aux XVIIe et XVIIIe siècles. Les engagés pour les Antilles (1634–1715)* (Paris: Société de l'Histoire des Colonies Françaises & Librairie Larose, 1952).

81. Bernard Bailyn, *The Peopling of British North America: An Introduction* (New York: Vintage Books, 1988), 85–86.

82. Christian Huetz de Lemps, "Indentured Servants Bound for the French Antilles in the Seventeenth and Eighteenth Centuries," in Altman and Horn, *To Make America,* 172–203: 174. Richard S. Dunn, *Sugar and slaves. The rise of the planter class in the English West Indies, 1624–1713* (Chapel Hill: The University of North Carolina Press, 1972), 57. Abbot Emerson Smith, *Colonists in Bondage: White Servitude and Convict Labor in America 1607–1776* (Chapel Hill: The University of North Carolina Press, 1947), 216.

83. W.J. Eccles, *The French in North America, 1500–1783* (revised 3rd ed., East Lansing: Michigan State University Press, 1998), 166. Smith, *Colonists in Bondage,* 233, 270. Hilary Beckles, "From Sea to Land: Runaway Barbados Slaves and Servants, 1630–1700," in *Out of the House of Bondage: Runaways, Resistance and Marronage in Africa and the New World,* Gad Heuman, ed. (London: Frank Cass, 1986), 79–94: 80. Dunn, *Sugar and Slaves,* 278. It has been suggested that indentured servitude prevented slavery from spreading in the Middle Colonies of British North America: Thomas M. Truxes, *Irish-American trade, 1660–1783* (Cambridge: Cambridge University Press, 1988), 145.

84. Jesús María G. López Ruíz, *Hernández de Serpa y su "hueste" de 1569 con destino a la Nueva Andalucía* (Caracas: Academia Nacional de la Historia, 1974), 214. Horn, *Adapting to a New World,* 48. David Steven Cohen, "How Dutch Were the Dutch of New Netherland?," *New York History* LXII/1 (1981), 43–60: Table 2.

85. Wolfgang v. Hippel, *Auswanderung aus Südwestdeutschland. Studien zur würtembergischen Auswanderung und Auswanderungspolitik im 18. und 19. Jahrhundert* (Stuttgart: Klett-Cotta, 1984), 31–33. Marianne Wokeck, "Harnessing the Lure of the "Best Poor Man's Country": The Dynamics of German-Speaking Immigration to British North America, 1683–1783," in Altman and Horn, *To Make America,* 204–243: 208–209.

86. Bailyn, Bernard, "The Idea of Atlantic History," *Itinerario: European Journal of Overseas History* 20:1 (1996), 19–44: 33.

87. John H. Elliott, *Imperial Spain, 1469–1716* (London: E. Arnold, 1963), 110.

88. P.E.H. Hair, "Discovery and Discoveries: The Portuguese in Guinea 1444–1650," in Hair, *Africa Encountered,* I: 15.

89. Linda A. Curcio-Nagy, "Faith and Morals in Colonial Mexico," in *The Oxford History of Mexico,* Michael C. Meyer and William H. Beezley, eds., (New York: Oxford University Press, 2000), 151–182: 169.

90. Alicia Piffer de Canabrava, *O Comércio Português no Rio da Prata (1580–1640)* (São Paulo: Universidade de São Paulo, 1944), 130. J.T. Medina, *Historia del Tribunal del Santo Oficio de la Inquisición en Chile* (2 vols., Santiago de Chile: Imprenta Ercilla, 1890), 99–100. Salo Wittmayer Baron, *A Social and Religious History of the Jews,* 2nd, revised and enlarged ed., XIII (New York and London: Columbia University Press, Philadelphia: The Jewish Publication Society of America, 1969), 136–143.
91. Maria Cristina Navarrete, *Historia Social del Negro en la Colonia Cartagena, siglo XVII* (Santiago de Cali: Universidad de Valle, 1995), 69. Seymour B. Liebman, *The Jews in New Spain: Faith, Flame, and the Inquisition* (Coral Gables, Florida: University of Miami Press, 1970), 225.
92. These Jews were joined by New Christians from Portuguese Brazil. José Antonio Gonsalves de Mello, *Gente de Nação. Cristãos-novos e judeus em Pernambuco 1542–1654* (Recife: Fundação Joaquim Nabuco, Editora Massangana, 1989).
93. Eltis, *Rise of African Slavery,* 240.
94. Richard Konetzke, *Süd- und Mittelamerika I. Die Indianerkulturen Altamerikas und die spanisch-portugiesische Kolonialherrschaft* (Frankfurt am Main: Fischer Taschenbuch Verlag, 1965), 220, 225, 231–233, 244–245.
95. John Vogt, *Portuguese Rule on the Gold Coast, 1469–1682* (Athens: The University of Georgia Press, 1979), 55, 184.
96. John Thornton, "The Development of an African Catholic Church in the Kingdom of Kongo, 1491–1750," *Journal of African History* 25:2 (1984), 147–168: 152–153.
97. Parry, *Age of Reconnaissance,* 134. Konetzke, *Indianerkulturen Altamerikas,* 241–242.
98. McAlister, *Spain and Portugal in the New World,* 175.
99. John W. O'Malley, *The First Jesuits* (Cambridge, Mass. and London: Harvard University Press, 1994), 79.
100. Maria Cândida D.M. Barros, "The Office of *Lingua:* A Portrait of the Religious Tupi Interpreter in Brazil in the Sixteenth Century," *Itinerario: European Journal of Overseas History* XXV:2 (2001), 110–140: 118–119. O'Malley, *First Jesuits,* 151.
101. O'Malley, *First Jesuits,* 77.
102. Brading, *First America,* 172–176.
103. John Thornton, *Africa and Africans in the Making of the Atlantic World, 1400–1680* (Cambridge: Cambridge University Press, 1992), 253, 260. Robin Law, *The Slave Coast of West Africa, 1550–1750: The Impact of the Atlantic Slave Trade on an African Society* (Oxford: Clarendon Press, 1991), 153.
104. Alice N. Nash, "The Abiding Frontier: Family, Gender and Religion in Wabanaki History, 1600–1763," (Ph.D. Dissertation, Columbia University, 1997), 211, 216–217.
105. Thornton, *Africa and Africans,* 255–260.
106. Kenneth Mills, *Idolatry and Its Enemies: Colonial Andean Religion and Extirpation, 1640–1750* (Princeton: Princeton University Press, 1997), 246–248, 255–257.
107. Nash, "Abiding Frontier," 107.
108. Fernández-Armesto, *Before Columbus,* 205.
109. 164,000 kilograms of gold were exported from Spanish America to Spain before 1660, whereas 82,000 left West Africa by land and sea in the period 1501–1650. In the end, substantial gold deposits were found in contemporary Colombia. From 1510 to 1660, these yielded twice as much gold as all of West Africa. Carla Rahn Phillips, "The growth and composition of trade in the Iberian empires, 1450–1750," in Tracy, *The Rise of Merchant Empires,* 34–101, 83; and Ward Barrett, "World bullion flows, 1450–1800," in Tracy, *Rise of Merchant Empires,* 224–254, 247 (Table 7.5).
110. Barbara Hadley Stein and Stanley J. Stein, "Financing Empire: The European Diaspora of Silver by War," in *Colonial Legacies: The Problem of Persistence in Latin American History,* Jeremy Adelman, ed., (New York and London: Routledge, 1999), 51–68: 63–65.
111. B.H. Slicher van Bath, *Indianen en Spanjaarden. Een ontmoeting tussen twee werelden. Latijns-Amerika 1500–1800* (Amsterdam: Bert Bakker, 1992), 161–165. Cf. Artur Attman, *American Bullion in the European World Trade 1600–1800* (Gothenburg: Acta

Regiae Societatis Scientiarum et Litterarum Gothoburgensis Humaniora 26. Kungl. Vetenskaps- och Vitterhets-Samhället, 1986).

112. Before 1700, 80–85% of the volume of goods transported between Spanish America and Spain, and 90–95% of their value, was shipped in fleets and galleons: Chaunu, Pierre, "Les routes espagnoles de l'Atlantique," *Anuario de Estudios Americanos* XXV (1968), 95–128: 116.

113. Phillips, "Growth and composition," 77–78. McAlister, *Spain and Portugal in the New World,* 202. Henry Kamen, *Spain in the later Seventeenth Century, 1665–1700* (London and New York: Longman, 1980), 132.

114. Huguette Chaunu and Pierre Chaunu, *Séville et l'Atlantique (1504–1650),* 8 vols. (Paris: Librairie Armand Colin, 1955–1959), VIII-1, 702–704, 706, 709. Manuel Carrera Stampa, "Las ferias novohispanos," *Historia Mexicana* II:3 (1953), 319–342: 321.

115. Murdo J. MacLeod, "Aspects of the internal economy," in *Colonial Spanish America,* Leslie Bethell, ed., (Cambridge: Cambridge University Press, 1987), 315–360: 355.

116. In 1598, Nombre de Dios was replaced by the equally insalubrious town of Portobelo as the southern end of the *carrera de Indias.* Chaunu and Chaunu, *Séville et l'Atlantique,* VIII-1, 927n, 929.

117. Parry, *Age of Reconnaissance,* 180.

118. Peter D. Bradley, *Society, Economy and Defence in Seventeenth-Century Peru. The Administration of the Count of Alba de Liste (1655–61)* (Liverpool: The Institute of Latin American Studies, University of Liverpool, 1992), 39. Carmen Cañero Báncora, "Las remesas de metales preciosas desde El Callao a España en la primera mitad del siglo XVII." *Revista de Indias* XIX (1959), 35–88: 39. Dionysio Alsedo y Herrera, *Memorial informativo, que pusieron en las reales manos del Rey Nuestro Señor (que Dios guarde) el Tribunal del Consulado de la ciudad de los reyes, y la Junta General del Comercio de las provincias del Peru* (s.l., ca. 1725), 75. Geoffrey J. Walker, *Spanish Politics and Imperial Trade, 1700–1789* (Bloomington: Indiana University Press, 1979), 143.

119. Ruth Pike, *Aristocrats and Traders: Sevillian Society in the Sixteenth Century* (Ithaca and London: Cornell University Press, 1972), 118.

120. Enriqueta Vila Vilar, *Los Corzo y los Mañara: Tipos y arquetipos del mercader con América* (Sevilla: Escuela de Estudios Hispano-Americanos, 1991), 41, 55.

121. Margarita Suárez, "Monopolio, comercio directo y fraude: la élite mercantil de Lima en la primera mitad del siglo XVII," *Revista Andina* 11:2 (December 1993), 487–502: 492.

122. Christopher Ward, *Imperial Panama: Commerce and Conflict in Isthmian America, 1550–1800* (Albuquerque: University of New Mexico Press, 1993), 78. Antonio Miguel Bernal, *La financiación de la Carrera de Indias (1492–1824). Dinero y crédito en el comercio colonial español con América* (Sevilla: El Monte, Banco de España, 1992), 224.

123. David A. Brading, *Miners and Merchants in Bourbon Mexico, 1763–1810* (Cambridge: Cambridge University Press, 1971), 95, 97. Walker, *Spanish Politics,* 77–78. John E. Kicza, *Colonial Entrepreneurs. Families and Business in Bourbon Mexico City* (Albuquerque: University of New Mexico Press, 1983), 55.

124. Slicher van Bath, *Indianen en Spanjaarden,* 150–151.

125. Carl Bridenbaugh and Roberta Bridenbaugh, *No Peace Beyond the Line. The English in the Caribbean 1624–1690* (New York: Oxford University Press, 1972), 3, 5.

126. J. Everaert, *De internationale en koloniale handel der Vlaamse firma's te Cádiz 1670–1700* (Brugge: De Tempel, 1973), 397. Kamen, *Spain in the Later Seventeenth Century,* 137. In 1751, an investigation showed that although most merchants in Cádiz were Spanish (218 against 162 foreigners), they could not claim more than 18% of all earnings: Richard Pares, *War and trade in the West Indies 1739–1763* (Oxford: Clarendon Press, 1936), 142.

127. Walker, *Spanish Politics,* 105.

128. Walker, *Spanish Politics,* 71–74, 111–113, 181–182, 189, 198.

129. Stuart B. Schwartz, *Sugar Plantations in the Formation of Brazilian Society. Bahia, 1550–1835* (Cambridge: Cambridge University Press, 1985), 181–182. Luiz Felipe de Alencastro, "The apprenticeship of colonization," in *Slavery and the Rise of the Atlantic System,* Barbara L. Solow, ed. (Cambridge: Cambridge University Press, 1991), 151–176: 164.

130. Evaldo Cabral de Mello, *Olinda Restaurada. Guerra e Açúcar no Nordeste, 1630–1654* (Rio de Janeiro: Editora Forense-Universitaria, São Paulo: Editora da Universidade de São Paulo, 1975), 83. Philips, "Growth and Composition," 64–65. Michel Morineau, *Incroyables gazettes et fabuleux métaux. Les retours des trésors américains d'après les gazettes hollandaises (XVIe-XVIIIe siècles)* (London: Cambridge University Press, and Paris: Éditions de la Maison des Sciences de l'Homme, 1985), 146–148, 163, 194–197.

131. Kenneth Maxwell, "The Atlantic in the eighteenth century: A southern perspective on the need to return to the 'big picture,'" *Transactions of the Royal Historical Society,* 6th series, III (1993), 209–236: 221–222.

132. Jordan Goodman, *Tobacco in History: The Cultures of Dependence* (London and New York: Routledge, 1993), 134–135, 141–142, 168, 175.

133. Johannes Jacobus Herks, *De geschiedenis van de Amersfoortse tabak* ('s-Gravenhage: Martinus Nijhoff, 1967), 70–73, 86–92. H.K. Roessingh, *Inlandse tabak. Expansie en contractie van een handelsgewas in de 17e en 18e eeuw in Nederland* (Zutphen: De Walburg Pers, 1976), 98–99, 245, 358–359, 404, 473.

134. Goodman, *Tobacco in History,* 162–164. Carl A. Hanson, "Monopoly and Contraband in the Portuguese Tobacco Trade, 1624–1702," *Luso-Brazilian Review* 19:2 (Winter 1982), 149–168.

135. Goodman, *Tobacco in History,* 182.

136. Robert C. Batie, "Why Sugar? Economic Cycles and the Changing of Staples in the English and French Antilles 1624–1654," in *Caribbean Slave Society and Economy: A Student Reader,* Hilary Beckles and Verene Shepherd, eds. (Kingston: Ian Randle and London: James Currey, 1991), 37–55: 44.

137. Fernando Ortiz, *Cuban Counterpoint: Tobacco and Sugar* (Durham, NC: Duke University Press, 1995. Original edition, 1916).

138. Carole Shammas, "The revolutionary impact of European demand for tropical goods," in *The Early Modern Atlantic Economy,* John J. McCusker and Kenneth Morgan, eds. (Cambridge: Cambridge University Press, 2000), 163–185: 169, 177–178. Robert Louis Stein, *The French Sugar Business in the Eighteenth Century* (Baton Rouge and London: Louisiana State University Press, 1988), ix.

139. Phillips, "Growth and Composition," 57.

140. Dunn, *Sugar and Slaves,* 189–190.

141. Anne Pérotin-Dumon, "French, English and Dutch in the Lesser Antilles; From Privateering to Planting, c. 1550 - c. 1650," in *General History of the Caribbean, Volume II: New Societies: The Caribbean in the Long Sixteenth Century,* P.C. Emmer and Germán Carrera Damas, eds. (London: UNESCO Publishing, Macmillan Education, 1999), 114–158, 154–155. By 1700, Brazil's sugar plantations had consumed 1,000 square kilometers of forest. Warren Dean, *With Broadax and Firebrand. The Destruction of the Brazilian Atlantic Forest* (Berkeley: University of California Press, 1995), 80.

142. Antonio García-Baquero González, *La Carrera de Indias: suma de la contratación y océano de negocios* (Sevilla: Sociedad Estatal para la Exposición Universal Sevilla 92 & Alagaida Editores, 1992), 204, 208–209. Bernal, *Financiación de la Carrera,* 352. Davis, Ralph, "English Foreign Trade, 1700–1774," *Economic History Review,* 2d series, XV no. 2 (December 1962), 285–303: 302–303.

143. Davis, "English foreign trade," 302–303. Eltis, *Rise of African Slavery,* 40–41.

144. In 1768–72, New England's exports to Britain were worth only £76,965. Chesapeake tobacco accounted for £756,128 per year, and West Indian sugar for £3 million. McCusker and Menard, *Economy of British America,* 108, 130, 160.

145. Peter V. Bergstrom, *Markets and Merchants. Economic Diversification in Colonial Virginia 1700–1775* (New York and London: Garland, 1985), Chapter 6. Middleton,

Arthur Pierce, *Tobacco Coast. A Maritime History of Chesapeake Bay in the Colonial Era* (Newport News: The Mariners' Museum, 1953), 104–106. Kenneth Morgan, *Bristol and the Atlantic Trade in the Eighteenth Century* (Cambridge: Cambridge University Press, 1993), 112, 114. Tobacco was also marketed by direct purchase by British merchants. American tobacco, as yet unharvested, was sold to British agents who would extend a line of credit to the planter for the purchase of European goods. It was the British firm which carried the risk for the shipment of both the European commodities to America and the tobacco to Europe. Port times, labor costs, and credit risks were thus reduced. A third system of tobacco marketing involved British or North American merchants who exported tobacco to their correspondents in Britain, receiving in turn two annual shipments of goods from London. Arthur Louis Jensen, *The Maritime Commerce of Colonial Philadelphia* (Madison: University of Wisconsin Press, 1963), 96. James H. Soltow, *The Economic Role of Williamsburg* (Charlottesville: The University Press of Virginia, 1965), 41–43. Jacob M. Price, *Capital and Credit in British Overseas Trade: The View from the Chesapeake, 1700–1776* (Cambridge and London: Harvard University Press, 1980), 6. Jacob M. Price, "Buchanan & Simpson, 1759–1763: A Different Kind of Glasgow Firm Trading to the Chesapeake," *William & Mary Quarterly,* Third Series XL no. 1 (1983), 3–41: 4.

146. A figure specific to the French sugar trade was the *commissionaire,* who formed a vital link between planters and French ship-owners. He gave credit to the planter, supplied him with European merchandise, and took care of the shipment and sale of his sugar crop. Dale Miquelon, *Dugard of Rouen: French Trade to Canada and the West Indies, 1729–1770* (Montreal and London: McGill-Queen's University Press, 1978), 92.

147. David Hancock, "'A revolution in trade': wine distribution and the development of the infrastructure of the Atlantic market economy, 1703–1807," in McCusker and Menard, *The Early Modern Atlantic Economy,* 105–153: 106–108.

148. Kenneth Morgan, "Shipping Patterns and the Atlantic Trade of Bristol, 1749–1770," *William and Mary Quarterly,* third series, XLVI no. 3 (1989), 506–538: 525–528. Morgan, *Bristol and the Atlantic Trade,* 66. Christopher J. French, "Productivity in the Atlantic shipping industry: a quantitative study," *Journal of Interdisciplinary History* 17 (1987), 613–638: 617.

149. James S. Pritchard, "The pattern of French colonial shipping to Canada before 1760," *Revue française d'Histoire d'Outre-Mer* LXIII (1976), 189–210: 191. Paul Butel, "France, the Antilles, and Europe in the seventeenth and eighteenth centuries: renewals of foreign trade," in Tracy, *Rise of Merchant Empires,* 153–173: 162. John G. Clark, *New Orleans, 1718–1812: An Economic History* (Baton Rouge: Louisiana State University Press, 1970), 64. The number of 392 is the average for 1749–55.

150. Lucien René Abénon, *La Guadeloupe de 1671 à 1759. Étude politique, économique et sociale,* 2 vols., (Paris: Éditions L'Harmattan, 1987), I: 278. Charles Frostin, *Histoire de l'autonomisme colon de la partie de St. Domingue aux XVIIe et XVIIIe siècles. Contribution à l'étude du sentiment américain d'indépendance* (Lille: Université de Lille III, 1973), 327n. Pares, *War and Trade in the West Indies,* 396–397.

151. Oliver M. Dickerson, *The Navigation Acts and the American Revolution* (Philadelphia: University of Pennsylvania Press, 1951), 76. Carole Shammas, "How self-sufficient was early America?" *Journal of Interdisciplinary History* 13 (1982), 247–272: 265n. Truxes, *Irish-American trade,* 44.

152. Curtis Nettels, "England and the Spanish-American Trade, 1680–1715," *The Journal of Modern History* III (1931), 1-32. Nuala Zahedieh, "The merchants of Port Royal, Jamaica, and the Spanish contraband trade, 1655–1692," *The William and Mary Quarterly,* 3d series 43 (1986), 570–592. Zacarías Moutoukias, *Contrabando y control colonial en el siglo XVII. Buenos Aires, el Atlántico y el espacio peruano* (Buenos Aires: Centro Editor de América Latina, 1988). Héctor R. Feliciano Ramos, *El contrabando inglés en el Caribe y el Golfo de México (1748–1778)* (Sevilla: Excma. Diputación Provincial de Sevilla, 1990). Wim Klooster, *Illicit Riches. Dutch Trade in the Caribbean, 1648–1795* (Leiden: KITLV Press, 1998). G.V. Scammell, "'A Very

Profitable and Advantageous Trade': British Smuggling in the Iberian Americas circa 1500–1750," *Itinerario. European Journal of Overseas History* XXIV:3-4 (2000), 135–172.

153. Canabrava, *Comércio português,* 130–140. Elena F.S. de Studer, *La trata de negros en el Río de la Plata durante el siglo XVIII* (Buenos Aires: Universidad de Buenos Aires, 1958), 89. Enriqueta Vila Vilar, *Hispanoamérica y el comercio de esclavos* (Sevilla: Escuela de Estudios Hispano-Americanos, 1977), 103. Alberto Crespo, *Esclavos negros en Bolivia* (La Paz: Academia Nacional de Ciencias de Bolivia, 1977), 58.

154. John Carter Brown Library, Providence, RI: Codex Du-1, "Beschrijvinge van de custen van Brasil, en verder zuidelijk tot Rio de la Plata, toestand der forten, enz. Getrokken uit scheepsjournalen, officiële verklaringen enz. van 1624–1637," statement by Henrick Coenraet, December 22, 1636.

155. Wim Klooster, "Subordinate but proud: Curaçao's free blacks and mulattoes in the eighteenth century," *New West Indian Guide* 68:3-4 (1994), 283–300.

156. Frostin, *L'autonomisme colon,* 365.

157. Julius Sherrard Scott III, "The Common Wind: Currents of Afro-American Communication in the Era of the Haitian Revolution" (Ph.D. dissertation, Duke University, 1986), 4–5, 20–21.

158. Schwartz, *Sugar Plantations,* 133–134.

159. Charles Verlinden, "The Transfer of Colonial Techniques from the Mediterranean to the Atlantic," in *The European Opportunity,* Fernández-Armesto, 225–254: 252–253.

160. Pike, *Aristocrats and Traders,* 172–175.

161. Philip D. Curtin, *Economic Change in Precolonial Africa: Senegambia in the Era of the Slave Trade* (Madison: The University of Wisconsin Press, 1975), 175.

162. N.I. Matar, "Muslims in Seventeenth-Century England," *Journal of Islamic Studies* 8:1 (1997), 63–82: 72–73.

163. Stephen Clissold, *The Barbary Slaves* (Totowa, New Jersey: Rowman and Littlefield, 1977), 4, 5, 53. Cf. Linda Colley, *Captives: Britain, Empire and the World, 1600–1850* (New York: Pantheon Books, 2002).

164. Paul E. Lovejoy, *Transformations in Slavery: A History of Slavery in Africa,* 2nd ed. (Cambridge: Cambridge University Press, 2000), 36.

165. Thornton, *Africa and Africans,* 87.

166. Wilks, *Forests of Gold,* 23–24.

167. William D. Phillips, Jr., "The Old World background of slavery in the Americas," in Solow, *Slavery and the Rise of the Atlantic System,* 43–61: 49–54. Verlinden, "Transfer of Colonial Techniques," 243. Birmingham, *Trade and Empire in the Atlantic,* 8–14.

168. Philip D. Curtin, *Death by Migration: Europe's Encounter with the Tropical World in the Nineteenth Century* (Cambridge: Cambridge University Press, 1989), 18, 42, 61, 159–160.

169. Russell-Wood, "Fluxos de emigração," 233.

170. Abdoulaye Ly, *La Compagnie du Sénégal* (s.l.: Présence Africaine, 1958), 257–263.

171. Curtin, *Senegambia in the Era of the Slave Trade,* 102–103.

172. P.E.H. Hair, "Protestants as Pirates, Slavers, and Proto-Missionaries: Sierra Leone 1568 and 1582," *Journal of Ecclesiastical History* XXXI:3 (July 1970), 203–224: 214–215.

173. Patrick Manning, "Contours of Slavery and Social Change in Africa," *American Historical Review* 88:4 (October 1983), 835–857.

174. Henk den Heijer, *Goud, ivoor en slaven. Scheepvaart en handel van de Tweede Westindische Compagnie op Afrika, 1674–1740* (Zutphen: Walburg Pers, 1997), 138, 116–118. James F. Searing, *West African Slavery and Atlantic Commerce: The Senegal River valley, 1700–1860* (Cambridge: Cambridge University Press, 1993), 68–69.

175. Herbert S. Klein, *The Atlantic Slave Trade* (Cambridge: Cambridge University Press, 1999), 90–91.

176. Law, *Slave Coast of West Africa,* 182.

177. Eltis, *Rise of African Slavery,* 59.

178. Stein, *French Sugar Business,* 29. Klein, *Atlantic Slave Trade,* 91–92.

179. Quote from: Bridenbaugh and Bridenbaugh, F. *No peace beyond the line*, 242n.
180. Historically, embargoes on individual cultural groups were nothing new. For example, after local slaves had displayed disorderly behavior, the Venetian Senate in 1368 put a temporary stop on the import of slaves of the Tatar language. Jacques Heers, *Esclaves et domestiques au Moyen-Age dans le monde méditerranéen* (Paris: Arthème Fayard, 1981), 131.
181. Brading, *First America,* 167.
182. Klein, *Atlantic Slave Trade,* 136–137.
183. Klein, *Atlantic Slave Trade,* 141–142.
184. Klein, *Atlantic Slave Trade,* 98–99. David Richardson, "Costs of Survival," *Explorations in Economic History* 24:2 (1987), 178–196. P.C. Emmer, *De Nederlandse slavenhandel 1500–1850* (Amsterdam, Antwerpen: De Arbeiderspers, 2000), 178.
185. Hair, "Protestants as Pirates," 217.
186. Martin A. Klein, "The Slave Trade and Decentralized Societies," *Journal of African History* 42:1 (2001), 49–65: 59.
187. David Eltis and Lawrence C. Jennings, "Trade between Western Africa and the Atlantic World in the Pre-Colonial Era," *American Historical Review* 93:4 (October 1988), 936–959: 942.
188. See for opposing views of the European impact: Patrick Manning, *Slavery, Colonialism and Economic Growth in Dahomey, 1640–1960* (Cambridge: Cambridge University Press, 1982), 226; and Law, *Slave Coast of West Africa,* 220.
189. British North America and the United States received well over half a million African slaves compared to well over 4 million Africans who were sent to Brazil, and more than 1.6 million who were shipped to Spanish America, the French Caribbean, and the British Caribbean each.
190. Klein, *Atlantic Slave Trade,* 210–211.
191. Klein, *Atlantic Slave Trade,* 162.
192. Philip D. Morgan, *Slave Counterpoint: Black Culture in the Eighteenth-Century Chesapeake and Lowcountry* (Chapel Hill and London: University of North Carolina Press, 1998), 271–272. Cf. Karl Jacoby, "Slaves by Nature? Domestic Animals and Human Slaves," *Slavery and Abolition: A Journal of Slave and Post-Slave Studies* 15:1 (April 1994), 89–99.
193. Michael A. Gomez, *Exchanging our Country Marks: The Transformation of African Identities in the Colonial and Antebellum South* (Chapel Hill and London: The University of North Carolina Press, 1998), 15. Judith A. Carney, *Black Rice: The African Origins of Rice Cultivation in the Americas* (Cambridge: Harvard University Press, 2001).
194. Claire Robertson, "Africa into the Americas? Slavery and Women, the Family, and the Gender Division of Labor," in *More than Chattel: Black Women and Slavery in the Americas,* David Barry Gaspar and Darlene Clark Hine, eds. (Bloomington and Indianapolis: Indiana University Press, 1996), 3–40: 18–19.
195. Ira Berlin, *Many Thousands Gone: The First Two Centuries of Slavery in North America* (Cambridge, Mass. and London: The Belknap Press of Harvard University Press, 1998), 104–105. David Northrup, "Igbo and Myth Igbo: Culture and Ethnicity in the Atlantic World, 1600–1850," *Slavery and Abolition: A Journal of Slave and Post-Slave Studies* 21:3 (December 2000), 1–20.
196. William D. Piersen, *Black Yankees: The Development of an Afro-American Subculture in Eighteenth Century New England* (Amherst: University of Massachusetts Press, 1988), 117–128. Thornton, *Africa and Africans,* 202–203. Berlin, *Many Thousands Gone,* 191–192. Elizabeth W. Kiddy, "Who Is the King of Congo? A New Look at African and Afro-Brazilian Kings in Brazil," in *Central Africans and Cultural Transformations in the American Diaspora,* Linda M. Heywood, ed. (Cambridge: Cambridge University Press, 2002), 153–182.
197. Mary Turner, "Religious beliefs," in *General History of the Caribbean,* Volume III: The slave societies of the Caribbean, Franklin W. Knight, ed. (London and Basingstoke: UNESCO Publishing/MacMillan Education, 1997), 287–321: 289.

198. Turner, "Religious beliefs," 294, 297, 306, 310, 315.
199. G. Debien, "Le marronage aux Antilles françaises au XVIIIe siècle." *Caribbean Studies* 5:3 (October 1966), 3–43: 3, 7.
200. In that year, 87,800 slaves and 24,000 maroons were counted: Acosta Saignes, Miguel, *Acción y utopia del hombre de las dificultades* (Havana: Casa de las Américas, 1977), 44.
201. See for the complexity of this rebellion: David Geggus, "The Haitian Revolution," in Beckles and Shepherd, *Caribbean Slave Society and Economy,* 402–418. The best monograph is: Carolyn E. Fick, *The Making of Haiti: The Saint Domingue Revolution from Below* (Knoxville: The University Press, 1990).
202. John K. Thornton, ""I Am the Subject of the King of Congo": African Political Ideology and the Haitian Revolution," *Journal of World History* 4:2 (1993), 181–214.
203. Jan Pachonski and Reuel K. Wilson, *Poland's Caribbean Tragedy: A Study of Polish Legions in the Haitian War of Independence 1802–1803* (Boulder: East European Monographs, distributed by New York: Columbia University Press, 1986).
204. The total death toll for European soldiers in the Caribbean in the period 1791–1815 has been estimated at 180,000. David Patrick Geggus, "Slavery, War, and Revolution in the Greater Caribbean, 1789–1815," in *A Turbulent Time: The French Revolution and the Greater Caribbean,* David Barry Gaspar and David Patrick Geggus, eds. (Bloomington and Indianapolis: Indiana University Press, 1997), 1–50: 25.
205. Horst Pietschmann, "Geschichte der europäischen Expansion-Geschichte des atlantischen Raumes–Globalgeschichte," in *Überseegeschichte. Berichte der jüngeren Forschung,* Thomas Beck, Horst Gründer, Horst Pietschmann, and Roderich Ptak, eds. (Stuttgart: Franz Steiner Verlag, 1999), 21–39: 30–31. Eltis, *Rise of African Slavery,* 280.
206. Edmund S. Morgan, "Those Sexy Puritans," *The New York Review of Books* 49:11 (June 27, 2002), 15–16.
207. François Furet, "De l'homme sauvage à l'homme historique: l'expérience américaine dans la culture française," in *La Révolution américaine et l'Europe. 21–25 février 1978, Paris-Toulouse,* Claude Fohlen and Jacques Léon Godechot, eds. (Paris: Éditions du Centre National de la Recherche Scientifique, 1979), 91–105. Cf. Susan Dunn, *Sister Revolutions: French Lightning, American Light* (New York: Faber and Faber, 1999).
208. Merrill D. Peterson, *Adams and Jefferson: A Revolutionary Dialogue* (Oxford: Oxford University Press, 1978), 46–47.
209. Ulrich Im Hof, *The Enlightenment. An Historical Introduction,* translated by William E. Yuill (Oxford and Malden, Mass.: Blackwell, 1994), 246.
210. Kenneth Maxwell, "The impact of the American Revolution on Spain and Portugal and their empires," in *The Blackwell Encyclopedia of the American Revolution,* Jack P. Greene and J.R. Pole, eds. (Cambridge, Mass. and Oxford: Blackwell, 1991), 528–543: 529–530. D.A.G. Waddell, "International politics and the Independence of Latin America," in *The Independence of Latin America,* Leslie Bethell, ed. (Cambridge: Cambridge University Press, 1987), 195–226: 197–204. Leslie Bethell, "The Independence of Brazil," in Bethell, *The Independence of Latin America,* 155–194: 169.
211. Simon Collier, *Ideas and Politics of Chilean Independence, 1808–1833* (Cambridge: Cambridge University Press, 1967), 203. *Biblioteca de Mayo. Colección de obras y documentos para la historia argentina* (Buenos Aires: Senado de la Nación, 1960), 6345, 6831, 6411.
212. Simón Bolívar, *Obras completas,* Vicente Lecuna ed. (3 vols., 2nd ed., Havana: Editorial Lex 1950), III: 685.
213. David Bushnell, *The Santander Regime in Gran Colombia* (Westport: Greenwood Press, 1970): 18. David Bushnell, "El ejemplo norteamericano y la generación colombiana de la independencia," *Boletín de Historia y Antigüedades* 63 (1976), 359–369: 366. Peggy K. Liss, *Atlantic Empires: The Network of Trade and Revolution, 1713–1826* (Baltimore and London: The Johns Hopkins University Press, 1983), 206,

208. José Luis Romero, "La independencia de Hispanoamérica y el modelo político norteamericano," *Inter-American Review of Bibliography* 26 (1976), 429–455: 447. O. Carlos Stoetzer, *El pensamiento político en la América española durante el período de la Emancipación (1789–1825)* (2 vols., Madrid: Instituto de Estudios Políticos, 1966), II, 68, 162.

214. Javier Ocampo López, *La independencia de los Estados Unidos de América y su proyección en Hispanoamérica. El modelo norteamericano y su repercusión en la independencia de Colombia. Estudio a través de la folletería de la independencia de Colombia* (Caracas: Instituto Panamericano de Geografía e Historia, 1979), 63–82.

215. Lester D. Langley, *The Americas in the Age of Revolution, 1750–1850* (New Haven and London: Yale University Press, 1996), 23. Glenn Thomas Curry, "The disappearance of the resguardos indígenas of Cundinamarca, Colombia, 1800–1863," Ph.D. thesis, Vanderbilt University, 1981, 63. Eric Van Young, *The Other Rebellion: Popular Violence, Ideology, and the Mexican Struggle for Independence, 1810–1821* (Stanford: Stanford University Press, 2001).

216. Miguel Izard, *El miedo a la revolución. La lucha por la libertad en Venezuela (1777–1830)* (Madrid: Editorial Tecnos, 1979).

217. Andrew Jackson O'Shaughnessy, *An Empire Divided: The American Revolution and the British Caribbean* (Philadelphia: University of Pennsylvania Press, 2000), 50–51, 76. Jorge I. Domínguez, *Insurrection or Loyalty: The Breakdown of the Spanish American Empire* (Cambridge, Mass. and London: Harvard University Press, 1980), 161. Likewise, the existence of a large slave and free black and mulatto population in Brazil helps to explain why the white elite was willing, for so long, to remain under colonial rule.

218. Eric Williams, *Capitalism and Slavery* (London: Andre Deutsch, 1964. Original edition, 1944), 52.

219. Kenneth Morgan, *Slavery, Atlantic Trade and the British Economy, 1660–1800* (Cambridge: Cambridge University Press, 2000), 28.

220. David Richardson, "The Slave Trade, Sugar, and British Economic Growth, 1748–1776," *Journal of Interdisciplinary History* 17 (1987), 739–769: 741.

221. Eltis, *Rise of African Slavery*, 265.

222. Williams, *Capitalism and Slavery*, 99–102.

223. Robin Blackburn, *The Making of New World Slavery: From the Baroque to the Modern 1492–1800* (London and New York: Verso, 1997), 547–548. Morgan, *Slavery, Atlantic Trade*, 59.

224. James Walvin, *England, Slaves and Freedom, 1776–1838* (Jackson: University of Mississippi Press, 1986), 97–100.

Life on the Margins: Boston's Anxieties of Influence in the Atlantic World by Mark A. Peterson

1. John Winthrop, "A Modell of Christian Charity," in *The Winthrop Papers*, 6 vols. to date (Boston: Massachusetts Historical Society, 1929–): 2: 295.

2. Alan Heimert, and Andrew Delbanco, eds., *The Puritans in America: A Narrative Anthology* (Cambridge: Harvard University Press, 1985), 7.

3. Christopher Hill, *God's Englishman: Oliver Cromwell and the English Revolution* (New York: Harper and Row, 1970), 158.

4. A Proclamation Giving Encouragement to such as shall Transplant themselves to Jamaica, 10 October 1655, in *British Royal Proclamations Relating to America, 1603–1783, American Antiquarian Society Transactions and Collections*, vol. 12 (Worcester: American Antiquarian Society, 1911): 96–100.

5. Winthrop, "Modell of Christian Charity," 283.

6. John Winthrop. Letter to his Wife, May 15, 1629. *In The Winthrop Papers*, 2: 91–92.

7. For an overview of the evolution of the concept of Atlantic history, see Bernard Bailyn, "The Idea of Atlantic History," *Itinerario* 20:1 (1996):19–44.

8. For an introduction to this process, see Patricia Seed, *Ceremonies of Possession in Europe's Conquest of the New World, 1492–1640* (New York: Cambridge University Press, 1995).

9. See Robin Blackburn, *The Making of New World Slavery: From the Baroque to the Modern, 1492–1800* (London: Verso, 1997); Philip D. Curtin, *The Rise and Fall of the Plantation Complex*, 2d ed. (Cambridge: Cambridge University Press, 1998); David Hancock, *Citizens of the World: London Merchants and the Integration of the British Atlantic Community, 1735–1785* (Cambridge: Cambridge University Press, 1995).

10. Exemplary studies include Paul Gilroy, *The Black Atlantic: Modernity and Double Consciousness* (Cambridge: Harvard University Press, 1993).

11. Thomas Hooker, *The Danger of Desertion* (1631) in George H. Williams, ed., *Thomas Hooker: Writings in England and Holland, 1626–1633* (Cambridge: Harvard University Press, 1975).

12. Kenneth Andrews, *Trade, Plunder, and Settlement: Maritime Enterprise and the Genesis of the British Empire, 1480–1630* (Cambridge: Cambridge University Press, 1984). For a brief overview of Stuart foreign policy, see J. P. Kenyon, *Stuart England* (New York: Penguin Books, 1978).

13. On the key geographical features of North America's relationship to the Atlantic world, see D.W. Meinig, *Atlantic America, 1492–1800* (New Haven: Yale University Press, 1986).

14. J. R. Jones, *The Anglo-Dutch Wars of the Seventeenth Century* (London: Longmans, 1996).

15. Neal Salisbury, *Manitou and Providence: Indians, Europeans, and the making of New England, 1500–1643* (New York: Oxford University Press, 1982).

16. The major exception to this generalization was the brief but bloody Pequot War of 1637, in which an alliance of English and native American warriors destroyed much of the Pequot nation, in a dispute that arose from conflicts precipitated by Dutch and English competition for the Connecticut River fur trade. See Alfred Cave, *The Pequot War* (Amherst: University of Massachusetts Press, 1996). On the origins of King Philip's War, see Francis Jennings, *The Invasion of America: Indians, Colonialism, and the Cant of Conquest* (New York: W. W. Norton, 1976); Douglas Leach, *Flintlock and Tomahawk: New England in King Philip's War* (New York: Macmillan, 1958); Jill Lepore, *The Name of War: King Philip's War and the Origins of American Identity* (New York: Alfred A. Knopf, 1998).

17. For a discussion of the imperial view of King Philip's War, see Stephen S. Webb, *1676: The End of American Independence* (Cambridge: Harvard University Press, 1985), 221–47.

18. Karen Ordahl Kupperman, *Providence Island, 1630–1641: The Other Puritan Colony* (New York: Cambridge University Press, 1993), 349–354.

19. On the rebellion against Andros and the Dominion of New England, see David S. Lovejoy, *The Glorious Revolution in America*, 2d ed. (Middletown, Conn.: Wesleyan University Press, 1987); Richard R. Johnson, *Adjustment to Empire: The New England Colonies, 1675–1715* (New Brunswick, N. J.: Rutgers University Press, 1981); Robert Earle Moody and Richard Clive Simmons, eds., *The Glorious Revolution in Massachusetts: Selected Documents, 1689–1692* (Boston: Colonial Society of Massachusetts; distributed by the University Press of Virginia, 1988).

20. Tony Claydon, *William III and the Godly Revolution* (Cambridge: Cambridge University Press, 1996); Stewart P. Oakley, *William III and the Northern Crowns during the Nine Years War, 1689–1697* (New York: Garland, 1987).

21. Cotton Mather, *Decennium Luctuosum* (Boston, 1699; reprint New York: Garland, 1978), provides a detailed and thoroughly biased account of the war from Puritan New England's perspective; for a modern account, see Philip S. Haffenden, *New England in the English Nation, 1689–1713* (Oxford: Clarendon Press, 1974).

22. Thomas Prince, *Extraordinary Events, the Doings of God . . .* (Boston, 1745).
23. Fred Anderson, *Crucible of War: The Seven Years War and the Fate of Empire in British North America, 1754–1766* (New York: Alfred A. Knopf, 2000).
24. Thomas Barnard, *A Sermon Preached Before His Excellency, Francis Bernard* (Boston, 1763).
25. The scholarly literature on the revolutionary transformation of Boston is vast, but some prominent titles include Bernard Bailyn, *The Ordeal of Thomas Hutchinson* (Cambridge: Harvard University Press, 1974); Benjamin Labaree, *The Boston Tea Party* (New York: Oxford University Press, 1964); Pauline Maier, *From Resistance to Revolution* (New York: Alfred A. Knopf, 1972); Edmund Morgan and Helen Morgan, *The Stamp Act Crisis* (Chapel Hill: University of North Carolina Press, 1953); Hiller B. Zobel, *The Boston Massacre* (New York: W. W. Norton, 1970). For an interesting transatlantic perspective, see Philip McFarland, *The Brave Bostonians: Hutchinson, Quincy, Franklin, and the Coming of the American Revolution* (Boulder: Westview Press, 1998).
26. John R. McNeill, *Atlantic Empires of France and Spain: Louisbourg and Havana, 1700–1763* (Chapel Hill: University of North Carolina Press, 1985).
27. On geography and economic development, see Meinig, *Atlantic America*, Part Two, 79–256.
28. For a popular history of the cod fisheries, see Mark Kurlansky, *Cod: A Biography of the Fish that Changed the World* (New York: Walker and Co., 1997).
29. For a later reiteration of Winthrop's social philosophy, see Cotton Mather, *Theopolis Americana: An Essay upon the Golden Street of the Holy City* (Boston, 1710).
30. Bernard Bailyn, "The Apologia of Robert Keayne," *William and Mary Quarterly*, 3d ser., 7 (1950): 568–87; Stephen Innes, "The Ethics of Exchange, Price Controls, and Robert Keayne," in *Creating the Commonwealth: The Economic Culture of Puritan New England* (New York: W.W. Norton, 1995), 160–191.
31. M. Halsey Thomas, ed., *The Diary of Samuel Sewall, 1674–1729*, 2 vols. (New York: Farrar, Straus, and Giroux, 1973), 2, 637–38; Mark A. Peterson, *The Price of Redemption: The Spiritual Economy of Puritan New England* (Stanford, Ca.: Stanford University Press, 1997), 87–88.
32. Samuel Eliot Morison, "John Hull of Boston, Goldsmith," in *Builders of the Bay Colony*, rev. ed. (Boston: Houghton Mifflin, 1958): 135–182.
33. Jr., Robert F. Dalzell, *Enterprising Elite: The Boston Associates and the World They Made* (New York: W.W. Norton, 1993).
34. Winthrop, "A Modell of Christian Charity," 284.
35. See G. B. Warden, *Boston, 1689–1776* (Boston: Little, Brown, 1970): 53–54, 76–77, 106–7, 117–21; Gary Nash, *The Urban Crucible: The Northern Seaports and the Origins of the American Revolution*, abridged ed. (Cambridge: Harvard University Press, 1986): 82–84; Cotton Mather, *Lex Mercatoria: or, The Just Rules of Commerce Declared* (Boston, 1705); Benjamin Colman, *Some Reasons and Arguments . . . for the setting up of Markets in Boston* (Boston, 1719).
36. Abram English Brown, *Faneuil Hall and Faneuil Hall Market, or, Peter Faneuil and His Gift* (Boston: Lee and Shepard, 1900).
37. My interpretation of the market controversies in Boston is informed by Sharon Rodgers, "Boston and the Atlantic World: One City's Dilemma," an unpublished paper presented at the International Seminar on the History of the Atlantic World, Harvard University, August, 1999, and by the seminar participants' discussion.
38. Samuel Sewall, *The Selling of Joseph: A Memorial* (Boston, 1700).
39. John Saffin, John Usher, Edward Shippen, James Whetcombe, and Andrew Belcher to William Welstead, 12 June 1681, in *The Jeffries Papers*, vol. 2, no. 149, ms. Massachusetts Historical Society, Boston.
40. George H. Moore, *Notes on the History of Slavery in Massachusetts* (New York: D. Appleton & Co., 1866): 48–50; Lorenzo Greene, *The Negro in Colonial New England* (New York: Atheneum, 1968): 79–95.

41. Jay Coughtry, *The Notorious Triangle: Rhode Island and the African Slave Trade, 1700–1807* (Philadelphia: Temple University Press, 1981).

42. *The Winthrop Papers*, 5, 38–39, 42–45.

43. Bernard Bailyn, *The New England Merchants in the Seventeenth Century* (Cambridge: Harvard University Press, 1955); Greene, *The Negro in Colonial New England.*

44. Sewall, *The Selling of Joseph.*

45. Joanne Pope Melish, *Disowning Slavery: Gradual Emancipation and "Race" in New England, 1780–1860* (Ithaca: Cornell University Press, 1998).

46. Edward G. Gray, *New World Babel: Languages and Nations in Early America* (Princeton: Princeton University Press, 1999).

47. Richard White, *The Middle Ground: Indians, Empires, and Republics in the Great Lakes Region, 1650–1815* (Cambridge: Cambridge University Press, 1991): 50. On "marchlands," see Bernard Bailyn, *The Peopling of British North America, An Introduction* (New York: Alfred A. Knopf, 1986):112ff.

48. Joseph Roach, *Cities of the Dead: Circum-Atlantic Performance* (New York: Columbia University Press, 1996).

49. Bailyn, *The Peopling of British North America*, 91–95; Virginia Anderson, *New England's Generation: The Great Migration and the Formation of Society and Culture in the Seventeenth Century* (Cambridge: Cambridge University Press, 1991).

50. Richard W. Cogley, *John Eliot's Mission to the Indians before King Philip's War* (Cambridge: Harvard University Press, 1999).

51. On New England Puritanism in transatlantic context, see Stephen Foster, *The Long Argument: English Puritanism and the Shaping of New England Culture, 1570–1700* (Chapel Hill: University of North Carolina Press, 1991); Francis J. Bremer, *Congregational Communion: Clerical Friendship in the Anglo-American Puritan Community, 1610–1692* (Boston: Northeastern University Press, 1994).

52. Jean-Christophe Agnew, *Worlds Apart: The Market and the Theater in Anglo-American Thought, 1550–1750* (Cambridge: Cambridge University Press, 1986).

53. Samuel Sewall to Isaac Addington, March 2, 1714, in *The Letter Book of Samuel Sewall*, 2 vols., Massachusetts Historical Society, *Collections*, 6th series, vols. 1–2 (Boston, 1886–88), II: 29–30.

54. T. A. Milford, "Boston's Theater Controversy and Liberal Notions of Advantage," *New England Quarterly* 72 (1999): 61–88.

55. For examples of two representative documents in this extended "moment," see Jonathan Belcher, *A Journal of My Intended Voyage and Journey to Holland, Hannover, &c*, July 8, 1704 to October 5, 1704, Ms., Massachusetts Historical Society, Boston, Massachusetts; Cotton Mather, *India Christiana* (Boston, 1721). For a general overview, see Mark A. Peterson, "The Selling of Joseph: Bostonians, Anti-Slavery, and the Protestant International," paper presented at the Organization of American Historians Annual Meeting, St. Louis, Missouri, April 2000; and Peterson, "Boston's 'Dutch' Moment: A Passage in the Shaping of Atlantic Aspirations, 1688–1733," paper presented at "Sometimes an Art," a symposium in celebration of Bernard Bailyn, Harvard University, May 2000.

56. Jon Butler, *The Huguenots in America: A Refugee People in New World Society* (Cambridge: Harvard University Press, 1983).

57. General accounts of the smallpox crisis of 1721–22 include Ola Elizabeth Winslow, *A Destroying Angel: The Conquest of Smallpox in Colonial Boston* (Boston: Houghton Mifflin, 1974); John B. Blake, *Public Health in the Town of Boston, 1630–1822* (Cambridge: Harvard University Press, 1959): 52–98; Perry Miller, *The New England Mind: From Colony to Province* (Cambridge: Harvard University Press, 1953): 345–366; Kenneth Silverman, *The Life and Times of Cotton Mather* (New York: Columbia University Press, 1985): 336–363. My own account of the crisis is drawn from these sources, and from the primary documents cited below.

58. Blake, *Public Health in Boston*, 54–55.

59. See Cotton Mather, *The Angel of Bethesda: An Essay upon the Common Maladies of Mankind*, Gordon W. Jones, ed. (Barre, Massachusetts: American Antiquarian Society,

1972), 107–112, for Mather's own account of the practice, including his ill-considered imitation of African dialect in recounting his slave's description of the process.

60. Emmanuel Timoni, "An Account, or History, of the Procuring the Small Pox by Incision, or Inoculation: as It Has for Some Time Been Practised at Constantinople," Royal Society of London, *Philosophical Transactions*, No. 339, XXIX (1714): 72; and Jacobus Pylarini, "Nova & Tuta Variolas Excitandi per Transplantationem Methodus, Nuper Inventa & in Usum Tracta," Royal Society, *Philosophical Transactions*, No. 347, XXIX (1716): 393–399.

61. Silverman, *Life and Times of Cotton Mather*, 264–265, 339.

62. Mather agonized in his diaries over whether and when to circulate his ideas on treating smallpox; see Cotton Mather, *Diary*, 2 vols., Massachusetts Historical Society, *Collections*, 7th series, vols. 7–8 (Boston, 1911–12) II: 620–629. Zabdiel Boylston published his own account of the events, *An Historical Account of the Small Pox Inoculated in New England* (London, 1726, reprinted Boston, 1730).

63. See *The New England Courant*, August 7, 14, 1721, and the *Boston Newsletter*, July 24, 1721. Douglass published a more sober critique of the Mather-Boylston method in *The Inoculation of the Smallpox as Practised in Boston* (1722).

64. Silverman, *Life and Times of Cotton Mather*, 350.

65. C. Mather, "The Way of Proceeding in the Small Pox Inoculated in New England," Royal Society, *Philosophical Transactions*, no. 370, XXXI (1722): 34.

66. Charles Maitland, *Mr. Maitland's Account of Inoculating the Small Pox Vindicated*, 2d ed., (London, 1722); Silverman, 352; Genevieve Miller, "Smallpox Inoculation in England and America: A Reappraisal," *William and Mary Quarterly*, 3d ser., 13 (1956): 476–492, evaluates the impact of the Mather-Boylston experiments on English practice.

Lisbon as a Strategic Haven in the Atlantic World
by Timothy Walker

1. In Portuguese, *Rio Tejo*.

2. Harold Livermore, *A New History of Portugal*, 2nd ed. (London: Cambridge University Press, 1976), 12–40.

3. Dava Sobel and William J. H. Andrewes, *The Illustrated Longitude* (New York: Walker & Co., 1998), diagram, 16.

4. Livermore, *New History*, 11 (although this name was first applied to the northern part of the country and the city of Oporto).

5. Joaquim Verrisimo Serrão, *História de Portugal*, Vol. VI (1750–1807) (Lisboa: Editorial Verbo, 1982), 398–400.

6. Vitor Serrão, *Lisboa Manerista* (Lisboa: Editora Verbo, 1998), 195–205.

7. A. J. R. Russell-Wood, "Portugal and the World in the Age of Dom João V," in *The Age of Baroque in Portugal*, Jay A. Levenson, ed. (New Haven: Yale University Press, 1993), 20.

8. Ibidem.

9. A. H. de Oliveira Marques, *History of Portugal*, 2 vols. (New York and London: Columbia University Press, 1972), I:165–168.

10. V. M. Godinho, "Portugal and Her Empire, 1680–1720," in *The New Cambridge Modern History*, J. S. Bromley, ed. (London: Cambridge University Press, 1970), VI: 533–536.

11. Kenneth Maxwell, *Pombal, Paradox of the Enlightenment* (Cambridge: Cambridge University Press, 1995), 131–132.

12. Godinho, "Portugal and Her Empire," 533–536.

13. Ibidem.

14. Kenneth Maxwell, "Eighteenth-Century Portugal: Faith and Reason, Tradition and Innovation During a Golden Age," in Levenson, *Age of Baroque*, 126–127.

15. Ibidem, 112.
16. David Francis, *Portugal, 1715–1808: Joanine, Pombaline and Rococo Portugal as seen by British Diplomats and Traders* (London: Tamesis Books, Ltd., 1985), chapters 4 and 5.
17. A.J.R. Russell-Wood, *A World on the Move: The Portuguese in Africa, Asia and America, 1415–1808* (Manchester, U.K.: Carcanet Press, 1992), 27–57.
18. Ibidem.
19. Ibidem.
20. H. E. S. Fisher, *The Portugal Trade* (London: Methuen & Company, 1971), 42.
21. Godinho, "Portugal and Her Empire," 509–515.
22. Ibidem, 536.
23. Ibidem, 509–510.
24. Ibidem.
25. Russell-Wood, "Portugal and the World in the Age of Dom João V," 27.
26. Maxwell, "Eighteenth-Century Portugal," 105–107.
27. Serrão, *História de Portugal*, 232–235, 428–429.
28. Douglas L. Wheeler, *Historical Dictionary of Portugal* (Metuchen, N.J.: The Scarecrow Press, 1993), 126–127.
29. Maxwell, "Eighteenth-Century Portugal," 106.
30. Timothy Walker, "Demands of Empire: The Portuguese Reaction to the American War of Independence (Early Trade Considerations and Diplomatic Relations between Portugal and the United States, 1750–1800)," Harvard University: Papers of the International Seminar on the History of the Atlantic World, August 1997, 6.
31. David Hancock, "'A revolution in trade': wine distribution and the development of the infrastructure of the Atlantic market economy, 1703–1807," in *The Early Modern Atlantic Economy*, John J. McCusker and Kenneth Morgan, eds. (Cambridge: Cambridge University Press, 2000), 105–153: 114: Table 5.2. A Madeira pipe equaled 110 gallons.
32. *Gazeta de Lisboa*, 6 January 1789; 18 January 1791; 26 March 1799.

Adventurers Across the Atlantic: English Migration to the New World, 1580–1780 by Meaghan N. Duff

1. Marcus Lee Hansen, *The Atlantic Migration, 1607–1860* (Cambridge: Harvard University Press, 1940), 3–52.
2. Numerous local studies produced in the 1970s and early 1980s posit that English communities were strikingly fluid while colonial communities were remarkably stable and cohesive, especially in their early generations. On early modern English society see Keith Wrightson's synthesis in *English Society, 1580–1680* (New Brunswick: Rutgers University Press, 1982). For reviews of scholarship on seventeenth-century America see John Murrin, "Review Article," *History and Theory, 2* (1972): 226–75, and James Henretta, "The Morphology of New England Society," *Journal of Interdisciplinary History, 2* (1971–72): 379–98.
3. Bernard Bailyn, "Introduction: Europeans on the Move, 1500–1800," in *Europeans on the Move: Studies on European Migration, 1500–1800*, Nicholas Canny, ed. (Oxford: Clarendon Press, 1994), 1–2.
4. This essay considers the voluntary and forced migration of British peoples to North America exclusively. For a comparative discussion of the transatlantic movement of Africans and Europeans see David Eltis, "Free and Coerced Transatlantic Migrations: Some Comparisons," *American Historical Review* 88:2 (1983): 251–280.
5. Russell R. Menard, "British Migration to the Chesapeake Colonies in the Seventeenth Century," in *Colonial Chesapeake Society*, Lois Green Carr, Philip D. Morgan, and Jean B. Russo, eds. (Chapel Hill: University of North Carolina Press, 1988), 131. Allan Kulikoff, *From British Peasants to Colonial American Farmers* (Chapel Hill: The University of North Carolina Press, 2000), 40–41.

6. Seymour Phillips, "The Medieval Background," in Canny, *Europeans on the Move,* 9–10. Phillips specifically notes the Viking discoveries, "the creation of trade links between regions as far apart as Ireland and Russia and the Caspian Sea by merchants and raiders from Scandinavia," and "the revival in international trade centered on the Mediterranean and led by Italian cities such as Genoa, Pisa, Venice, and Amalfi."

7. Ibid., 20–22.

8. Ibid., 23–25.

9. Wrightson, *English Society,* 41–44.

10. Kulikoff, *From British Peasants to Colonial American Farmers,* 22–23. For a further explanation of rural servitude see Ann Kussmaul, *Servants in Husbandry in Early Modern England* (Cambridge: Cambridge University Press, 1981).

11. Ibid., 26.

12. Allan Kulikoff, "Migration and Cultural Diffusion in Early America, 1600–1860: A Review Essay," *Historical Methods,* 19 (Fall 1986):156.

13. Nicholas Canny, "England's New World and the Old, 1480s to 1630s," in *The Origins of Empire: British Overseas Enterprise to the Close of the Seventeenth Century,* Nicholas Canny, ed. (New York: Oxford University Press, 1998), 149–50.

14. Kulikoff, *From British Peasants to Colonial American Farmers,* 40–41.

15. Nicholas Canny, "English Migration into and across the Atlantic during the Seventeenth and Eighteenth Centuries," in Canny, *Europeans on the Move,* 63–65; Henry A. Gemery, "Emigration from the British Isles to the New World: Inferences from Colonial Populations," *Research in Economic History,* 5 (1980): 196–98, 215; Menard, "British Migration," 102–105; James Horn, *Adapting to a New World: English Society in the Seventeenth-Century Chesapeake* (Chapel Hill: The University of North Carolina Press, 1994): 24–25; Richard S. Dunn, *Sugar and Slaves: The Rise of the Planter Class in the English West Indies, 1624–1713* (Chapel Hill: The University of North Carolina Press, 1972): 55.

16. James Horn, "Tobacco Colonies: The Shaping of English Society in the Seventeenth-Century Chesapeake," in Canny, *Origins of Empire,* 176–177.

17. Ibid.,177–179.

18. Kulikoff, *From British Peasants to Colonial American Farmers,* 20–21, 57. Kulikoff describes yeomen as small landowners or tenants renting substantial farms from gentlemen. They typically cultivated fifty to hundred acres and some built estates worth £100 to £200.

19. Ibid., 56–57.

20. Horn, "Tobacco Colonies," 182.

21. Ibid., 182–183.

22. Kulikoff, *From British Peasants to Colonial American Farmers,* 63.

23. Ibid., 66; Virginia DeJohn Anderson, *New England's Generation: The Great Migration and the Formation of Society and Culture in the Seventeenth Century* (New York: Cambridge University Press, 1991): 19.

24. Stephen Innes, *Creating the Commonwealth: The Economic Culture of Puritan New England* (New York: W.W. Norton, 1995): 23; Jim Potter, "Demographic Development and Family Structure," in *Colonial British America: Essays in the New History of the Early Modern Era,* Jack P. Greene and J.R. Pole, eds. (Baltimore: The Johns Hopkins University Press, 1984): 134–136.

25. David Cressy, *Coming Over: Migration and Communication Between England and New England in the Seventeenth Century* (New York: Cambridge University Press, 1987); John Frederick Martin, *Profits in the Wilderness: Entrepreneurship and the Founding of New England Towns in the Seventeenth Century* (Chapel Hill: The University of North Carolina Press, 1991); Canny, "English Migration," 41–42, 50. See also H.A. Gemery, "Emigration from the British Isles to the New World, 1630–1700: Inferences from Colonial Populations," *Research in Economic History,* 5 (1980): 179–231.

26. Hilary McD. Beckles, "The 'Hub of Empire': The Caribbean and Britain in the Seventeenth Century," in Canny, *Origins of Empire,* 222.

27. Ibid., 223.
28. Ibid., 227.
29. James Horn, "British Diaspora: Emigration from Britain, 1680–1815," in *The Eighteenth Century*, P.J. Marshall, ed. (New York: Oxford University Press, 1998), 31. See also *Europeans on the Move,* Canny, 39–149; Henry A. Gemery, "European Emigration to North America, 1700–1820: Numbers and Quasi-Numbers," *Perspectives in American History,* 1 (1984): 283–342; and Aaron Fogelman, "Migrations to the American Colonies," *Journal of Interdisciplinary History,* 32 (Spring 1992): 691–709.
30. Marianne Wokeck, "German and Irish Immigration to Colonial Philadelphia," in *The Demographic History of the Philadelphia Region, 1600–1800,* S.E. Kleep, ed. (Philadelphia: American Philosophical Society, 1989): 128–144. See also A.G. Roeber, " 'The Origin of Whatever Is Not English among Us': The Dutch-speaking and the German-speaking Peoples of Colonial British America," in *Strangers Within the Realm: Cultural Margins of the First British Empire*, Bernard Bailyn and Philip D. Morgan, eds. (Chapel Hill: University of North Carolina Press, 1991), 220–283.
31. Ned C Landsman, "The Middle Colonies: New Opportunities for Settlement, 1660–1700," in Canny, *Origins of Empire,* 373.
32. Bernard Bailyn, *Voyagers to the West: A Passage in the Peopling of America on the Eve of Revolution* (New York: Vintage Books, 1986), 126–203.
33. Ibid., 147–166.
34. A. Roger Ekirch, *Bound for America: The Transportation of British Convicts to the Colonies, 1718–1775* (New York: Oxford University Press, 1987), 22–24, 112–114.
35. Horn, "British Diaspora," 30; Canny, "English Migration," 50.
36. Examples of these competing interpretations abound. Two comprehensive works which illustrate these approaches are D.W. Meinig, *The Shaping of America: A Geographical Perspective on 500 Years of History, Volume I: Atlantic America, 1492–1800* (New Haven: Yale University Press, 1986); and David Hackett Fischer, *Albion's Seed: Four British Folkways in America* (New York: Oxford University Press, 1989).
37. Kulikoff, "Migration and Cultural Diffusion," 158.
38. Alison Games, *Migration and the Origins of the English Atlantic World* (Cambridge: Harvard University Press, 1999), 191.

Searching for Prosperity: German Migration to the British American Colonies, 1680–1780 by Rosalind J. Beiler

1. "Ein kortzer bericht von Caspar Wistar," Wistar Family Papers, Historical Society of Pennsylvania, Philadelphia, Pa. (hereafter "A Short Report," HSP).
2. "A Short Report," HSP. For descriptions of transatlantic journeys, see "Diary of the Rev. Samuel Guldin, Relating to His Journey to Pennsylvania, June to September, 1710," *Journal of the Presbyterian Historical Society* 14 (1930): 28–41, 64–73; R. W. Kelsey, ed., trans., "An Early Description of Pennsylvania: Letter of Christopher Sower. Written in 1724, Describing Conditions in Philadelphia and Vicinity, and the Sea Voyage from Europe," *Pennsylvania Magazine of History and Biography* 45 (1921): 243–54; Gottlieb Mittelberger, *Gottlieb Mittelberger's Journey to Pennsylvania in the Year 1710 and Return to Germany in the Year 1754.* Translated and Edited by Oscar Handlin and John Clive. (Cambridge, Mass.: University of Harvard Press, 1960.)
3. "A Short Report," HSP.
4. Georg Fertig, *Lokales Leben, atlantische Welt: Die Entscheidung zur Auswanderung vom Rhein nach Nordamerika im 18. Jahrhundert* (Osnabrück: Universitätsverlag Rasch, 2000): 69–80; and "Transatlantic Migration from German-Speaking Parts of Central Europe, 1600–1800: Proportions, Structures, and Explanations," in *Europeans on the Move: Studies on European Migration, 1500–1800*, Nicholas Canny, ed. (Oxford: Clarendon Press: 1994): 196–203. Fertig summarizes and revises the work of previous historians, especially Marianne Wokeck, *Trade in Strangers: The Beginnings of*

Mass Migration to North America (University Park, Pa.: Penn State University Press, 1999); and Aaron Fogleman, "Progress and Possibilities in Migration Studies: The Contributions of Werner Hacker to the Study of Early German Migration to Pennsylvania," *Pennsylvania History* 56 (1989): 318–329; and "Migrations to the Thirteen British North American Colonies, 1700–1775: New Estimates," *Journal of Interdisciplinary History* 22 (1992): 691–709.

5. Wokeck, *Trade in Strangers,* 1–7.
6. Fertig, *Lokales Leben,* 65–81; Aaron Fogleman, *Hopeful Journeys: German Immigration, Settlement, and Political Culture in Colonial America, 1717–1775* (Philadelphia: University of Pennsylvania Press, 1996): 15–28; Wokeck, *Trade in Strangers,* 1–23.
7. William I. Hull, *William Penn and the Dutch Quaker Migration to Pennsylvania* (Philadelphia: Patterson and White, 1935): 178–258; Richard MacMaster, *Land, Piety, Peoplehood: The Establishment of Mennonite Communities in America, 1683–1790* (Scottdale, Pa.: The Herald Press, 1985): 88–110; Fogleman, *Hopeful Journeys,* 4–11, suggests a different periodization for German immigration. Two significant factors differentiate his categories from Wokeck's: he divides migration into periods based on the immigrants motives for leaving, and he includes immigrants to all colonies rather than focusing exclusively on Pennsylvania. While I have chosen to use Wokeck's breakdown, Fogleman's examination of motivations is particularly helpful in understanding those who arrived between 1683 and the 1720s.
8. For a recent study of the New York immigrants, see Philip Otterness, "The Unattained Canaan: The 1709 Palatine Migration and the Formation of German Society in Colonial America" (Ph.D. Dissertation, University of Iowa, 1996). See also Walter Knittle, *Early Eighteenth Century Palatine Emigration: A British Government Redemptioner Project to Manufacture Naval Stores* (Philadelphia: Dorrance and Company, 1937).
9. Wokeck, *Trade in Strangers,* 40–42; Marianne Wokeck, "The Flow and the Composition of German Immigration to Philadelphia, 1727–1775," *Pennsylvania Magazine of History and Biography* 105 (1981): 249–278.
10. Fogleman, *Hopeful Journeys,* 28–35.
11. Wokeck, *Trade in Strangers,* 40–42; Wokeck, "Flow and Composition," 271–273. Fogleman, *Hopeful Journeys,* 6–11.
12. Fogleman, *Hopeful Journeys,* 8–11.
13. Daniel B. Thorp, *The Moravian Community in Colonial North Carolina: Pluralism on the Southern Frontier* (Knoxville, Tenn.: University of Tennessee Press, 1989); George Jones, *The Georgia Dutch: From the Rhine and Danube to the Savannah, 1733–1783* (Athens, Ga.: University of Georgia Press, 1992); A.G. Roeber, *Palatines, Liberty, and Property: German Lutherans in Colonial British America* (Baltimore: The Johns Hopkins University Press, 1993): 158–174.
14. Andreas Brink, *Die deutsche Auswanderungswelle in die britischen Nordamerikakolonien um die Mitte des 18. Jahrhunderts* (Stuttgart: Franz Steiner Verlag, 1993), 260–266; Fogleman, *Hopeful Journeys,* 6.
15. "A Short Report," HSP.
16. The responses are part of interviews government officials conducted with emigrants from Nassau-Weilburg. The original documents are in the Preussisches Staatsarchiv Wiesbaden, Bestand VI 1. Nassau-Weilburg, Gen. XIV c., Nr. 17. Microfilmed copies are in the Library of Congress, Manuscript Division. German transcriptions of the interviews are published in Julius Goebel, ed., "Neue Dokumente zur Geschichte der Massenauswanderung im Jahre 1709," *Deutsch-amerikanische Geschichtsblätter* 13 (1913): 181–201. Excerpts from the interviews are translated in Henry Z. Jones, *The Palatine Families of New York, 1710* (University City, Calif.: Henry Z. Jones, 1985): 1: iv–v.
17. Jones, *Palatine Families,*1: v.
18. *Some Account* is reprinted in Albert Cook Myers, ed., *Narratives in Early Pennsylvania, West New Jersey and Delaware, 1630–1707* (New York: C. Scribner's Sons, 1912); 202–215.

19. Myers, *Narratives,* 199–201. Richard S. Dunn, "Penny Wise and Pound Foolish: Penn as a Businessman," in *The World of William Penn,* Richard S. Dunn and Mary Maples Dunn, eds. (Philadelphia: University of Pennsylvania Press, 1986): 43; Gary Nash, *Quakers and Politics: Pennsylvania, 1681–1726* (Princeton: Princeton University Press, 1968; reprint 1993): 11–15; Sally Schwartz, *"A Mixed Multitude: The Struggle for Toleration in Colonial Pennsylvania"* (New York: New York University Press, 1987): 23–24; Hull, *William Penn,* 236.

20. For a summary of Pennsylvania's promotional literature, see Julius Sachse, "Pennsylvania: The German Influence in its Settlement and Development," *The Pennsylvania German Society Proceedings and Addresses* 14 (1905): 8–12. Facsimiles of the title pages for promotional literature are reprinted in an appendix in Julius Sachse, "Title Pages of Book and Pamphlets that Influenced German Emigration to Pennsylvania," *The Pennsylvania German Society Proceedings and Addresses* 7 (1897): 201–256.

21. The most influential of these was *Umständige Geographische Beschreibung Der zu allerletzt erfundenen Provintz Pensylvaniae, In denen End-Gräntzen Americae In der West-Welt gelegen Durch Franciscum Danielem Pastorium, J.U. Lic. und Friedens-Richtern daselbsten. Wobey angehecket sind einige notable Begebenheiten, und Bericht-Schreiben an dessen Herrn Vatern Melchiorem Adamum Pastorium Und andere gute Freunde,* published in 1700 and reprinted in translation in Myers, *Narratives,* 360–448. Pastorius' *Umständige Beschreibung* was usually bound together with a German translation of Gabriel Thomas' *Historical and Geographical Account of Pensilvania and of West-New-Jersey* (London, 1698), and Daniel Falkner's *Curieuse Nachricht.* Myers, *Narratives,* 359.

22. Julius Sachse, *Daniel Falkner's Curieuse Nachricht von Pensylvania: The Book that stimulated the Great German Emigration to Pennsylvania* (Lancaster, Pa.: The Society, 1905), 37.

23. Sachse, *Falkner's Curieuse Nachricht,* 23–28.

24. Knittle, *Palatine Emigration,* 14–19; Jones, *Palatine Families,* 1: 471–472; Introduction to reprint of Josua Kochertal, *Außführlich- und umständlicher Bericht von der berühmten Landschafft Carolina In den Engelländischen America gelegen* (Frankfurt, 1709); Philip Otterness, "The 'Poor Palatines' of 1709: The Origins and Characteristics of Early Modern Mass Migration," Working Paper No. 96–26, International Seminar on the History of the Atlantic World, 1500–1800, Harvard University, September 1996.

25. Myers, *Narratives,* 356.

26. Sachse, *Falkner's Curieuse Nachricht,* 22–25.

27. Knittle, *Palatine Emigration,* 14–19.

28. Bernard Bailyn, in *The Peopling of British North America: An Introduction* (New York: Vintage Books, 1986), 65–86, addresses the role of land speculators in luring settlers to the British colonies.

29. Myers, *Narratives,* 374.

30. Kochertal, *Außführlich- und umständlicher Bericht,* 10.

31. Sachse, *Falkner's Curieuse Nachricht,* 102–103.

32. Kochertal, *Außführlich- und umständlicher Bericht,* 12.

33. Sachse, *Falkner's Curieuse Nachricht,* 104–105.

34. Kochertal, *Außführlich- und umständlicher Bericht,* 12–13.

35. Rosalind J. Beiler, "The Transatlantic World of Caspar Wistar: From Germany to America in the Eighteenth Century," (Ph.D. Dissertation, University of Pennsylvania, 1994): 35–71; Wokeck, *Trade in Strangers,* 1–18. For first-hand accounts of the war's devastation, see Jones, *Palatine Families,* 1: i–ii.

36. Myers, *Narratives,* 436.

37. Myers, *Narratives,* 377.

38. Myers, *Narratives,* 437.

39. Beiler, "The Transatlantic World of Caspar Wistar," 72–132.

40. Kochertal, *Außführlich- und umständlicher Bericht,* 11.

41. Beiler, "The Transatlantic World of Caspar Wistar," 72–132. For discussions of the tensions between villagers and the state in the Kraichgau, see Fogleman, *Hopeful Journeys,* 36–65.
42. Myers, *Narratives,* 377.
43. Sachse, *Falkner's Curieuse Nachricht,* 201.
44. Kochertal, *Außführlich- und umständlicher Bericht,* 9–10.
45. Samuel W. Pennypacker, "The Settlement of Germantown, Pennsylvania and the Causes which led to it," *Historical and Biographical Sketches* (Philadelphia: R.A. Tripple, 1883): 17; Sachse, *Falkner's Curieuse Nachricht,* 31–43.
46. Rosalind J. Beiler, "Distributing Aid to Believers in Need: The Religious Foundations of Transatlantic Migration," *Pennsylvania History,* Special Supplemental Issue 64 (1997): 79–81.
47. Beiler, "Transatlantic World," 134–185.
48. Beiler, "Distributing Aid," 73–79; MacMaster, *Land, Piety, Peoplehood,* 33–49.
49. Beiler, "Distributing Aid," 79–87; MacMaster, *Land, Piety, Peoplehood,* 50–59.
50. Harold Bender, ed., "Palatinate Mennonite Census Lists, 1664–1774, I," *Mennonite Quarterly Review* 14 (1940): 14–15. See also "1706 Religionsverzeichnis," Badisches Generallandesarchiv Karlsruhe (hereafter GLA) 61/5479. A 1717 census indicates that they were located in sixteen villages within Amt Dilsberg, including Bruchhausen, where Wistar was a hunter's apprentice at the time. The villages were: Zuzenhausen, Bammenthal, Meckesheim, Eschelbronn, Mauer, Langenzell, Helmstadt, Angelloch, Hof Hohenhardt, Daisbach, Schatthausen, Kloster Lobenfeld, Ochsenbach, Bayerthal, Biederbach, and Bruchhausen. Bender, "Palatine Mennonite Census," 20–23.
51. Beiler, "The Transatlantic World," 273–275; "Distributing Aid to Believers in Need," 73–87.
52. Sachse, *Falkner's Curieuse Nachricht,* 22–25.
53. Max Goebel, *Geschichte des christlichen Lebens in der rheinisch-westphälischen evangelischen Kirche,* 2, Das siebenzehnte Jahrhundert (Coblenz, in Commission bei Karl Bädeker, 1862): 811–813; Donald Durnbaugh, *European Origins of the Brethren* (Elgin, Ill: Brethren Press, 1958): 36.
54. Sachse, *Falkner's Curieuse Nachricht,* 22–30; Durnbaugh, *European Origins,* 38–79, 281–320.
55. Knittle, *Palatine Emigration,* 14–19, 32–46; Kochertal, *Außführlich- und umständlicher Bericht,* introduction. Documents from German Archives concerning the 1708–1710 migrations are reprinted in Julius Goebel, ed., "Briefe Deutscher Auswanderer aus dem Jahr 1709," *Deutsch-Amerikanische Geschichtsblätter* 12 (1912):124–189.
56. Jones, *Palatine Families,* 1: 388–390, 402–403, 437–438. While they emigrated prior to Wistar's apprenticeship, some of their friends and relatives who remained behind crossed the Atlantic in later years. Jost Schwab, the father-in-law of Abraham Rhiem, the only "friend" Wistar had on the ship, had sponsored the baptism of Herchheimer's son in 1700. For the genealogy of Abraham (Eberhard) Rhiem and Johann Jost Schwab, see Elmer Denniston, *Genealogy of the Stukey, Ream, Grove, Clem and Denniston Families* (Harrisburg, Pa.: The author, 1939): 245–250; and Emily S. Morse and Winifred M. McLachlan, *The Swope Family Book of Remembrance* (Provo, Utah: J.T. Smith, 1972): 2: 1289–1296.
57. Henckel's conflicts with Catholic officials occurred while he was the pastor at Breitenborn and Daudenzell. He became the pastor at Neckargemünd and the Meckesheimer Cent in 1714. The records from his ministry there are in the Evangelische Oberkirchenrat, Karlsruhe (hereafter EOK). For a history of his life and the reproduction of many documents concerning his ministry in the Palatinate, see articles by Burt Brown Barker, in *Henckel Family Records* 3 (1928): 90–116; 4 (1929): 118–130; 6 (1931): 212–230; 8 (1932): 314–340. See also Ann Hinckle Gable, *The Pastoral Years of Rev. Anthony Henckel, 1692–1717* (Camden, Me.: Penobscot Press, 1991).
58. July 1, 1717; GLA 229/71466 II. A facsimile of the original is reproduced in Gable, *Pastoral Years,* 116–121.

59. John George Käsebier to Count Casimir, Nov. 7, 1724, translated and reprinted in *The Brethren in Colonial America: A Source Book on the Transplantation and Development of the Church of the Brethren in the Eighteenth Century*, Donald Durnbaugh, ed. (Elgin, Ill.: Brethren Press, 1967), 30.
60. Christopher Sauer to Friends in Germany, Dec. 1, 1724, in Kelsey, "An Early Description of Pennsylvania," 250.
61. Kelsey, "An Early Description of Pennsylvania," 250–251.
62. Anna Maria and Johannes Müller, Burnetsfield, Albany County, NY, to relatives in Germany, July 10, 1749, excerpted in Fertig, *Lokales Leben,* 406.
63. Donald Durnbaugh, "Two Early Letters from Germantown," *Pennsylvania Magazine of History and Biography* 84 (1960): 228–229.
64. John George Käsebier to Count Casimir, Nov. 7, 1724, in Durnbaugh, *Brethren in Colonial America,* 30–31.
65. John George Käsebier to Count Casimir, Nov. 7, 1724, in Durnbaugh, *Brethren in Colonial America,* 30.
66. Durß Thommen, Quitopahilla, Pennsylvania, to government officials in Basel, Switzerland, Oct. 3, 1737, in Leo Schelbert, "Von der Macht des Pietismus: Dokumentarbericht zur Auswanderung einer Basler Familie im Jahre 1736," *Baseler Zeitschrift für Geschichte und Altertumskunde* 75 (1975): 104.
67. Johann Diedrich Fahnenstuck to his wife's parents, Oct. 25, 1728, translation, HSP.
68. Hans Martin to his daughters in Brattelen, close to Basel, Switzerland, Sept. 6, 1735, GLA 74/9847.
69. Andreas Boni to his cousin Martin, Oct. 16, 1735, GLA 74/9847.
70. Caspar Wistar, Philadelphia, to [Georg Friederich Hölzer?], Sept. 25, 1737, Wistar Family Papers, HSP.
71. Fahnenstock to his wife's parents, Oct. 25, 1728, translation, HSP.
72. Kelsey, "An Early Description," 243–254.
73. Sauer, Germantown, to friends and acquaintances in Schwarzenau, Berleburg, Laasphe, and Christianseck, Aug. 1, 1725, in Durnbaugh, *Brethren in Colonial America,* 37.
74. Caspar Wistar, Philadelphia, to [Georg Friederich Hölzer?], Sept. 25, 1737, Wistar Family Papers, HSP.
75. *Records of the Court of Admiralty held in Philadelphia, Pennsylvania,* I, 1735–1747, 65–107, Manuscript Division, Library of Congress, Washington, DC. The ship *Princess Augusta* included 118 immigrant men who were over the age of 16. See Wokeck, *Trade in Strangers,* 241. For further discussion of the legal issues facing German-speaking immigrants who participated in Atlantic trade, see Rosalind J. Beiler, "Smuggling Goods or Moving Households? Eighteenth-Century Emigrants and Commerce in the First British Empire," forthcoming.
76. Caspar Wistar, Philadelphia, to Georg Friederich Hölzer, Neckargemünd, May 4, 1732, Wistar Family Papers, HSP.
77. Rosalind J. Beiler, "From the Rhine Valley to the Delaware Valley: The Eighteenth-Century Transatlantic Trade Channels of Caspar Wistar," in *In Search of Peace and Prosperity: New Settlements in Eighteenth-Century Europe and America*, Hartmuth Lehman, Hermann Wellenreuther, and Renate Wilson, eds. (University Park, Pa.: Penn State University Press, 2000), 172–188.
78. Wokeck, *Trade in Strangers,* 59–112.
79. Georg Friederich Hölzer, Neckargemünd, to Baltes Langhaer, April 28, 1735, Wistar Family Papers, HSP.
80. Wistar, Philadelphia, to [Georg Friederich Hölzer?], Sept. 25, 1737, Wistar Family Papers, HSP.
81. Wokeck, *Trade in Strangers,* 30–34; Fertig, *Lokales Leben,* 113–135. For Mittelberger's description, Mittelberger, *Journey to Pennsylvania.*
82. An original draft of Wistar's letter (undated) is in Wistar Family Papers, HSP. This letter was published in several places in Europe in 1733 and 1734. See two different

translations in *Pennsylvania German Society Proceedings and Addresses* 8 (1897): 141–144; and *The Perkiomen Region, Past and Present* 2 (1899): 119–120.

83. Durnbaugh, *Brethern in Colonial America,* 41–53.
84. The number of published warnings increased significantly in the 1730s and later. See the bibliography of published pamphlets concerning the British colonies in Fertig, *Lokales Leben,* 416–421.

Identity and Migration: The Atlantic in Comparative Perspective by David Eltis

1. Heather Pringle, "Hints of Frequent Pre-Columbian Contacts," *Science,* 288 (2000): 783–784. The earliest sea-borne contacts with China appear to have been by Arab, Persian, and Indian navigators and did not result in settlement. The first overseas Chinese settlements involving ocean voyages—in the Malay Peninsula and Sumatra—date from the early fourteenth century, though intermittent trading contacts go back to BCE. See Victor Purcell, *The Chinese in Southeast Asia* (London: Oxford University Press, 1965): 11–16; Wang Gungwu, "Merchants Without Empire: the Hokkinen Sojourning Communities," in *The Rise of Merchant Empires: Long-Distance Trade in the Early Modern World, 1350–1750,* James D. Tracy, ed. (Cambridge: Cambridge University Press, 1990): 400–421.
2. Robin Law, "Ethnicity and the Slave Trade: 'Lucumi' and 'Nago' as ethonyms in West Africa," *History in Africa* 23 (1997): 1–16.
3. Marianne S. Wokeck, *Trade in Strangers: The Beginnings of Mass Migration to North America* (University Park, Pa.: Penn State University Press, 1999).
4. See <http://www.cilt.org.uk/commlangs/intro.htm>.
5. Peter Linebaugh and Marcus Rediker argue that a "multiethnic class . . . was essential to the rise of capitalism and the modern global economy." *The Many-Headed Hydra: The Hidden Story of the Revolutionary Atlantic* (Boston: Beacon Press, 2000): 6–7.
6. For this argument see David Eltis, *The Rise of African Slavery in the Americas* (Cambridge: Cambridge University Press, 2000), 137–192.
7. Ida Altman points to heavy representation of hidalgos, artisans, and professionals from two cities in southwestern Spain: Ida Altman, "A New World in the Old: Local Society and Spanish Emigration to the Indies," in Ida Altman and James Horn, eds., *To Make America': European Emigration in the Early Modern Period* (Berkeley and Los Angeles: University of California Press, 1991), 39–40, 43–47.
8. Nicolás Sánchez-Albornoz, *The Population of Latin America,* trans. W.A.R. Richardson (Berkeley: University of California Press, 1974): 86–112. The Brazilian population, however, has yet to reverse this decline. See John Hemmings, *Red Gold: The Conquest of Brazilian Indians* (London: MacMillan, 1978): 487–501.
9. Stuart Schwartz, *Sugar Plantations in the Formation of Brazilian Society* (Cambridge: Cambridge University Press, 1985); Eltis, *Rise of African Slavery,* 193–223.
10. David Eltis, "The Slave Economies of the Caribbean: Structure, Performance, Evolution and Significance," in Franklin W. Knight, ed., *General History of the Caribbean,* Volume III: The slave societies of the Caribbean (London and Basingstoke: UNESCO Publishing/MacMillan Education, 1997).
11. Ian K. Steele, *The English Atlantic, 1675–1740: An Exploration of Communication and Community* (Oxford: Oxford University Press, 1986); and Kenneth J. Banks, *Communications and Imperial Absolutism in the French Atlantic, 1713–1763* (Montreal: McGill-Queens Press, 2003). For the rapidly increasing literature on the black Atlantic see Ira Berlin, *Many Thousands Gone: The First Two Centuries of Slavery in North America* (Cambridge: Harvard University Press, 1998): especially 29–63.
12. Thus, children of convicts in New South Wales were born free, unlike the children of slaves. See D.J. Neal, *Rule of Law in a Penal Colony: Law and Power in early New*

South Wales (Cambridge: Cambridge University Press, 1991), 15, and for other comparisons of slave and convict status, see 34–41.

13. For the full account, see Pruneau de Pommegorge, *Description de la 'Nigritie'* (Paris, 1789), 104–118.

14. Stephen Behrendt, David Eltis, and David Richardson, "The Costs of Coercion: African Agency in the History of the Atlantic World," *Economic History Review* 54 (2001): 454–476.

15. Philip D. Curtin, *Economic Change in Precolonial Africa: Senegambia in the Era of the Slave Trade* (Madison: The University of Wisconsin Press, 1975), 93.

16. T.H. Breen, *Puritans and Adventurers: Change and Persistence in Early America* (New York: Oxford University Press, 1980): 107–108; Carole Shammas, "English-Born and Creole Elites in Turn of the Century Virginia," in *The Chesapeake in the Seventeenth Century: Essays on Anglo-American Society*, Thad W. Tate and David Ammerman, eds. (Chapel Hill, N.C.: University of North Carolina Press, 1979): 274–296.

17. James Horn, *Adapting to a New World: English Society in the Seventeenth Century Chesapeake* (Chapel Hill, N.C., and London: University of North Carolina Press, 1994): 39–48, 109–111; Russell R. Menard, "British Migration to the Chesapeake Colonies in the Seventeenth Century," in *Colonial Chesapeake Society*, Lois Green Carr, Philip D. Morgan, and Jean B. Russo, eds. (Chapel Hill: University of North Carolina Press, 1988): 122–126.

18. "Extracts from Henry Whistler's Journal of the West India Expedition," in *The narrative of general Venables, with an Appendix of Papers Relating to the Expedition to the West Indies and the Conquest of Jamaica, 1654–1655*, Charles H. Firth, ed. (London: Longmans, Green, and Co., 1900): 146.

19. G. Debien, "Les engagés pour les Antilles (1634–1715)," *Revue d'Histoire des Colonies* 38 (1951): 98–112.

20. Cornelis Ch. Goslinga, *The Dutch in the Caribbean and in the Guianas, 1680–1791* (Assen, Maastricht, and Dover, N.H.: Van Gorcum, 1985), 231–266.

21. Peter Wilson Coldham, *The Complete Book of Emigrants, 1607–1660* (4 vols., Baltimore: Genealogical Pub. Co., 1987–1993). See, for example, "The humble Peticon of Rene Petit yo maj agent at Rouen . . .," 1679 (arranging the settlement of several hundred Huguenots in South Carolina), British Public Record Office, CO1/43, f. 246–251.

22. Robert Stein, "The Free Men of Colour and the Revolution in Saint Domingue, 1789–1792," *Histoire Sociale* 14 (1981): 14.

23. See, most recently, Hilary McD. Beckles, "A 'riotous and unruly lot': Irish Indentured Servants and Fremen in the English West Indies, 1644–1713," *William and Mary Quarterly* 47 (1990): 503–522: 508–509.

24. Donald H. Akenson, *If the Irish Ran the World: Montserrat, 1630–1730* (Montreal: McGill-Queen's University Press, 1997): 117–53; quote is from p. 149; Richard S. Dunn, *Sugar and slaves. The rise of the planter class in the English West Indies, 1624–1713* (Chapel Hill: The University of North Carolina Press, 1972): 130; Trevor Burnard, "European Migration to Jamaica, 1655–1780," *William and Mary Quarterly* 53 (1996): 769–796: 780.

25. Thomas Sowell, *Ethnic America: A History* (New York: Basic Books, 1981): 35–41; See the Irish names in Allen J. Kuethe, "Los Llorones Cubanos: The Socio-Military Basis of Commercial Privilege in the American Trade Under Charles IV," in *The North American Role in the Spanish Imperial Economy, 1760–1819*, Jacques A. Barbier, and Allan J. Kuethe, eds. (Manchester: Manchester University Press, 1984): 142–57. For the 1650s migration see Abbot Emerson Smith, *Colonists in Bondage: White Servitude and Convict Labor in America, 1607–1776* (Chapel Hill, N.C.: The University of North Carolina Press, 1947).

26. Sheldon J. Godfrey and Judith C. Godfrey, *Search Out the Land: The Jews and the Growth of Equality in British Colonial America, 1740–1867* (Montreal: McGill-Queen's University Press, 1995): 38; British Public Record Office, "Barbados Minutes, 1654–58," 1: 60, Jan 9, 1655.

27. Michael Angels and Denis de Carli, "A Curious and Exact Account of a Voyage to Congo In the Years 1666 and 1667," in Awnsham Churchill and John Churchill, *A Collection of Voyages and Travels* (6 vols., London, 1744–1746): 1: 491–492.
28. Godfrey and Godfrey, *Search Out the Land*, 38; Stephen A. Fortune, *Merchants and Jews: The Struggle for British West Indian Commerce, 1650–1750* (Gainesville, Fla.: University Press of Florida, 1984).
29. Trevor Burnard, "Who Bought Slaves in Early America? Purchasers of Slaves from the Royal African Company in Jamaica, 1674–1708," *Slavery and Abolition*, 17 (1996): 74, 79–80; Allan D. Meyers, "Ethnic Distinctions and Wealth among Colonial Jamaican Merchants, 1685–1716," *Social Science History* 22 (1998): 54–75. Meyers stresses the disabilities of Jews in Jamaica, but the broader imperial perspective suggests an opposite conclusion, at least in relative terms.
30. This paragraph is based on Godfrey and Godfrey, *Search Out the Land*, 34–61. The stress here on the differences between slave and non-slave colonies is, however, my own interpretation.
31. John Thornton, *Africa and Africans in the Making of the Atlantic World, 1400–1680* (Cambridge: Cambridge University Press, 1992), 197–201, especially the discussion of marriage on the Remire estate in Cayenne in the late 1680s.
32. Richard Ligon, *True and Exact History of the Island of Barbados* (London, 1657), 55.
33. Dunn, *Sugar and Slaves*, 258. For a full account see CO1/28: 200–205.
34. See *Calendar of State Papers. Colonial Series. America and West Indies*, 1685–88 (London: Her Majesty's Stationery Office, 1899): docs 299, 311, 330, 339, 445, 560, 623, 869, 883, 965, 1,286; and ibid, 1689–1692, doc 1,041. References to the prominent role of Gold Coast slaves in slave resistance all appear to come from the eighteenth century, even though they refer in some cases to events in the previous century.
35. Orlando Patterson, *The Sociology of Slavery: An Analysis of the Origins, Development and Structure of Negro Slave Society in Jamaica* (London: MacGibbon & Key, 1967): 267–268; idem, "Slavery and Slave Revolts: A Sociohistorical Analysis of the First Maroon War," in *Maroon Societies: Rebel Slave Communities in the Americas*, Richard Price, ed. (2 ed., Baltimore: The Johns Hopkins University Press, 1979): 254–259; Michael Craton, *Testing the Chains: Resistance to Slavery in the British West Indies* (Ithaca: Cornell University Press, 1982): 74–80.
36. The next three paragraphs are based on Behrendt, Eltis, and Richardson, "Costs of Coercion."

Trans-Atlantic Transformations: The Origins and Identity of Africans in the Americas by Paul E. Lovejoy

1. The research for this paper was supported by a grant from the Social Sciences and Humanities Research Council of Canada and was undertaken in the context of the UNESCO Slave Route Project through the York/UNESCO Nigerian Hinterland Project, York University.
2. Maureen Warner-Lewis, "Genealogical Evidence of Ethnic and Religious Plurality among African Immigrants to Trinidad," in: *Identifying Enslaved Africans: Proceedings of the UNESCO/SSHRC Summer Institute*, Paul E. Lovejoy, ed. (Toronto: York University, 1997).
3. See my "Situating Identities in the African Diaspora: Islam and Slavery in the Americas," Conference on " 'More than Cool Reason': Black Responses to Enslavement, Exile, and Resettlement," University of Haifa, Israel, January 18–22, 1998, and published as "Cerner les identités au sein de la diaspora africaine, l'islam et l'esclavage aux Ameriques," *Cahiers des Anneaux de la Mémoire*, 1, 1999, 249–278. Also see the various contributions in *Trans-Atlantic Dimensions of Ethnicity in the African Diaspora*, Paul Lovejoy and David Trotman, eds. (London: Continuum, 2002).

4. Karen Fog Olwig, "African Cultural Principles in Caribbean Slave Societies," in *Slave Cultures and the Cultures of Slavery*, Stephan Palmié, ed. (Knoxville: University of Tennessee Press, 1995): 23–39. Also see Sidney Mintz and Richard Price, *The Birth of African-American Culture: An Anthropological Perspective* (Boston: Beacon Press, 1992 [1956]).

5. Paul E. Lovejoy, "The Muslim Factor in the Trans-Atlantic Slave Trade," in *Slavery on the Frontiers of Islam*, Paul E. Lovejoy, ed. (Princeton: Markus Wiener, 2002). Also see my "Background to Rebellion: The Origins of Muslim Slaves in Bahia," *Slavery and Abolition*, 15:2 (1994): 151–180; and "Jihad e Escravidão: As Origens dos Escravos Muculmanos de Bahia," *Topoi: Revista de História* (Rio de Janeiro), 1 (2000): 11–44.

6. See my "The African Diaspora: Revisionist Interpretations of Ethnicity, Culture and Religion under Slavery," *Studies in the World History of Slavery, Abolition and Emancipation*, 2:1 (1997); and "Identifying Enslaved Africans in the African Diaspora," in *Identity in the Shadow of Slavery*, Paul E. Lovejoy, ed. (London: Cassell Academic, 2000): 1–29.

7. Ira Berlin, "From Creole to African: Atlantic Creoles and the Origins of African-American Society in Mainland North America," *William and Mary Quarterly*, 53:2 (1996): 251–288.

8. Douglas Chambers, "Eboe, Kongo, Mandingo: African Ethnic Groups and the Development of Regional Slave Societies in Mainland North America," International Seminar, "The History of the Atlantic World," Harvard University, September 3–11, 1996.

9. Berlin, "From Creole to African," 253–254.

10. For a discussion of the interaction between *orisha* worship, Islam, and Christianity in nineteenth-century Yorubaland, see J.D.Y. Peel, *Religious Encounter and the Making of the Yoruba* (Bloomington: Indiana University Press, 2000).

11. Many studies consider ethnicity, although rarely in detail and without an attempt to explore the meaning of different ethnic identities in Africa and the Americas at the time. See, for example, Daniel C. Littlefield, *Rice and Slaves: Ethnicity and the Slave Trade in Colonial South Carolina* (Baton Rouge: Louisiana State University Press, 1981); Peter M. Wood, *Black Majority: Negroes in Colonial South Carolina from 1670 through the Stono Rebellion* (New York: Alfred Knopf, 1974). Demographic data including ethnic identification of slaves in the British Caribbean has been tabulated by B.W. Higman; see *Slave Populations in the British Caribbean, 1807–1834* (Baltimore: The Johns Hopkins University Press 1984), but the meaning of the different ethnic labels in historical context has yet to be studied. Similarly, David Geggus has explored French shipping and plantation records to identify ethnic patterns, but without analyzing the historical origins in Africa in detail; see "Sex Ratios, Age and Ethnicity in the Atlantic Slave Trade: Data from French Shipping and Plantation Records," *Journal of African History*, 30 (1989): 23–44. Mary Karasch's study of ethnicity in Rio de Janeiro is largely static as well; see *Slave Life in Rio de Janeiro, 1808–1850* (Princeton: Princeton University Press, 1987).

12. Michael Mullin, *Africa in America: Slave Acculturation and Resistance in the American South and the British Caribbean, 1736–1831* (Urbana, Ill., and Chicago: University of Illinois Press, 1992), 14.

13. Gwendolyn Midlo Hall, *Africans in Colonial Louisiana: The Development of Afro-Creole Culture in the Eighteenth Century* (Baton Rouge: Louisiana State University Press, 1992).

14. Gwendolyn Midlo Hall, "African Ethnicities and the Meanings of Mina," in Lovejoy and Trotman, *Trans-Atlantic Dimensions of Ethnicity*.

15. David Eltis, David Richardson, Stephen Behrendt, Herbert S. Klein, *Atlantic Slave Trade. A Database on CD-ROM* (Cambridge: Cambridge University Press, 1999). For an analysis, see Lovejoy, *Transformations in Slavery: A History of Slavery in Africa* (2d ed., Cambridge: Cambridge University Press, 2000).

16. For a discussion, see Michael A. Gomez, "A Quality of Anguish: The Igbo Response to Enslavement in the Americas," in Lovejoy and Trotman, *Trans-Atlantic Dimensions of Ethnicity*.

17. For an analysis, see Maria Inês Côrtes de Oliveira, "The Reconstruction of Ethnicity in Bahia: The Case of the Nago in the Nineteenth Century;" and João José Reis, "Ethnic Politics among Africans in Nineteenth-Century Bahia," both in Lovejoy and Trotman, *Trans-Atlantic Dimensions of Ethnicity.*

18. For an analysis of the Trinidad data, see David V. Trotman, "Africanizing and Creolizing the Plantation Frontier of Trinidad, 1787–1838," in Lovejoy and Trotman, *Trans-Atlantic Dimensions of Ethnicity.*

19. For a preliminary analysis of some aspects of the demographic material in relation to ethnicity, see my "Ethnic Designations of the Slave Trade and the Reconstruction of the History of Trans-Atlantic Slavery," in Lovejoy and Trotman *Trans-Atlantic Dimensions of Ethnicity.*

20. See Paul E. Lovejoy, "Identifying Enslaved Africans: Methodological and Conceptual Considerations in Studying the African Diaspora," in Lovejoy, *Identifying Enslaved Africans.* Also see my "Methodology through the Ethnic Lens: The Study of Atlantic Africa," in *African Historical Research: Sources and Methods,* Toyin Falola and Christian Jennings, eds. (Rochester: University of Rochester Press, 2002).

21. In constructing "the world they made together," Mechal Sobel, for example, relies extensively on twentieth-century anthropological accounts to gain insight into eighteenth-century events and developments; see *The World They Made Together: Black and White Values in Eighteenth-Century Virginia* (Princeton: Princeton University Press, 1987).

22. Albert J. Raboteau, *Slave Religion: The "Invisible Institution" in the Antebellum South* (New York: Oxford University Press, 1978).

23. Even such classic studies as Eugene Genovese, *Roll Jordan Roll: The World the Slaves Made* (New York: Pantheon Books, 1974) fall into this trap. Consequently, the juxtaposition of the African religious tradition and Christian conversion is an inadequate mechanism for examining the development of slave culture. At its worst, this approach fails to grasp the major developments in the historical reconstruction of the role of religion in Africa in the specific context of the slave trade.

24. Sterling Stuckey, *Slave Culture, Nationalist Theory and the Foundations of Black America* (New York: Oxford University Press, 1987).

25. Raboteau observes that "religion, particularly religious myth and ritual, might be among the most conservative elements of culture." See *Slave Religion in the Antebellum South,* 325–326 fn.

26. Until recently, the failure to examine contemporary religious expressions and experience within Africa during the period of slave exports can be partially excused for want of historical study by Africanist historians, but is no longer the case; see, for example, the excellent research of Robin Law, *The Slave Coast of West Africa, 1550–1750: The Impact of the Atlantic Slave Trade on an African Society* (Oxford: Clarendon Press, 1991). For other studies, see George Brandon, *Santeria from Africa to the New World* (Bloomington: Indiana University Press, 1993); and Guérin Montilus, *Dieux en diaspora. Les Loa Haïtiens et les Vaudou du Royaume d'Allada (Bénin)* (Niamey: CELHTO, 1988).

27. Cf. John Thornton, *Africa and Africans in the Making of the Atlantic World, 1400–1680* (Cambridge: Cambridge University Press, 1992), although at times Thornton may have overstated his case with respect to the extent to which Africans from the interior of west-central Africa were already Christians before reaching the Americas.

28. See my "Methodology through the Ethnic Lens."

29. Earl Lewis, "To Turn as on a Pivot: Writing African Americans into a History of Overlapping Diasporas," *American Historical Review,* 100:3 (1995). Also see Berlin, "Creole to African."

30. As Berlin ("Creole to African," 253fn) notes, "creole" has been extended to "native-born free people of many national origins, including both Europeans and Africans, and of diverse social standing. It has also been applied to people of partly European but mixed racial and national origins in various European colonies and to Africans who entered Europe. In the United States, creole has also been specifically applied to people of

mixed but usually non-African origins in Louisiana. Staying within the bounds of the broadest definition of Creole and the literal definition of African America, I use both terms to refer to black people of native American birth." See also John A. Holm, *Pidgins and Creoles: Theory and Structure* (2 vols., Cambridge: Cambridge University Press, 1988–1989). For the thesis that the term is Bantu in origin, see Maureen Warner-Lewis, "Posited Kikoongo Origins of Some Portuguese and Spanish Words from the Slave Era," *América Negra*, 13 (1997).

31. Kamau Edward Brathwaite, *The Development of Creole Society in Jamaica, 1770–1820* (Oxford: Clarendon Press, 1971), 306. The book is based on his Ph.D. thesis.

32. Brathwaite, *Creole Society*, 309–311. Brathwaite was responding in particular to M.G. Smith's conception of plural society; see *The Plural Society in the British West Indies* (Berkeley: University of California Press, 1965).

33. Philip D. Curtin, *Two Jamaicas, 1830–1865: The Role of Ideas in a Tropical Colony* (Cambridge: Harvard University Press, 1955).

34. Mintz and Price, *African American Cultures*, 42.

35. According to Mintz and Price (*African American Cultures*, 48), "to document our assertions that fully formed African-American cultures developed within the earliest years of settlement in many New World colonies involves genuine difficulties. These stem from the general shortage of descriptive materials on slave life during the initial period, as well as from the lack of research regarding the problem."

36. See, e.g., Karen Fog Olwig, *Cultural Adaptation and Resistance on St. John: Three Centuries of Afro-Caribbean Life* (Gainesville: University Press of Florida, 1985). The fact that Olwig studies three centuries would have the effect of emphasizing the adaptation and ultimate creolization of the population.

37. George Brooks, *Landlords and Strangers: Ecology, Society, and Trade in Western Africa, 1000–1630* (Boulder: Westview Press, 1993); and Akintola J.G. Wyse, *The Krio of Sierra Leone: An Interpretative History* (Washington, D.C.: Howard University Press, 1991).

38. Berlin, "Atlantic Creole," 254. Also see Mintz's description of the process of creolization, "The Socio-Historical Background to Pidginization and Creolization," in *Pidginization and Creolization of Languages: Proceedings of a Conference held at the University of the West Indies, Mona, Jamaica, April 1968*, Dell H. Hymes, ed. (Cambridge: Cambridge University Press, 1971), 481–496.

39. Stephan Palmié, "A Taste for Human Commodities: Experiencing the Atlantic System," in Palmié, *Slave Cultures and Cultures of Slavery*, 40–54.

40. Stephan Palmié, "Ekpe/Abakuá in Middle Passage: Time, Space and Units of Analysis in African-American Historical Anthropology," in *The Atlantic Slave Trade in African and Diaspora Memory*, Ralph Austen and Kenneth Warren, eds. (Durham, N.C.: Duke University Press, forthcoming).

41. Fernando Ortiz, *Cuban Counterpoint: Tobacco and Sugar* (Durham, N.C.: Duke University Press, 1995), 101–102. According to Ortiz, Africans "brought with them their diverse cultures, some as primitive as that of the Ciboneys, others in a state of advanced barbarism like that of the Tainos, and others more economically and socially developed, like the Mandingas, Yolofes [Wolofs], Hausas, Dahomeyans, and Yorubas, with agriculture, slaves, money, markets, trade, and centralized governments ruling territories and populations as large as Cuba; intermediate cultures between Taino and the Aztec, with metals, but as yet without writing. The Negroes brought with their bodies their souls, but not their institutions or their implements. They were of different regions, races, languages, cultures, classes, ages, sexes, thrown promiscuously into the slave ships, and socially equalized by the same system of slavery. They arrived deracinated, wounded, shattered, like the cane of the fields, and like the cane they were ground and crushed to extract the juice of their labor. No other human element has had to suffer such a profound and repeated change of surroundings, cultures, class, and conscience. They were transferred from their own to another more advanced culture." Also see Fernando Ortiz, *Hampa afro-cubana. Los Negros Esclavos: estudio sociológico y*

de derecho público (Havana: Revista bimestre cubana, 1916 [1975]), especially Chapter 2, "Los negros afrocubanos," 37ff. Ortiz drew on an extensive amount of documentation for 1916. For a listing of ethnic categories in Cuba in 1916, see ibid., 40–66.

42. Palmié, "Ekpe/Abakua."
43. Douglas Chambers, " 'My own nation:' Igbo Exiles in the Diaspora," *Slavery and Abolition*, 18:1 (1997): 72–97.

Whose Centers and Peripheries? Eighteenth-Century Intellectual History in Atlantic Perspective
by Jorge Cañizares-Esguerra

1. Diego Durán, *Historia de las Indias de Nueva España, 1581,* M. Garibay, ed., 2 vol. (México: Porrua, 1967).
2. Ibidem, 2:556.
3. *The London Review and Literary Journal* (August 1787): 16, 17.
4. Guillaume-Thomas Abbé Raynal, *Histoire philosophique et politique, des etablissemens et du commerce des Europeens dans les deux Indes,* 10 vol. (Genève: Jean Leonard Pellet, 1781), book 6, ch. xx, 3:255–256.
5. Guillaume-Thomas Abbé Raynal, *Histoire philosophique,* 7 vols. (Maestricht: Jean-Edme Dufour, 1774), book 6, ch. I, 3:3.
6. Jean-Jacques Rousseau, *Discourse on the origins and foundations of inequality among men, 1755,* in *The Collected writings of Rousseau*, Roger D. Masters and Christopher Kelly, eds. (Hanover, N.H.: University Press of New England, 1990–): vol. 3: note 8 in Rousseau's original, pp. 84–86.
7. Joannes Cornelius De Pauw, *Recherches philosophiques sur les américains, ou Mémoires intéressants pour servir à l'histoire de l'espèce humaine, 1768–1769,* (3 vols., Berlin: G. J. Decker, 1770), 2:195–203.
8. De Pauw, *Recherches philosophiques,* vol 1.
9. On European perceptions of Spain, see William S. Maltby, *The Black Legend in England: The Development of Anti-Spanish Sentiment, 1558–1660* (Durham: Duke University Press, 1971); Julian Juderias, *La leyenda negra* (9th ed., Barcelona: Editorial Araluce, 1943); and Ricardo García Cárcel, *La leyenda negra. Historia y opinión* (Madrid: Alianza, 1992).
10. On this tradition in the Spanish Enlightenment, see Antonio Mestre, *Mayans y la España de la Ilustración* (Madrid: Instituto de España/Espasa Calpe, 1990).
11. For a partial description of the collection, see *Catálogo de la colección de Juan Bautista Muñoz,* 3 vols. (Madrid: Real Academia de Historia, 1954–1956). The catalogue describes in detail the contents of seventy-six of ninety-five folio volumes of documentation collected by Muñoz now located at the Academy of History in Madrid. The remaining nineteen volumes can be found today at the Royal Library in Madrid. The catalogue also includes a short description of eighteen quarto volumes, most of which are located at the Royal Library as well. Muñoz was also responsible for pressing the Spanish authorities in Mexico to collect thirty-five additional volumes known as *Colección Memorias de Nueva España,* which is also housed at the Academy of History. The collection that Muñoz assembled totals one hundred forty-eight volumes.
12. On founding of the Archive of the Indies, see Margarita Gómez Gómez, "El Archivo General de Indias, génesis histórica de sus ordenanzas," *Archivo General de Indias. Ordenanzas* (Seville: Junta de Andalucia, 1986); and Francisco de Solano, "El Archivo de Indias y la promoción del americanismo científico," in *Carlos III y la ciencia de la Ilustración,* Manuel Selles, José Luis Peset, and Antonio Lafuente, eds. (Madrid: Alianza, 1988): 277–296.
13. For the principles organizing Muñoz's collection and the Archive of the Indies, see Muñoz's "Idea de una obra cometida," Nov. 28, 1783. *[A]rchivo del {R]eal [J]ardín*

[B]otanico, división 13, legajo 5, 8, # 9; and "Razón de una obra cometida," Nov. 16, 1785, *ARJB,* división 13, legajo 5, 8, #10.

14. José Flores, *Específico nuevamente descubierto en el reino de Guatemala para la curación del horrible mal de cancro y otros mas frecuentes (experimentado ya favorablemente en esta capital de Mexico)* (México: Felipe Zuñiga de Ontiveros, 1782).

15. Antonio León y Gama, *Instruccion sobre el remedio de las lagartijas. Nuevamente descubierto para la curacion del cancro y otras enfermedades* (México: Felipe de Zuñiga y Ontiveros, 1782).

16. Antonio León y Gama, *Descripción histórica y cronológica de las dos piedras que con occasion del Nuevo empedrado que se esta formando en la plaza principal de México se hallaron en ella en el año de 1790* (vol 1. 1792), Carlos María de Bustamante, ed. (2 vols., México: Imprenta de Alejandro Valdés, 1832), 2:29–32 (par. 105–109). In the text, León y Gama never identified the provenance of the examples he cited. After a painstaking survey of the copies of codices he owned, I have identified the codices from which he drew most of his examples.

17. León y Gama, *Descripción Histórica,* 2:41–45 (par. 117–119).

18. For a more detailed account of the debates sketched here, see Jorge Cañizares-Esguerra, *How to Write the History of the New World. Histories, Epistemologies, and Identities in the Eighteenth-Century Atlantic World* (Stanford: Stanford University Press, 2001).

The Purpose of Pirates, or Assimilating New Worlds in the Renaissance by Benjamin Schmidt

1. The mystery sources are Bartolomé de Las Casas and Alexander Olivier Exquemelin, both of whom will be discussed in greater detail later in the essay. Here I am citing their best-known works, which are readily available in English editions: B. de Las Casas, *A Short Account of the Destruction of the Indies,* edited and translated by Nigel Griffen, introduction by Anthony Pagden (London: Penguin, 1992), first and final quotations at pp. 15 and 35, respectively; and A.O. Exquemelin, *The Buccaneers of America,* William S. Stallybrass ed. (London, [1935]; rep. Williamstown, Mass.: Croner House, 1976), third quotation on p. 156. The second quotation comes from the Dutch-language edition (and my own translation): Alexander Olivier Exquemelin, *De Americaensche zee-rovers. Behelsende een pertinente en waerachtige beschrijving van alle de voornaemste roveryen, en onmenschelijcke wreedheden, die de Engelse en Franse rovers, tegens de Spanjaerden in America gepleeght hebben* (Amsterdam, 1678): 42.

2. The controversy over Exquemelin's origins is discussed by H. de la Fontaine Verwey, "De scheepsschirurgijn Exquemelin en zijn boek over de flibustiers," in *Drukkers, Liefhebbers en Piraten in de Zeventiende Eeuw,* 2 vols. (Amsterdam: N. Israel, 1976): 2; and Michel-Christian Camus, "Une note critique à propos d'Exquemelin," *Revue francaise d'histoire d'outre-mer* 77, no. 286 (1990): 79–90. In summarizing the debates over Exquemelin's biography, Fontaine Verwey sensibly points out that, whatever the author's personal background, the *Americaensche zee-rovers* certainly grew out of the milieu of Holland publishing. In all events, the book's original printer, Jan ten Hoorn, oversaw its production, including the images that will be discussed later in this essay.

3. On the politics of the late-sixteenth-century Netherlands, see Geoffrey Parker, *The Dutch Revolt,* rev. ed. (London: Penguin, 1985). For more general historical context, see Jonathan I. Israel, *The Dutch Republic: Its Rise, Greatness, and Fall, 1477–1806* (Oxford: Oxford University Press, 1995).

4. The classic version of this narrative—still well worth reading—is John Lothrop Motley, *The Rise of the Dutch Republic,* 3 vols. (New York: Harper and Bros., 1855). A similarly heroic recitation of the Revolt tacking from the other side may be found in

William H. Prescott, *History of the Reign of Philip the Second, King of Spain* (Boston: Phillips, Sampson, and Co., 1858).

5. See the "Verbintenis van eenige Eedelen," in J. W. Te Water, *Historie van het verbond en de smeekschriften der Nederlandsche edelen ter verkrijging van vrijheid in den godsdienst en burgerstaat in de jaren 1565–1567,* 4 vols. (Middelburg, 1779–1796), 4: 61.

6. Las Casas was, of course, himself a propagandist, who exaggerated the bad treatment of the Indians in his campaign to end native slavery in Spanish America.

7. For Las Casas, see the *Spieghel vande Spaensche tyrannie beeldelijcken afgemaelt* (Amsterdam, 1609), the images of which were reproduced in dozens of later editions. The Gijsius engravings discussed here come from a 1620 reduction of the *Oorsprong en voortgang der Neder-landtscher beroerten ende ellendicheden* (Leiden, 1616), which was published anonymously under the title *Tweede deel van den Spiegel der Spaensche tyrannye gheschiet in Nederlandt* (Amsterdam, 1620).

8. For more detail, see Israel, *Dutch Republic;* and, particularly for the rivalry of the Netherlands and England, Pieter Geyl, *Orange and Stuart, 1641–72* (London: Weidenfeld and Nicolson, 1969). Dutch colonial history lacks an adequate English-language overview. The most recent Dutch summary, with a full bibliography, is Henk den Heijer, *De geschiedenis van de WIC* (Zutphen: Walburg Pers, 1994).

9. The name derives from the French *boucan,* itself a variation of the indigenous Tupi word *mukém,* or barbecue, and it suggested the manner in which the pirates roasted their enormous, post-plunder feasts on wooden frames of sticks resembling a grill.

10. See, for example, Lois Potter, "Pirates and 'Turning Turk' in Renaissance Drama," in *Travel and Drama in Shakespeare's Time,* Jean-Pierre Maquerlot and Michèle Willems, eds. (Cambridge: Cambridge University Press, 1996); and Barbara Fuchs, "Faithless Empires: Pirates, Renegadoes, and the English Nation," *English Literary History* 67 (Spring 2000): 45–69.

11. See Joseph Sabin's monumental *Bibliotheca Americana: A Dictionary of Books Relating to America, from its Discovery to the Present Time,* 29 vols. (New York: Sabin and Bibliographical Society of America, 1868–1936), no. 23468, which also cites the great Dutch bibliographer, Frederick Muller, to a similar effect: "There is certainly no other book of that time which experienced a popularity similar to that of the 'Buccaniers of America.'" For possible runners-up, cf. *'t Begin, midden en eynde der see-roveryen, van den alder-fameusten zee-roover, Claes G. Compaen van Oostsanen in Kennemerlant* (1659); and Willem Ysbrandtsz Bontekoe, *Journael ofte gedenckwaerdige beschrijvinge van de Oost-Indische reyse van Willem Ysbrandtsz. Bontekoe van Hoorn* (Hoorn, 1646), both of which went through dozens of editions.

INDEX